FIRST IN FLIGHT

STEPHEN KIRK

FIRST IN FLIGHT

THE WRIGHT BROTHERS
IN NORTH CAROLINA

John F. Blair Publisher   Winston-Salem, North Carolina

The paper in this book meets
the guidelines for permanence
and durability of the Committee
on Production Guidelines for
Book Longevity of the
Council on Library Resources.

C 2

Library of Congress Cataloging-in-Publication Data

Kirk, Stephen, 1960–

    First in flight : the Wright brothers in North Carolina / Stephen Kirk.

        p.   cm.

    Includes bibliographical references and index.

    ISBN 0-89587-127-0 (alk. paper)

    1. Wright, Orville, 1871–1948. 2. Wright, Wilbur, 1867–1912.

  3. Aeronautics—United States—Biography. 4. Aeronautics—United

States—History. I. Title.

TL540.W7K57   1995

629.13'0092'273—dc20   95–6039

Design by Debra Long Hampton

Map by Jonathan Phillips

Printed and Bound by R. R. Donnelley & Sons

To Mary, Elizabeth, and Rebecca

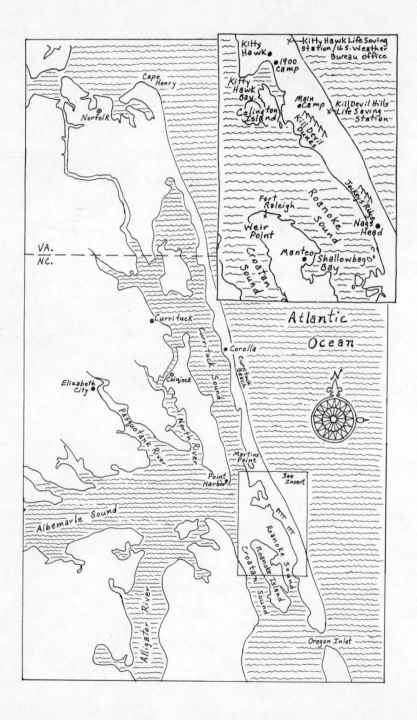

CONTENTS

Acknowledgments

The excerpts from Bruce Salley's 1908 dispatches included in this book appear courtesy of the Southern Historical Collection at UNC-Chapel Hill.

I owe thanks to many people for the help they provided during this project: the staff at Wright Brothers National Memorial, especially Darrell Collins and Warren Wrenn; Dawne Dewey at Wright State University; Steve Massengill at the North Carolina State Archives; Michael Halminski of the Chicamacomico Historical Association; Daniel W. Barefoot of Lincolnton, North Carolina, who generously shared unpublished material; Peggy A. Haile at the Norfolk Public Library; Steven Hensley of Greeneville, Tennessee; Barry Reynolds, southern Virginia's baddest librarian; Jonathan Phillips of Wake Forest, North Carolina, mapmaker and friend; Marion Strode and Pamela C. Powell at the Chester County (Pa.) Historical Society; Monica Hoel and Thelma Hutchins at Emory and Henry

College; Nellie Perry of the National Park Service; Doug Twiddy, Carole Thompson, and Jody Gibson of Twiddy and Company Realtors on the northern Outer Banks; the staff of the Maud Preston Palenske Memorial Library in St. Joseph, Michigan; Betty Husting of Locust Valley, New York; Thomas C. Parramore of Raleigh, North Carolina; Rodney Barfield at the North Carolina Maritime Museum in Beaufort; and Brenda O'Neal at the Museum of the Albemarle in Elizabeth City, North Carolina.

The staff at the Outer Banks History Center in Manteo was of great help. Curator Wynne Dough gave my manuscript a careful reading. Hellen Shore and Sarah Downing answered numerous questions and located photographs for me.

Thanks is also due Judy Breakstone, Sue Clark, Margaret Couch, Debbie Hampton, Liza Langrall, Carolyn Sakowski, Anne Schultz, Dr. Heath Simpson, Lisa Wagoner, and Andrew Waters at John F. Blair, Publisher.

Lastly, I should credit my mother, Pat Kirk, whose interest in books inspired mine; my father, Ed Kirk, who got close enough to Chuck Yeager to actually reach out and touch him, but wisely refrained from doing so; and my wife, Mary, and daughters, Elizabeth and Rebecca, for their support through more than a few lost weekends.

Introduction

Admittedly, this is the kind of book Orville Wright wouldn't have liked.

During his later years, a number of writers went to great lengths to win his approval for their biographies of the Wrights, the primary results being hurt feelings and even an attempt by Orville to pay one writer to kill his project. It took Fred Kelly, the Wrights' authorized biographer, more than a quarter-century to earn Orville's confidence.

The rub was always Orville's insistence on separating the invention of the airplane from the personality of its inventors. He wanted the story to be heavy in technical explanation and light on personal detail. As far as he was concerned, the development of the airplane was a tale fraught strictly with engineering hurdles, but contrary to his wishes, the public found the image of two self-taught geniuses in suits and stiff collars chasing gliders in the dunes as appealing as the invention itself.

Neither does this book attempt to do justice to the career of the Wright brothers.

Experts agree that their experiments in Ohio, Virginia, and Europe were more important to the development of aviation than what they did on North Carolina's Outer Banks, the focus here. But just as the Wrights' personal traits had a definite bearing on the solution of the flight problem—whether Orville liked it or not—so did the Outer Banks exert an influence on the Wrights. It is far from certain they would have succeeded elsewhere.

I got the idea for this project upon seeing a photograph captioned "World's First Flight Crew" in an old book I bought for twenty-five cents at a library sale. The photograph showed seven mustached, hard-looking men of the United States Lifesaving Service standing before a plain wall. These were men whose job it was to guard the welfare of sailors along one of the most dangerous sections of the Atlantic coast. As a sidelight, they gave aid to a couple of visiting bicycle builders and posed for their camera, looking about as natural as figures in a wax museum. I wanted to learn how these men found themselves parties to one of the great events of the century; how their lives were affected when the Wright brothers came to "town"; how their help, along with that of other local residents and a variety of visitors to the Outer Banks, figured in the Wrights' success.

People like Dan Tate, Augustus Herring, Alf Drinkwater, and Bruce Salley are remembered only as footnotes to the Wright brothers' story—when they are remembered at all. But that is not to say they have no stories to tell. One ten-year-old Kitty Hawk boy went aloft in a Wright brothers glider nearly two years before Orville Wright—

the world's first heavier-than-air pilot—ever did. One local man was so well respected by the Wrights that he remained in contact with Orville for more than four decades after the famous flights. Others parlayed a rather scanty association with the brothers into fame and public appearances. One of the early aeronauts who witnessed the Wrights' experiments on the Outer Banks was distinctly unimpressed, disparaging them as mere "bicycle mechanics" to his dying day. Another started out their friend and ended up claiming they appropriated some of their most important ideas from him.

Pieces of the Wrights—a sewing machine, bits of wing fabric, the wood from their camp buildings, papers they left behind—are scattered around the Outer Banks, in fact and legend, well beyond the bounds of Wright Brothers National Memorial.

This book seeks to describe the full range of the Wright brothers' experiences on the Outer Banks—their experiments, their leisure-time pursuits, the lifesaving personnel and local citizens they associated with, the other outsiders who came hoping to fly with them or cover them in the press. It also seeks to present the Wrights' trips to North Carolina in the broader context of what was happening on the Outer Banks at the turn of the century. Other events of note took place while the Wrights were in residence, including the ground-breaking work of another experimenter, now as obscure as the Wrights are famous, who changed the world nearly as much as did Wilbur and Orville.

If the Wright brothers' story can be boiled down to one essential fact, it is that on December 17, 1903, they made four powered airplane flights at Kill Devil Hills, North Carolina, the first in history. But depending on how far you care to read into dubious sources, you can find that they made three flights that day, or only one, or that they flew successfully three days earlier, or that they never left the ground at all until 1908. And that doesn't begin to examine the claims of people who counted themselves responsible in some way for the brothers' success. There is no part of the Wrights' story that hasn't been disputed by someone.

The appearance of Wilbur and Orville Wright on the North Carolina coast marked an unlikely convergence of two of the most original of men and one of the most fascinating of places. With the approach of the centennial anniversary of the first powered flights, interest in the Wrights will be stronger than ever. Perhaps attention is also due their lesser-known Outer Banks associates, along with some of the local rumors, contrary claims, and fanciful tales that have followed in the wake of a great event.

FIRST IN FLIGHT

CHAPTER 1

1900

World's fairs now vie with one another more in their side-show or "Midway" attractions than in their true objects, and each succeeding one has to outreach its predecessors in strange and startling sensations. One of the shocks that is to be given at the Buffalo Pan-American Exposition next year is a spectacular "trip to the moon." You go aboard the airship Luna; when all is ready the cables are thrown off and you rise into the upper regions, (for so it appears to the passengers). It is night and the stars shine brightly above. . . . You see the moon, too, at first far away but gradually nearer; and at length you land on it.

Elizabeth City North Carolinian,
October 11, 1900

The State of Affairs

The good people of Elizabeth City, North Carolina, need not have looked five hundred miles to the north for a fantasy flying story. The actual chain of events had already begun just across Albemarle Sound. Wilbur and Orville Wright, camping in a tent half a mile south of Kitty Hawk, spent the day the above article appeared repairing their first man-carrying glider, damaged by a gust of wind the previous day. Wilbur had made his first glides about a week earlier, probably on October 3.

Yet no one in coastal North Carolina guessed that they were about to host one of the great achievements in an age of technological advances.

Many of those advances had made it as far as the remote place the Wright brothers chose for their experiments. Elizabeth City was a prime beneficiary. As the southern terminus of the rail route from Norfolk, Virginia, it was enjoying a prosperity brought by technology. And thanks to a new telegraph line, even citizens of the Outer Banks—who had long set a standard for isolation—could swap messages with Norfolk, and then the rest of the world, at the speed of light.

In North Carolina and elsewhere, the older citizens of that era had seen the world shrink more in their lifetimes than it had in all previous recorded history. Advances in transportation were perhaps the foremost reason why people felt a greater ability to exert control over their world than ever before. Automobiles, only about ten years old at the turn of the century, were still few and plagued by mechanical troubles. But trolleys and "safety bicycles"—a familiar subject to the Wright brothers—simplified getting around in cities. And with trains traveling at unheard-of speeds of sixty to seventy miles per hour, and with five-hundred-foot floating palaces making swift, safe, regular passage across the ocean, it was possible to travel halfway around the world in a week and a half.

Advances like these came into popular use before the memory of traveling by horse over washboard roads had begun to fade. People were prepared to believe anything was possible.

Anything except human flight, that is. John Trowbridge captured the sentiment of the era in a well-traveled poem called "Darius Green and His Flying Machine." The poem describes a country bumpkin who uses thimble and thread, a bellows, umbrellas, and "a hundred other things" to build a contraption for flying. On the Fourth of July, he hurls himself from a window and, predictably enough, falls in a heap in the barnyard, amid the straw and chaff "and much that wasn't so sweet by half."

The name Darius Green was recognized by reading people all over the country. The poem probably struck such a chord because it contained an element of the familiar. Until the latter part of the nineteenth century, aeronautics was the province of barnyard engineers. Though many were talented, they were hampered by a lack of scientific data to guide their work, and they generally operated without any contact with, or knowledge of, other experimenters in the field. They stood no chance of achieving flight. It was their low status in the public eye that defined flying as a fringe pursuit, with would-be aeronauts held in about as high regard as the builders of perpetual-motion machines.

The best-known example in eastern North Carolina was James Henry Gatling, who lived near Murfreesboro, about eighty-five miles northwest of Kitty Hawk. A literal Darius Green, Gatling began as a boy in the 1820s and 1830s by observing birds and designing kites, then graduated to jumping from a barn loft holding an umbrella or wearing wings made of fodder and corn leaves. Ridicule from neighbors and even his family's slaves soon drove him to pursue his passion in secret.

As an adult, laboring in the considerable shadow of his younger brother Richard Gatling—inventor of the Gatling gun—he built a craft powered by twin, manually operated blowers that directed air at the underside of the wings, which he believed would sustain him aloft. He intended to call his machine the *Gatling Flyer*, but once he put it on public display, someone wryly christened it the *Old Turkey Buzzard*, and it was that name that stuck.

There were many things James Henry Gatling didn't know about the flight problem. He didn't know what sort of wings he needed to support the weight of his machine: how long from tip to tip, how broad from front to back, how deep from top to bottom, and what kind of curvature they should have, if any. He didn't know what wind velocity and what horsepower would be necessary to sustain him aloft. He didn't even know how many horsepower his engine delivered, or the most efficient means for using that horsepower to propel him through the air. In fact, he likely didn't know he needed to know such things.

Nonetheless, Gatling optimistically mapped himself out a mile-long course for the day in 1873 when he was to test his machine. Launched from a twelve-foot-high cotton-gin platform, the *Old Turkey Buzzard* suffered an unscheduled meeting with an oak tree at the edge of the yard. Gatling never attempted to fly again.

In fairness, it should be noted that Gatling was well ahead of most of his contemporaries. At least he built a full-scale prototype. Most independent experimenters never progressed beyond drawings and small models, yet they continued to believe they were within a hairsbreadth of a man-carrying, powered machine.

Experimenters like James Henry Gatling inhabited many parts of the map. Local newspapers sometimes printed their claims without close examination, but by and large, people recognized them for what they were—dreamers. Whatever public exposure they got tended to emphasize their folly, rather than the honest effort—and sometimes the blood—they spent in pursuit of flight.

The turning point came in the 1880s, when trained engineers began to take a serious interest in aeronautics. The principal figures in the United States were Octave Chanute and Samuel Langley.

Octave Chanute was the great benefactor of early aviation. Born in Paris in 1832, he moved to New Orleans during his boyhood years, then to New York. Chanute grew interested in engineering just as the railroad boom was opening up the West. Too impatient to learn his craft sitting in a classroom, he presented himself to a track-laying crew of the Hudson River Railroad in 1849 and offered to work for nothing. It wasn't long before he made his way onto the payroll and up the company ladder. He did his most notable work in Illinois, Missouri, and Kansas; among his major credits were the stockyards of Chicago and Kansas City and the first bridge over the Missouri River. Chanute enjoyed a stellar national reputation, his professional accomplishments and fine character receiving ample play in the newspapers.

Chanute caught the aeronautical bug in the mid-1870s, when he traveled to Europe and learned that human flight was coming to be considered a real possibility by engineers there. When Chanute thought back on his own career, he remembered times when the destruction of a bridge or the lifting off of a roof in a storm could not be accounted for by the wind velocity alone. He wanted to learn about the mechanics of lift and how it might be applied to the flight problem.

His method was not to begin experimenting immediately, but to make a thorough survey of all the serious efforts at human flight. Chanute believed that the technical problems connected with flight were so complex that they could never be solved by lone experimenters. He felt that only a cooperative effort among many scientists and engineers could achieve success. Toward that end, he began establishing contact with a variety of flight enthusiasts on both sides of the ocean. Soon, experimenters were learning of Chanute's interest and writing him for information and advice, for which he rewarded them with news of their colleagues scattered far and wide. Not only did Chanute help liberate experimenters from the isolation that had doomed them to failure, he also contributed personal finances toward the work of individuals he found particularly promising.

This portion of Chanute's career reached its peak in the early 1890s with the publication of his classic work, *Progress in Flying Machines*. The book begins with brief accounts of early experimenters like the French locksmith Besnier, whose 1678 craft consisted of a pole slung over either shoulder with a broad paddle attached at each end— four paddles in all. Besnier strove to beat his way through the air by brute force, jumping first from a chair, then a table, then a window sill, then a second story, and finally a garret, from which he succeeded in paddling over the roof of the cottage next door. Chanute soberly characterized these efforts as "short downward flights aided by gravity."

Covering everything from muscle-powered craft to the sophisticated gliders of Germany's Otto Lilienthal, *Progress in Flying Machines* tells a tale paved with good intentions but bad ideas. Thanks to Octave Chanute, prospective aeronauts now had a thorough survey of early experiments in flight and a much clearer notion of which paths showed promise and which would certainly end in failure.

It was at an 1886 conference Chanute helped organize that Samuel Langley had his first formal contact with the aeronautical community. Initially, both men were hesitant to let their interest in the subject become public knowledge. Chanute revealed his passion for flight only to his aeronautical correspondents and a few friends. Langley conducted his early experiments in aerodynamics behind a fence and referred to them as his "work in pneumatics." They both had reputations to protect. Aligning themselves with the long tradition of cranks who wanted to fly could only expose them to ridicule.

Born in 1834, Samuel Langley was one of the country's foremost astronomers. He was best known for his study of sun spots and his measurement of the heat generated by the sun.

As a scientist, Langley approached aeronautics in a different way from Octave Chanute. Rather than surveying what had previously been done in the field, he set about designing experiments to determine how much horsepower would be needed to sustain a wing in the air. Toward that end, he built what he called a "whirling table"— a long, horizontal arm mounted on a vertical pole and driven by a steam engine. When the "table" was turning at top speed, the tips of the arm attained speeds of nearly seventy miles an hour.

Langley mounted a variety of measuring instruments, wing surfaces, and stuffed birds—a buzzard, a California condor, an albatross—on the arm and set it to spinning. When his results were in, he concluded that flight was not only attainable, but that as speed increased, less and less horsepower would be needed to sustain a craft in the air. Further study into the nature of wind action led him to envision a day when airliners would be able to circle the globe, firing their engines only during times when there was no wind.

The scientific community scoffed at such notions. Langley saw that his only chance to make his ideas more palatable was to build a workable flying model.

He began tinkering with models as early as 1887, but his real work in aeronautics began in 1891. By then, Langley had been chosen secretary of the Smithsonian Institution, the highest position at the national museum. As such, he had considerable resources at his disposal, and the backstage areas at the museum were gradually transformed into aeronautical workshops. Langley served as chief designer and administrator for the project, doing none of the actual building himself.

He called his large-scale models "Aerodromes." The staff at the Smithsonian built a total of seven, the largest weighing thirty pounds and boasting a wingspan of nearly thirteen feet. Langley favored a tandem-wing design, with one set of wings behind and in the same geometric plane as with the other—like a dragonfly—and the steam engine that drove the propellers between the forward and rear wings. The launching system consisted of a twenty-foot catapult mounted on top of a houseboat floating on the Potomac River. Langley thought such a system would allow the Aerodromes a slight loss of altitude until they attained flying speed. Landing in water would also minimize damage to the craft.

The year 1896 marked the high point of aeronautics before the Wright brothers. After five years of buckling wings, faulty launches, engine troubles, and staff turnover, Langley and his assistants brought two of the Aerodromes to the houseboat on the Potomac for testing on May 6. With the great Alexander Graham Bell as a witness, the first craft sheared off a wing on launching, but the second made an astounding flight of over half a mile. After it was retrieved and allowed to dry, it was launched again and flew nearly as far. Another test was conducted in late November, one of the Aerodromes covering forty-two hundred feet at a speed of thirty miles per hour.

Samuel Langley's views on flight and his principles of aeronautical design appeared to have been vindicated, and he set his sights on building a full-scale Aerodrome that could carry human passengers.

Meanwhile, Octave Chanute was also enjoying a remarkable year. After nearly two decades of studying the flight problem, trading ideas with many of the world's top aeronauts, and inspiring numerous young men to take to the air, he was finally ready to apply his experience toward building a glider.

His master design was for a "multiplane" craft with a maximum of sixteen wings, eight of which could be stacked on either side of the fuselage. Chanute's plan allowed for the wings to be stacked either at the front or back of the craft in a variety of configurations, nearly all of which were tried: four wings in front and eight in back; two in front and eight in back; twelve in front; two in front and ten in back; and eight in front and four in back, which proved to be the best arrangement. Each of the six-foot wings was mounted on a spring that allowed it to rotate slightly in a gust of wind, giving the glider a measure of stability. With a nod to its insectlike appearance, the craft was called the *Katydid*.

Chanute's second glider, developed almost as an afterthought midway through his flight trials, was far simpler. It also proved to be the best glider in the world to that date. Planned as a triplane, it was soon converted into a biplane. Like the *Katydid*, it was a hang glider; its pilot did not fly the craft from an internal position, but hung suspended by his arms and controlled lateral movement by swinging his legs. One of its principal features was a cruciform tail designed to give slightly with the wind.

The testing site was the desolate sand dunes at the southern end

Octave Chanute (center) and the Katydid
NATIONAL AIR AND SPACE MUSEUM

Samuel Langley
NATIONAL AIR AND SPACE MUSEUM

of Lake Michigan near Miller, Indiana, thirty miles east of Chicago. Photographs show Chanute on the dunes standing in the pilot's position beneath his gliders. W. H. Williamson, author of a biographical pamphlet for the dedication of Chanute Field in Illinois in 1940, claimed Chanute made a "few flights" during the trials, his reasoning being that a man of Chanute's character would never ask other men to do something he would not do first himself. The *Chicago Tribune* took speculation to an extreme in its obituary of Chanute: "In making 2000 flights long before the Wrights or any of the other heroes of the present day began their experiments, Mr. Chanute escaped without a serious accident."

That was not much of an accomplishment, since Chanute likely witnessed all those flights from a safe distance. He was sixty-five years old in 1896, and the consensus today is that he never flew in the Indiana dunes or anywhere else, but only posed for a few pictures.

The first set of trials took place in June and July of 1896. Augustus Herring, Chanute's chief assistant and builder, achieved a best glide of a modest eighty-two feet in the *Katydid*.

The second trials, in late August and early September, were far more encouraging, the new biplane assuming the leading role. Herring and another young pilot made numerous well-controlled glides over 200 feet, the longest extending 359 feet. During the 2,000 glides that summer—the rough total for all the pilots in attendance—the greatest mishap occurred when Chanute's son Charles split the seat of his pants. It was a safety record of which Chanute was justly proud.

To flight enthusiasts, it seemed that the age of Darius Green was past. The flight problem was being systematically attacked by trained scientists and engineers, and there was a sense that a major breakthrough was immediately at hand.

That breakthrough never came.

Samuel Langley believed he was only a couple of years from a man-carrying Aerodrome, but he soon discovered that the task was far more complicated than simply scaling-up the design of his model craft. His efforts consumed seven years and vast sums of money. He made his final effort at powered flight the same month the Wright brothers made their historic attempts—December 1903. His venture into aeronautics ultimately brought him the kind of ridicule he'd been wary of from the start, damaging his reputation in the scientific community and his position of public trust as head of the Smithsonian.

Octave Chanute's interpretation of his glider trials was a mixed bag. On one hand, he understood the flight problem well enough to recognize that neither he nor anyone else was close to developing a powered craft. On the other hand, his further aeronautical research contradicted the evidence he'd seen with his own eyes: he focused on variations of the *Katydid*, to the neglect of his highly successful biplane. The trials in the Indiana dunes were the high point of his career in flight.

After the brief promise of 1896, the prospects for flight were as dim as ever.

Unlike many inventions of the Industrial Age, glider construction was not technology-dependent, requiring only inexpensive materials that had been available for centuries. Yet despite a wide variety of experiments, little progress had been made since Leonardo da Vinci.

Though early experimenters were important in laying the ground-work for flight, the fact remains that when the Wright brothers came to Kitty Hawk, they had few positive examples to guide them in a field where defeat was the norm.

The Wrights

There are few points in the story of the Wright brothers that have not been the subject of competing claims and fanciful tales. In some tellings, Wilbur can't even get off the train and set foot on North Carolina soil for the first time without becoming the subject of rumor.

His trunks packed with the pieces of the brothers' first man-carrying glider, Wilbur left home in Dayton, Ohio, on Thursday, September 6, 1900, and laid over in Norfolk, Virginia, Friday night. Late Saturday afternoon, he boarded a train for the last overland leg of his journey, which took him through the Dismal Swamp to Elizabeth City.

According to Outer Banks writer Milford Ballance, he happened to find himself sitting across the aisle from a lovely young girl named Nell Cropsey. A little over a year later, "Beautiful Nell" made national headlines when she turned up missing from her home under suspicious circumstances. She was found in the Pasquotank River six weeks later, most likely the victim of murder at the hands of her boyfriend, Jim Wilcox. Nell Cropsey's murder had a lasting effect on local people, who endured weeks of tension during which the river was dragged and cannons were fired along shore in an effort to shake her body loose from the depths. But it is unlikely in the extreme that her life really intersected Wilbur Wright's.

Actually, rumors about the Wright brothers in North Carolina go back even farther than that. In 1889, precocious fourteen-year-old farm boy John Maynard Smith of Belhaven, seventy miles southwest of Kitty Hawk, invented a model airplane powered by a clock motor and a tractor propeller—one mounted in front of the wings. Within four years, Smith's model made it as far as President Grover Cleveland, who, unfortunately, was less than impressed, disparaging the craft on the grounds that "any fool knows that if you put a propeller on the front of a ship, it would push a ship backwards."

One afternoon in 1897, two strangers stopped unexpectedly at the Smiths' home and were invited to stay the night. After dinner, the model airplane was brought in from the barn and demonstrated in the living room. The strangers departed early the next morning, stealing the model and John Maynard Smith's drawings.

Once the Wright brothers achieved powered flight at Kill Devil Hills, some of the citizens of Belhaven thought back to the airplane theft of 1897 and came up with a pair of suspects: agents of the Wrights, or even Wilbur and Orville themselves.

John Maynard Smith and the people of Belhaven had little to worry about from Wilbur and Orville Wright in 1897. To that date, the brothers' interest in aeronautics had not developed beyond browsing the family bookshelves and the local library. It was the height of the bicycle boom. Just the previous year, the Wrights had graduated from selling and repairing a variety of bicycle makes to custom-building their own line.

When they entered the field, the bicycle was seen as one of the great inventions of the nineteenth century. Bicycles were liberating. They were fast, reliable, exciting, and relatively inexpensive. But the bicycle business was also highly competitive; at one point, there were three other shops within two blocks of the Wrights' establishment. And the brothers may have sensed that they were partaking of a kind of intermediate technology. Bicycles set travelers free from their dependence on horses, but their potential could not rival that of the automobile. Wilbur was among those who poked fun at the first cars that rattled around Dayton, Ohio, but the future was at hand.

Yet if the Wrights were dissatisfied with what was outwardly a

Orville and Wilbur Wright
LIBRARY OF CONGRESS

productive life, the real reason was personal. Wilbur in particular had some inkling of his talent, and at age thirty, he was squandering it on a machine already perfected by others. He was a man in search of a great problem to solve.

Wilbur was born near Millville, Indiana, on April 16, 1867, Orville in the family's longtime home at 7 Hawthorn Street in Dayton on August 19, 1871.

Over the years, their personalities have merged in the public consciousness to such an extent that they are often seen as a single entity. In *Six Great Inventors*, for example, author James G. Crowther flatly refuses to draw any distinction between the two: "For the purpose of this book, the Wright brothers have been regarded as one composite inventive personality. Their achievement was the result of mutual inspiration and discussion, and their respective contributions cannot be separated."

This attitude was sanctioned by Wilbur himself, who once claimed that from the time they were children, he and Orville "lived together, played together, worked together, and, in fact, thought together. We usually owned all of our toys in common, talked over our thoughts and aspirations so that nearly everything that was done in our lives has been the result of conversations, suggestions, and discussions between us."

But according to Wright biographer Tom Crouch, such a partnership may have been more a conscious decision than a natural development. The Wrights often squabbled during their early business dealings, with one or the other brother feeling he was saddled with an unfair share of the work or was receiving too little credit for his efforts. It was mainly to avoid ill feelings resulting from their work with gliders that they resolved to blur the distinctions between them and present all their ideas as joint conceptions. This attitude grew on them to the point that they even signed their checks "Wright

Brothers," with a simple "W. W." or "O. W." the only indication of the signer.

Differences between the two are not difficult to find.

Wilbur was older, balder, and a more avid correspondent. He was the more visionary of the two. As their father, Milton Wright, put it when he learned that Wilbur and Orville had ascended in a balloon together at the height of their fame, "Wilbur ought to keep out of all balloon rides. Success seems to hang on him." But Wilbur was also prone to depression. One of the defining incidents of his life came in his late teens, when he was inadvertently clubbed in the face while playing a hockey-type game with neighborhood boys. His injuries drove him into a three-year-long withdrawal from friends and family. Aside from the risks he later took in his flight experiments, he seems to have considered himself a kind of invalid-in-waiting from that point. Worn down by lawsuits and stricken with typhoid at age forty-five, he died rather easily.

Orville was probably closer to his younger sister, Katharine, than he was to Wilbur. He was more shy than Wilbur, but also more of a prankster. A dapper dresser, he wore a mustache and had a touch of vanity. Disliking the suntanned look he acquired on the Outer Banks, he would adjourn to the bathroom with a lemon every morning upon getting back to Dayton and set to rubbing his face with its juice, with the result that his skin returned to its normal paleness weeks before Wilbur's. Though younger than Wilbur, Orville was the leader in their printing and newspaper-publishing ventures before they turned to bicycles.

Building gliders was initially Wilbur's dream, but some of their breakthrough ideas were Orville's. And since Orville outlived Wilbur by over thirty-five years, he was the one who stayed in the public's mind as the patriarch of aviation through the first half of the twentieth century.

It isn't known exactly why the Wrights took to the flight problem. They experienced no epiphany. Their interest developed slowly over a period of twenty years.

They received their introduction to aeronautics in 1878, when their father, a bishop in the United Brethren Church, bought them a rubber-band-powered helicopter toy during one of his many trips. Designed by French aeronautical pioneer Alphonse Pénaud, such toys could rise to a height of nearly fifty feet or hover for almost half a minute. Fascinated, eleven-year-old Wilbur and seven-year-old Orville fashioned successful small-size copies, but failed when they tried to scale-up their design.

When he was in his early teens, Orville built kites and sold them to friends. This short-lived venture was only one of a number of youthful entrepreneurial schemes.

A more important influence came in the great aeronautical year of 1896. Sandwiched between the reports of Samuel Langley's Aerodrome tests on the Potomac and Octave Chanute's glides in the Indiana dunes came news that the great German Otto Lilienthal had died in a glider crash.

It is unknown how taken the Wrights were with Langley and Chanute at that date, but like many others of their generation, they had followed news accounts of Lilienthal's exploits with relish. From 1891 until his death, Lilienthal made about two thousand glides in the Rhinow Mountains north of Berlin in a number of batlike, birdlike, and biplane hang gliders. These glides routinely stretched into the hundreds of feet. He was without question the world's preeminent glider designer and pilot.

To the many people who pinned their hopes for the future of aeronautics on Lilienthal, his death hit hard. Orville Wright was himself severely ill with typhoid at the time, and Wilbur withheld the news of Lilienthal's passing until he judged his brother strong enough to take it. The German's tragic accident got Wilbur thinking seriously about the flight problem for the first time, but in the short term, it didn't inspire him to do anything more momentous than adjourn to the family library to examine Etienne Jules Marey's *Animal Mechanism*, a book covering bird flight that he had already read several times.

His own ambitions took shape slowly over the next two and a half years. By late May 1899, Wilbur was ready for more in-depth information than the public library in Dayton could provide. Sounding like a believer in Octave Chanute's theory of cooperative experimentation, he wrote Samuel Langley's Smithsonian for its recommendations on reading material. It was his first communication on the subject of flight:

> I am about to begin a systematic study of the subject in preparation for practical work to which I expect to devote what time I can spare from my regular business. I wish to obtain such papers as the Smithsonian Institution has published on the subject, and if possible a list of other works in print in the English language. I am an enthusiast, but not a crank in the sense that I have some pet theories as to the proper construction of a flying machine. I wish to avail myself of all that is already known and then if possible to add my mite to help on the future worker who will attain final success.

Richard Rathbun, the assistant secretary of the Smithsonian, responded by sending a handful of pamphlets and a list of other publications. Within a few weeks, Wilbur was already on the verge of contributing more than a "mite" of knowledge to the field.

At the most basic level, three things were necessary to achieve powered flight: wings that generated sufficient lift, a light yet powerful motor, and a control system. Different experimenters approached the problem with different orientations. Otto Lilienthal, who compiled extensive tables showing the lifting capacity of various wing surfaces, considered lift the primary element. Samuel Langley, who oversaw the construction of one of the most sophisticated lightweight engines in the world for his full-sized Aerodrome, thought the power plant was foremost. Wilbur Wright put the emphasis on a control system. With access to the important but flawed work of Lilienthal, he also mistakenly believed that the lift part of the equation had been solved.

Designing a control system for an airplane presented a puzzling problem. Here, for the first time, was a machine that had to be controlled in three axes of motion: the yaw axis, in which the nose of the airplane turns left or right; the pitch axis, in which the nose moves up or down; and the roll axis, in which one wing banks higher than the other. Every experimenter understood the necessity of turning left and right and moving up and down, but roll was something new—and, in the popular view, something to be avoided. When early aeronauts experienced the sensation of having a gust of wind push one wing higher than the other, they felt dangerously out of control. To combat the problem, they built their wings in a "dihedral" configuration, meaning that they sloped upward toward their tips in a kind of flattened V. This had the effect of making the craft stable; if one wing started to rise higher than the other, the wind tended to push it back down. But it also meant that such craft were limited to broad, flat turns, like those of a boat.

Wilbur Wright had seen how birds banked in turning. As a bicycle builder and rider, he had also noted how cyclists naturally leaned into a turn. Now, in applying his observations to the flight problem, he was the first to understand the advantage in maneuverability that could be had by initiating a roll.

One day in July 1899, while working in the bicycle shop, he began idly manipulating an empty inner-tube box in his hands. He suddenly saw how, with a simple twist, the opposite ends of the box could be presented at different angles to the wind: here was a way to control an airplane in the roll axis. If, for example, the right wing were to be angled above the horizontal and the left wing below the horizontal, the right wing would rise, initiating a left-hand turn. Wilbur was still three years from understanding the importance of rudder controls in turning, but his breakthrough with the inner-tube box was the basis for tightly banked airplane turns. The Wrights' method of presenting their wings at different angles to the wind came to be known as "wing warping." The principle behind it was not entirely new. Other experimenters had considered presenting the wings at different angles, but mainly as a means of correcting for roll and restoring a straight-and-level course. Wilbur thought in more aggressive terms.

That same month, he and Orville set about building a biplane kite that bore a basic similarity to the craft they would construct through most of their career. It had a five-foot wingspan and was wired so that the wings could be warped, or twisted, by means of levers the Wrights operated on the ground. When they tested it, with ten or twelve local schoolboys as witnesses, the kite banked left and right just as they had envisioned.

Now ready to try a man-carrying kite, the Wrights needed a place with the kind of stiff, reliable winds the Dayton area did not offer. On November 27, 1899, Wilbur wrote the United States Weather Bureau asking for information on wind velocities in the Chicago area.

With his reply of December 4, Willis Moore, the head of the Weather Bureau, went one better than that. He sent a couple of copies of the *Monthly Weather Review*, which included tables of average hourly wind velocities at all the weather stations in the country. This was the means by which the Wrights first became aware of the existence of Kitty Hawk, North Carolina, though the place was not of immediate interest to them.

By May 1900, Wilbur was ready to approach Octave Chanute, beginning a correspondence that encompassed more than ten years and several hundred letters. His introductory statement must have seemed as striking to Chanute as it remains today: "For some years I have been afflicted with the belief that flight is possible to man. My disease has increased in severity and I feel that it will soon cost me an increased amount of money if not my life."

Despite Wilbur's protest that "the problem is too great for one man alone," the letter is a testament to the confidence and understanding he had gained through his reading. A complete unknown, he gently criticized the methods of one acknowledged master, Otto Lilienthal, to another, Chanute, and managed to do so without conceit simply because he was right. The letter also outlined Wilbur's basic design principles, stated his intention to tether his proposed man-carrying kite to a 150-foot tower, and asked "for advice as to a suitable locality where I could depend on winds of about fifteen miles per hour without rain or too inclement weather."

With Wilbur's consistent use of "I" and references to "my plan," the letter also suggests what a peripheral role Orville played in the early work.

Wilbur Wright was joining a long line of would-be aeronauts who had come to Chanute for advice. On the other hand, he had an unusual grasp of the flight problem and was self-assured without puffing himself up. Responding on May 17 with his customary courtesy, Chanute told Wilbur where he might read of other experimenters who had tried tethering their machines, but he cautioned that he himself considered the practice complicated and dangerous. As for possible testing sites, he recommended San Diego, California, and Pine Island, Florida. "These, however," he noted, "are deficient in sand hills, and perhaps even better locations can be found on the Atlantic coasts of South Carolina or Georgia."

That latter portion of the country was looking better and better.

The Chicago area offered more-than-adequate winds, but Chanute's experience with big-city media during his experiments in northern Indiana had demonstrated the need of conducting glider trials in private. California and Florida were simply too far away. But as noted in the *Monthly Weather Review*, isolated, obscure Kitty Hawk, North Carolina, had the sixth-highest average wind in the United States.

On August 3, Wilbur wrote to the Weather Bureau station at Kitty Hawk for information about local wind conditions and topography. According to an article in the *Durham Morning Herald*, Orville later claimed that an identical letter was sent to Myrtle Beach, South Carolina, but that the brothers never received a reply.

Exactly what became of the original letter to Kitty Hawk is uncertain. In the popular version, it was received by the Kitty Hawk Weather Bureau officer, Joe Dosher, who wrote a brief reply and then passed Wilbur's letter to Bill Tate. Dosher was not a native of the area, and he felt that Tate, a lifelong resident and the best-connected man in the community, could better address Wilbur's concerns.

But Dosher's reputation has taken some lumps in a couple of North Carolina accounts. According to the Durham paper, he gave Tate the withering instruction, "You answer these nuts." A latter-day article in the *Raleigh News and Observer* is even less flattering, describing how Dosher sailed Wilbur's letter into a trash basket with the comment, "It's from a couple of cranks who want to know about the weather down here. They want to fly big kites or something." Tate then rescued the letter from the ash heap of history and presumably shamed Dosher into replying.

Actually, both these accounts are dubious, with their implication that the letter came jointly from the brothers. Wilbur was writing all the flight-related correspondence at that stage.

Joe Dosher's answer was dated August 16: "In reply to yours of the 3rd, I will say the beach here is about one mile wide, clear of trees or high hills and extends for nearly sixty miles same condition. The wind blows mostly from the north and northeast September and October. . . . I am sorry to say you could not rent a house here, so you will have to bring tents. You could obtain board."

Whether passed along with Joe Dosher's blessing or pulled from a trash can, Wilbur's letter fell into the right hands when it reached local businessman, political leader, and one-man chamber of commerce Bill Tate.

According to Elmer Woodard, Jr., Bill's grandson, in a tape-recorded interview with the National Park Service in 1990, the Tate family got a foothold in Kitty Hawk in the time-honored Outer Banks fashion: Bill's father was a shipwreck victim who decided to stay and take up residence.

Born in 1869, Bill Tate did not have an easy early life. His mother died when he was eight. Three years later, in 1880, his father was on his way back to Kitty Hawk from Currituck Courthouse on the mainland when his boat capsized in rough water. He managed to lash himself to the bottom of the boat but was frozen to death by the time he drifted ashore. Bill then lived with his uncle Dan, a Kitty Hawk storekeeper, for two years before being sent to an orphanage in the North Carolina Piedmont. He later graduated from Atlantic Collegiate Institute, located in Elizabeth City.

A fisherman, a county commissioner, a notary public, and a former postmaster, Bill Tate was the definition of a self-made man. He addressed a more encouraging reply to a stranger in Dayton, Ohio, than Wilbur Wright had reason to hope for:

> You would find here nearly any type of ground you could wish; you could, for instance, get a stretch of sandy land one mile by five with a bare hill in center 80 feet high, not a tree or bush anywhere to break the evenness of the wind current. This

in my opinion would be a fine place; our winds are always steady,
generally from 10 to 20 miles velocity per hour.

. . . If you decide to try your machine here & come I will
take pleasure in doing all I can for your convenience & success &
pleasure, & I assure you you will find a hospitable people when
you come among us.

Thanks to his new and only Outer Banks friend, Wilbur was sold.
He didn't even write a reply, but simply showed up with his bags on
Tate's doorstep almost eight weeks later.

First Season

Nearly as much is known about Wilbur's trip across Albemarle
Sound in 1900 as about the Wrights' gliding experiments that year.
The brothers are noted for their meticulous organization, but
organization was sorely lacking on that first trip to the Outer Banks.

Outside of attending an exhibition in Chicago in 1893, Wilbur
and Orville had always stuck close to home. They were new to scientific experimentation and unsure of their abilities. What they expected to achieve is a bit ambiguous. In a September 3, 1900, letter
to his father, who was traveling, Wilbur announced his upcoming
venture with surprising confidence:

I am intending to start in a few days for a trip to the coast
of North Carolina in the vicinity of Roanoke Island, for the
purpose of making some experiments with a flying machine. It
is my belief that flight is possible and, while I am taking up the
investigation for pleasure rather than profit, I think there is a
slight possibility of achieving fame and fortune from it. . . . I am

certain I can reach a point much in advance of any previous workers in this field even if complete success is not attained just at present.

His tone was more sober by the time he reached the Outer Banks and came face to face with having to test his ideas in the field. He wrote his father from Kitty Hawk on September 23 that he had no "strong expectation of achieving the solution at the present time or possibly any time. My trip would be no great disappointment if I accomplish practically nothing."

The Wrights generally cast their first visit to North Carolina as a kind of sportsmen's vacation, and only secondarily as an opportunity for serious study. Even if their ideas on flight proved unworthy, they still wanted the trip to be the adventure of a lifetime.

That attitude is reflected in an error in judgment Wilbur made in his preparations. In one of his letters to Chanute, he had asked for advice on obtaining eighteen-foot-long spruce spars for his glider's wings, and Chanute had responded with the name and address of a Chicago lumberyard that could fill his order. Meanwhile, Wilbur decided to postpone action, assuming he could find exactly what he needed during his layover in Norfolk. As it turned out, sixteen-foot spars were the best he could obtain, the result being that his glider's wings were shorter and had less lifting capacity than planned. It was an oversight he never would have allowed in subsequent years.

Another oversight came in assuming he could easily obtain passage from Elizabeth City to the Outer Banks. Wilbur had sought out Kitty Hawk partly for its privacy, but he must have been surprised to discover how truly isolated it was. It took him two days to travel from western Ohio to Elizabeth City—nearly halfway across the continent—but more than twice that time to make it across Albemarle Sound to Kitty Hawk.

Bill Tate's advice on coastal passage was tortuously worded: "You

can reach here from Elizabeth City, N.C. (35 miles from here) by
boat direct from Manteo 12 miles from here by mail boat every
Mond., Wed & Friday."

But Joe Dosher's letter left no doubt: "The only way to reach
Kitty Hawk is from Manteo Roanoke Island N.C. in a small sail
boat."

Wilbur stepped off the train in Elizabeth City late in the afternoon on Saturday, September 8. Having missed the regular Friday
boat to Manteo, he made his way to the waterfront to inquire about
passage to Kitty Hawk. To his amazement, no one had heard of the
place. It was Tuesday, September 11, before he stumbled across a
ragged skiff captained by a man named Israel Perry, who offered to
take him across the water.

The Elizabeth City waterfront in the early years of the century
MUSEUM OF THE ALBEMARLE

Despite the fact that he came close to drowning one of the great men of the twentieth century, Israel Perry remains one of the most obscure figures connected with the Wright brothers' story. There are no known photographs of him or his infamous boat, the *Curlicue*. As Orville put it when he arrived on the Outer Banks that year, "Will has even rescued the name of Israel Perry, a former Kitty Hawker, from oblivion."

Where facts are lacking, fancy has filled in the gaps.

Perry had a helper on his boat, possibly a young black man. According to Wright biographer Fred Howard, a 1952 Warner Brothers movie script reincarnated this humble helper as a buxom brunette with romantic designs on Wilbur. Thankfully, that script was never brought to production.

In Milford Ballance's local re-creation, Perry rows his skiff to the dock right at Wilbur's feet, tosses up a rope for him to hold, and introduces himself rather stiffly: "I am Captain Israel Perry. And who might you be?" The real Perry was probably saltier than that.

Just after dinner on September 11, Perry and his anonymous helper loaded Wilbur's lumber and heavy trunk on the skiff and made for Perry's larger vessel, the *Curlicue*, a flat-bottomed fishing schooner anchored three miles down the Pasquotank River, which empties into Albemarle Sound. Wilbur soon saw he was in for a difficult time: the skiff was so overloaded that it dipped water, while the schooner was so underloaded that it was pushed backward by the headwind.

One constant was the porousness of both boats. Though the water was calm, continual bailing was necessary aboard the skiff, Wilbur chipping in with the vigor of a man saving his own life. It was with relief that he reached the anchored *Curlicue*. But his hopes never got too high. As Wilbur put it, "When I mounted the deck of the larger boat I discovered at a glance that it was in worse condition if possible than the skiff. The sails were rotten, the ropes badly worn and the rudderpost half rotted off, and the cabin so dirty and vermin-infested that I kept out of it from first to last." In fact, Wilbur preferred sleeping on the open deck to braving the cabin.

The trip started off with clear weather and a light westerly breeze, but once the *Curlicue* passed out of the Pasquotank and into the open sound, the water proved unexpectedly rough and the wind swung around south and then east, ominous changes noted by the uneasy Israel Perry. The waves picked up as darkness fell, and the bailing began anew, what with the *Curlicue* springing a leak and water washing over the bow. By eleven o'clock, the wind was blowing at gale force and the boat was being pushed dangerously toward shore. There was little choice but to run for protection up the North River, which empties into Albemarle Sound several miles east of the Pasquotank. Wilbur described what happened next:

> In a severe gust the foresail was blown loose from the boom and fluttered to leeward with a terrible roar. The boy and I finally succeeded in taking it in though it was rather dangerous work in the dark with the boat rolling so badly. . . . The mainsail also tore loose from the boom, and shook fiercely in the gale. The only chance was to make a straight run over the bar under nothing but a jib, so we took in the mainsail and let the boat swing round stern to the wind. This was a very dangerous maneuver in such a sea but was in some way accomplished without capsizing. . . . Israel had been so long a stranger to the touch of water upon his skin that it affected him very much.

It was a difficult stay on the North River, the *Curlicue* not getting under way again until Wednesday afternoon. Wilbur was by then a hungry man. In the galley, Perry prepared what Milford Ballance identifies as "some sort of hash," probably as good a guess as any. Wilbur wanted none of it. In his trunk was a jar of jelly packed for him by his sister. It was the only food he ate for two days, and a preview of the rough life he would find camping on the Outer Banks.

The *Curlicue* limped into Kitty Hawk Bay around nine o'clock Wednesday night. Given the lateness of the hour, Wilbur had to spend another night on board.

His duty discharged, Israel Perry became a longstanding subject of humor among the Wright family. One letter—now lost—that Wilbur sent home on the subject was supposedly the funniest thing he ever wrote. Since Wilbur's observations are nearly all that survive of Perry, he has gone down as a man who kept a dangerously decrepit boat and a filthy kitchen and never bathed. Taking the cue, Orville wrote jokingly of Israel Perry before he ever made his acquaintance.

In fairness to Perry, it should be noted that Wilbur was a landlubber with little knowledge of sailing on so large a body of water as Albemarle Sound. Having to bail sound boats was more a matter of course than a harbinger of doom. As for Perry's boatmanship, he proved he could handle his craft under extreme conditions. As for his personal hygiene, the main local water supply came from cisterns, and Outer Banks residents sometimes found themselves having to dispense with the niceties due to water shortage toward the end of a long summer, as when Wilbur arrived. But perhaps the most telling thing to be said in Perry's behalf, Wilbur's written record notwithstanding, is that the Wright brothers crossed the sound aboard the *Curlicue* again.

Wilbur finally set foot on Outer Banks soil Thursday morning, nearly a full week after he'd left Ohio. He was greeted by Elijah Baum, a boy of fourteen or fifteen who was supposedly amusing himself by sailing model boats in Kitty Hawk Bay. Baum lived in a frame house overlooking the bay. In contrast to the heavy oceanfront development at Kitty Hawk today, the village was spread out along the sound side at the turn of the century.

Learning that Wilbur was headed to Bill Tate's house, located about a mile inland, Baum took him there. "He offered to pay me for showing him how to reach Captain Tate's home, but I wouldn't take the money," Baum recalled years later. "We did not charge people for doing favors like that when I was a boy."

Formally dressed as always, Wilbur greeted the surprised Bill Tate in typically formal fashion. Tate described the meeting this way: "I answered a knock at the door of my humble domicile, and found a neighbor's boy, Elijah W. Baum, and a strange gentleman who took off his cap and introduced himself as Wilbur Wright of Dayton, Ohio, 'To whom you wrote concerning this section'."

Invited inside, Wilbur told Tate about his difficult journey from Elizabeth City—how his back hurt from sleeping on deck, how his arms and shoulders ached from hugging the sorry sides of the *Curlicue*, and how he had gone nearly without food for two days. "This last statement," Tate later noted,

called for action. To me the account of the trip was of small moment. In my mind it was a lesson in a mode of travel that a stranger needed to harden him up for a vacation on the coast; but to have a stranger within your gates who had been without food for 48 hours was a horse of another color. It being the breakfast hour, about 9:30 A.M., a hasty fire was made in the kitchen stove. Mrs. Tate got busy—the aroma of ham and eggs was soon permeating the house, a meal soon made ready. Mr. Wright was seated and done a he-man's part by that humble breakfast. I didn't ask him if he enjoyed it—that question would have been superfluous. Actions speak louder than words, you know.

After his meal, Wilbur asked if he could board with the Tates. As he had not been expecting company, Bill adjourned to another room to talk with his wife, Addie, his successor as the local postmaster.

With just two upstairs bedrooms in the home at that time—a third was later added over the kitchen—all four Tates would have to share a single room. Addie expressed concern over whether Wilbur would be satisfied with what the family could provide.

As Bill recalled it, Wilbur overheard the conversation, came to the door, and made his case, again in rather formal terms: "I should not expect you to revolutionize your domestic system to suit me, but I should be considerate enough to subordinate myself to your system so as not to entail any extra hardship on you."

He followed with a translation: "I'll be satisfied to live as you live."

The Tates were won over.

Wilbur had only one request. Having seen Orville nearly die of typhoid, and having heard cautionary tales from his father, who trav-

Bill and Addie Tate (seated), their two daughters, and an unidentified woman on the porch of the Tate home, which doubled as the local post office

eled a great deal on church business, he was concerned about the quality of drinking water in strange locales. Tate showed him the family's well "very reluctantly," by his own admission. Sure enough, the fastidious Wilbur found it lacking. He asked that the Tates boil a gallon of water for him each morning and put it in a pitcher in his room.

Wilbur had found an excellent friend in Bill Tate, who once described turn-of-the-century Outer Banks people this way: "Denied the advantages of good schools, subsisting upon the fruits of a battle with the sea, having little or no transportation, and being out of touch with the outside world, the average man had become immune to the fact that there was anything new."

More to the point, he offered this opinion on the subject of flying: "At the time the Wrights arrived in our community, we were set in our ways. We believed in a good God, a bad Devil, and a hot Hell, and more than anything else we believed that the same good God did not intend man should ever fly."

Had he been less modest, Tate would have exempted himself from his statement. He listened carefully to what the Wrights had to say and saw merit in their ideas. Before that first season was over, he was a believer. As Orville put it, Tate wanted "to spend his remaining days—which may be few—in experimenting with flying machines. . . . Tate can't afford to shirk his work to fool around with us, so he attempts to do a day's work in two or three hours so that he can spend the balance with us and the machine."

That enthusiasm never faded. Tate maintained a lifelong friendship with Orville after Wilbur's death, exchanging correspondence and visits for over forty years. Having invited the Wright brothers to Kitty Hawk and nurtured them during their early experiments, he is one of the legitimate heroes of their story.

Fittingly enough, the Tates' front yard was the site where the Wrights' first full-size glider was assembled, under a canvas shelter erected for protection from the elements. Addie Tate donated her sewing machine to the cause; Wilbur needed it to restitch the French sateen wing coverings, which had to be modified because of his inability to obtain eighteen-foot spars in Norfolk. Addie did some of the sewing herself, though she once admitted the Wrights "didn't need much help. Both Orville and Wilbur were as good a seamstress as I am."

Wilbur was nearly done with the glider by the time his brother arrived.

Orville left Dayton on Monday, September 24, and arrived in Kitty Hawk on Friday, cutting more than two days off Wilbur's travel time. He brought camping equipment—cots, blankets, an acetylene lamp—along with such items as coffee, tea, and sugar, which Wilbur had informed him were unavailable in Kitty Hawk.

Both of the Wrights boarded with the Tates until October 4, at which time they pitched a tent in the sand about half a mile to the south, tying one end of it to a scraggly oak tree so it wouldn't blow

The Wrights' tent on the sand near Kitty Hawk
LIBRARY OF CONGRESS

away. They took a couple of pictures of this forlorn camp, among the first scenes in their classic visual testimony of their life and experiments on the Outer Banks.

A photographic record was important to the Wrights from the start. Not long before they began their aeronautical experiments, they purchased their first camera. Notoriously frugal in building everything from printing presses to gliders, they chose one of the best, most expensive cameras on the market: a Korona-V, made by Ernst Gundlach, a German immigrant. At a price of eighty-five dollars, it cost nearly six times as much as their original man-carrying glider. It was worth the price. The airplane was the first major invention whose development was fully documented on film. And the Wrights' camera was perhaps the only one on the Outer Banks in 1900.

In typically meticulous fashion, they kept a written record of each picture's f-stop, date, subject, and type of plate. All the same, the photographs they took that first season suggest that their commitment to the flight problem was less than wholehearted. Young men on a vacation, they took pictures of Kitty Hawk, Kitty Hawk Bay, Kill Devil Hills, the Tates, the Kitty Hawk Lifesaving Station, the men who staffed it—but only three of their glider, none of which shows it manned. And one of the three is a view of the craft after it was wrecked by the wind on October 10.

So, too, is the record of their flight tests from 1900 incomplete. The glider was flown as an unmanned kite during most of the trials. No one knows for certain what day it first went aloft, though it was most likely the day before they left the Tates'. The number of free glides is also unknown. The Wrights estimated Wilbur spent a total of about two minutes in the air in that capacity.

Once Orville arrived, Wilbur left most of the chronicling of life on the Outer Banks to his younger brother. Though Orville often

The crew of the Kitty Hawk Lifesaving Station in 1900.
As identified at Wright Brothers National Memorial, they are, from left,
Robert Griggs; Robert Sanderlin; Thomas Hines; Joseph Baum;
keeper S. J. Payne, who watched the powered flights of December 17, 1903,
through a spyglass; James Best; and Thomas Sanderlin.
LIBRARY OF CONGRESS

said he disliked writing, readers have long enjoyed his letters from Kitty Hawk. A city boy whose adventures had always taken place within a few miles of home, he liked to entertain his sister with tales of how hard-bitten he and Wilbur were, roughing it in the dunes. He wrote of trying to sleep in freezing conditions, of going to bed without knowing whether their thin tent would be picked up and carried away by the wind during the night, and them with it. He wrote of rations so poor that eating condensed milk off a spoon was a good dessert.

In Orville's estimation, the Wrights' pantry at home "in its most depleted state would be a mammoth affair compared with our Kitty Hawk stores. Our camp alone exhausts the output of all the henneries within a mile. What little canned goods, such as corn, etc., is of such a nature that only a Kitty Hawker could down it."

As for the livestock that roamed freely through the marshes, he noted that "the poor cows have such a hard time scraping up a living that they don't have any time for making milk. You never saw such poor pitiful-looking creatures as the horses, hogs and cows are down here. The only things that thrive and grow fat are bedbugs, mosquitoes, and wood ticks."

The Wrights understood the Outer Banks as a land of poverty amid plenty, remarking on the residents' wishful attempts at making beans, corn, and turnips grow from the sand, while simultaneously marveling at the woods filled with game, the eagles, buzzards, and sea gulls so abundant in the sky that Wilbur grew sick of watching them, and the fish "so thick you see dozens of them whenever you look down in the water."

That last fact told a great deal about the local state of affairs: the Wrights found that in Kitty Hawk, a fishing village, there were no fish they could buy. "It is just like in the north," Orville wrote, "where our carpenters never have their houses completed, nor the painters their houses painted; the fisherman never has any fish."

Or perhaps it said something about the local tradition of self-reliance. If the Wright brothers wanted fish, they could catch them themselves. And so they did.

Wilbur quickly understood how far Kitty Hawk existed outside the mainstream. He wrote his father a description of Bill Tate's house, noting that while it was the best in town, it was unpainted, unplastered, and unvarnished, and had sparse furnishings, no carpets, and no pictures. Nonetheless, he came to the conclusion that there was no real suffering among the Tates or anyone else in the area. As Orville once put it, the residents of Kitty Hawk "never had anything good in their lives, and consequently are satisfied with what they have."

In some obvious ways, the Wrights remained unaffected by the local environment. Regardless of the weather, they wore suits and stiff collars. And as they had promised their father, they did not experiment on Sundays, even when the weather was favorable.

But they were much less set in their ways than is generally believed. These were men who, at home in Dayton, had once taken the front wheels from two high-wheel bicycles and used them in an oversized tandem, which they rode through the streets together to the amusement of townspeople. At various times on the Outer Banks, they rigged a balloon-tire bicycle to carry them effortlessly across the dunes, washed their dishes with sand, hunted mice indoors with guns, and ran up and down the beach flapping their arms in imitation of the birds.

The first day they tested their 1900 craft, they intended only to fly it as an unmanned kite, but it wasn't long before Wilbur felt the urge to climb aboard. On the beach near the Kitty Hawk Lifesaving Station, he apparently flew for a matter of minutes, Orville and Bill Tate holding lines that kept him a few feet off the ground. Orville and Tate then played out the lines, and Wilbur attained a height of perhaps fifteen feet before the craft began to bob. According to Orville, Wilbur brought the session to an abrupt end with his first utterance on the experience of flight: "Let me down!" They then returned to unmanned tests.

Notwithstanding a suggestion in one of Orville's letters that "we"— both he and Wilbur—flew aboard the glider that first day of testing, it is generally believed that Wilbur did all the flying in 1900, as well as in 1901. If that is true, the reason is not immediately clear. The Wrights were close in size, so a difference in weight is not the explanation. Perhaps Wilbur still considered the project primarily his; in fact, he continued to write nearly all the technical correspondence related to flight for years.

But even if he was an adjunct member of the partnership initially, Orville quickly grew beyond that. At one point that season, after a

The 1900 glider being flown as a kite

day spent tinkering with the position of the glider's elevator, he wrote his sister that "Will was so mixed up he couldn't even theorize. It has been with considerable effort that I have succeeded in keeping him in the flying business at all." Wilbur got the Wrights started on the flight problem, but Orville in many ways sustained the effort.

The Wrights' gliders from 1900 and 1901 are easy to identify in photographs. The wings had a broad chord—the distance from the front edge to the back edge—giving them a short, stubby look. Those early gliders also had no tail. More accurately, they had half a tail—the horizontal portion, the elevator, which directed the craft up or down—but it was positioned in front of the glider, not behind.

The short wing spars left the Wrights with 165 square feet of wing area, rather than the planned 200 square feet, which meant that they needed a wind of nearly 25 miles per hour to sustain the craft with a 150-pound man aboard.

A light wind was blowing during their second day of trials—date unknown—so they were restricted to kiting the craft once more. Wilbur wasn't prepared to go airborne without further unmanned tests anyway.

That day, in one of the first instances of what was to become a trademark—the careful gathering of data on the forces acting on their gliders—they loaded the craft with chains of different weights and rigged a fish scale to measure the air resistance under a variety of wind speeds, as determined by a hand-held wind gauge loaned to them by Joe Dosher at the Weather Bureau station. Though the Wrights' information-gathering procedures always retained a home-built character, their results were invariably more accurate than those of their predecessors, one of the main keys to their success.

Their third day of testing was Wednesday, October 10. They spent the morning kiting the glider in thirty-mile-per-hour winds but in the afternoon moved to a small dune south of Kitty Hawk and erected a derrick. It was a humble affair compared with the 150-foot model Wilbur had proposed in his first letter to Octave Chanute.

They made just one test with the glider tethered to the derrick, during which the craft rose to a height of about twenty feet. While they had the craft on the ground making adjustments, a gust of wind lifted it and threw it twenty feet across the sand, breaking a number of wires, ribs, and struts. The Wrights carried the shattered machine back to camp.

Their disappointment ran deeper than just the accident of October 10. Progress was proving extremely slow. Operating the wing warping and the elevator in tandem proved so difficult that they reconciled themselves to trying to master the elevator alone.

And their wings were not producing nearly the lift that Otto Lilienthal's tables said they should. Though the process was not completely understood at the time, a wing generates lift because the wind moving over its curved upper surface travels faster than the wind moving over its flat lower surface. The slower-moving air has a greater pressure than the faster-moving air; in rising, a wing is moving toward the area of less pressure.

But simply perceiving that a curved wing generates lift did not solve the problem for glider designers. Lifting efficiency varies according to a wing's chord, its camber (the ratio of its thickness to its chord), the placement of its thickest point, its span (the distance from tip to tip), the shape of its leading edge, and other factors.

Otto Lilienthal was the man who had taken the fledgling science of wing design farther than anyone. The Wrights' problems with lift were partly of their own making, as they had built their wings with a flatter curvature than that recommended by Lilienthal. But still, the tables suggested that they should have been able to maintain their craft in the air with its wings angled just three degrees above the horizontal; in practice, they found the actual angle to be a whopping twenty degrees, a major discrepancy.

Their lack of success with the derrick was another blow. Otto Lilienthal, history's greatest aeronaut to that date, had spent five full years accumulating a scant five hours in the air, and had died in the process. Tethering their manned glider to a derrick was to have been the Wrights' means of spending hours, rather than seconds, in the air, an infinitely better opportunity for working out the problems of control. But as Octave Chanute had warned, the practice was patently dangerous; without forward progress to help sustain it in the air, the craft would crash immediately should the wind die. Like Lilienthal, the Wrights would have to amass flight time second by second.

In mid-October, they received word from their sister that she had found it necessary to dismiss the man they had left tending their bicycle shop. Concerned about the state of their business—Wilbur had been absent since September 6—the Wrights decided to make a couple of last attempts at meaningful progress and return home.

On Thursday, October 18, they headed for some steep dunes a mile from camp, intending to try their first free glides. Their craft would produce more lift moving forward into the wind than tethered to the ground by ropes, meaning that it would support a man in a lighter breeze. However, by the time they reached their destination, the wind was blowing at only ten miles per hour. Not wanting to waste the trip, they spent the day tossing the glider from the dunes and carefully observing its progress until it would, in Orville's words, "whack the side of the hill with terrific force." They then patched the damage and carried the craft back up for another throw. Though the glider took a beating, they were pleased with its durability.

Their last day of testing—it may have been either October 19 or 20—salvaged the entire season. For the first time, they made the four-mile trip south to Kill Devil Hills, most likely with the aid of a horse and cart procured by Bill Tate, who accompanied them. Though only seven or eight miles above the resort of Nags Head, Kill Devil Hills was isolated from vacationers in those days, as was Kitty Hawk. All local traffic passed east and west between Manteo and Nags Head, with few beachcombers making it as far as Kill Devil Hills.

The Wrights liked the high dunes at Kill Devil Hills so well that they never flew again at Kitty Hawk. Standing at either wingtip, Orville and Bill Tate started the glider down the slope of one of the big dunes and ran with it, holding the wings level until they could no longer keep pace. Though many aeronauts considered it suicidal, Wilbur lay prone, a position the Wrights chose because the pilot's air resistance was only half that of a man sitting upright; in practice, it proved safe for landing in the sand. The elevator control worked perfectly. Wilbur was able to maintain the craft about five feet above the sand until he brought it smoothly back to earth.

Though they didn't record the exact length of the glides that day, they later estimated that Wilbur's last efforts stretched three to four hundred feet. Few men had ever flown farther. And with the pilot controlling the craft from an internal position—controlling it by using his brain, rather than by swinging his legs—they were already moving beyond their forerunners.

The Wrights were entirely unsentimental about their early gliders. They had gotten their use out of the 1900 craft, and they knew they could design a better one next time. When the day was done, Bill Tate expressed interest in the patched-up craft, and they told him he could have it.

Addie Tate later made the trip to the glider's resting place with her pair of scissors. Using the same sewing machine Wilbur had borrowed to stitch the French sateen into wing coverings, she fashioned it into dresses for her daughters, Irene and Pauline, ages four and three.

The Outer Banks had left a mark on the Wright brothers, but the Wright brothers had not yet left much of a mark on the Outer Banks. When the Kitty Hawkers came "peering around the edge of the woods and out of their upstairs windows," as Orville put it, it was not to watch the Wrights' experiments but to see whether their miserable camp had survived the latest storm. Local residents were more interested in the Wrights' camp stove—fueled by what is believed to have been the first gasoline ever brought to the Outer Banks—than in their glider.

Except for the Tate family, that is. The bond established between the Wright brothers and the Tates that year grew through three generations.

Though never a pilot, Bill Tate in later years became a member of the National Aeronautic Association. During the time he worked as a lighthouse keeper, he printed business cards saying he was the "Original N.C. Aviation Booster" and the "First Lighthouse Employee to Inspect Navigational Aids by Air." He organized the first American monument to the Wright brothers, a replica of which still stands in what was once his front yard. A fixture at commemorative ceremonies honoring the Wrights, he introduced Amelia Earhart on the day the cornerstone was laid for the national memorial at Kill Devil Hills.

His nephew Tom Tate did even better than that. Sometime after Wilbur's aborted attempt at flying the glider as a manned kite that first season, when his plans for tethering the craft and accumulating hours of practice were falling apart, the Wrights hit upon the idea of sending ten-year-old, seventy-pound Tom aloft. Different dates have been offered for Tom's ascents. It was not recorded how many

times, or for how long, he went up. And of course, the Wrights
controlled the craft from the ground. It very likely flew at a height
of ten feet or less. All the same, Tom Tate experienced what only a
handful of men—and certainly no one else so young—could claim.
Orville once described him as "a small chap . . . that can tell more
big yarns than any kid of his size I ever saw." But the best story of
his life—that he flew aboard a Wright brothers glider nearly two
years before Orville Wright, the world's first heavier-than-air pilot,
ever did—was no tall tale.

Tom Tate and his fish, with part of the 1900 glider in the background

Bill Tate's half-brother Dan assisted the Wrights during three seasons on the Outer Banks, helping launch their gliders hundreds of times.

In 1908 or 1911, one of Bill's young sons followed in Tom Tate's footsteps by gliding briefly aboard a Wright craft. His other son later started a small museum to the Wrights and became a pilot.

One of Bill's daughters married a New Jersey aviator and flew over fifty thousand miles with him, many of them on trips home to see her parents in coastal North Carolina.

Though the Wright brothers didn't know a soul in North Carolina before their first visit, they made one good set of friends by the time they headed back home in 1900.

CHAPTER 2

1901

If report is to be credited, there is building on an unfrequented part of Carolina's coast an air-ship which is to put Santos Dumont's now far-famed flying machine to the blush. An Ohio inventor with two companions and fellow-workmen, it is stated, have located with their various constructive material and appliances at a quiet spot near Nags Head . . . and have been there busied for some time in the perfection of a machine with which they expect to solve the problem of aerial navigation. The utmost secrecy is being maintained in regard to the same and the aerial craft itself is kept within an enclosed structure. Scant courtesy is shown and but meagre information doled out to the few inhabitants who have been led by curiosity to this isolated spot.

Elizabeth City North Carolinian,
August 1, 1901

Mixed Reviews

Though there were four small newspapers in Elizabeth City at the turn of the century, there was no competition over the Wright brothers' story. In fact, members of the press made no attempt to contact the brothers or witness their activities on the Outer Banks until after their powered flights of 1903. Even secondhand reports were few.

Perhaps that says something about the status of aeronautics. A little hyperbole for the benefit of the townsfolk notwithstanding, it was generally understood that attempts at flying came to nothing. Idly predicting that a local experiment might put the famous Alberto Santos-Dumont "to the blush" was easy. But when it came time to allocate newsmen's time, it was unanimously agreed among the local papers that investigating such an experiment wasn't worth the trip across Albemarle Sound.

Perhaps the Wright brothers would have been a bigger drawing card if they'd conducted their experiments after the manner of Alberto Santos-Dumont. A wealthy young Brazilian living in France, the heir to a coffee fortune, Santos-Dumont cultivated an obsession with flying that was highly public. Beginning in 1898, people in and around Paris turned to the skies as he navigated a series of small dirigibles of his own design. The winner in October 1901 of one of aviation's first great prizes, awarded for flying a circuit from the outskirts of Paris around the Eiffel Tower, Santos-Dumont was the world's most famous aeronaut at the turn of the century.

For the public, captivated by the achievements of Santos-Dumont but not understanding the difference between lighter-than-air and heavier-than-air craft, the reasons for conducting experiments in private were less than obvious. It was only those who knew the limitations of dirigibles—their poor maneuverability, the degree to which they were subject to the wind, their small lifting capacity despite their great size—who understood that the race for true flight was far from won.

The "utmost secrecy" and "scant courtesy" of Wilbur and Orville Wright are taken as articles of faith among their detractors, who feel that the Wrights borrowed what they could from Octave Chanute and other believers in community effort, yet jealously tried to keep their own contributions from becoming public knowledge. Even the Wrights' simplest actions—like constructing a shelter to protect their gliders from wind, rain, and sand—have at times been given a sinister slant.

Those who actually knew them in North Carolina saw them differently. While it's true that Wilbur selected Kitty Hawk partly because of its isolation, it's equally true that the Wrights were freely visited at their camps by a number of local people, some of whom not only asked questions but also assisted in handling the gliders.

Beginning in 1901, other aeronauts began visiting the Wrights on the Outer Banks and experimenting with them. The brothers saw this as an intrusion and took a personal dislike to a couple such interlopers, but all the same, they were more than willing to discuss the flight problem at length with their peers.

The Wrights didn't issue invitations to members of the aeronautical community to come and experience life on the Outer Banks. Octave Chanute did it for them.

After the 1900 season, Wilbur wrote Chanute from Dayton informing him of the progress of his recent experiments. Chanute was sufficiently interested to want to include a mention of the Wrights in a paper he was writing and to arrange a personal visit. That visit took place in Dayton on June 26 and 27, 1901, as the brothers were preparing for their second trip to North Carolina.

Two days after the visit, Chanute wrote Wilbur asking if a protégé of his, Edward Huffaker of Chuckey City, Tennessee, could accompany the brothers to the Outer Banks to test a glider he was building. In the same letter, Chanute extended a similar request on behalf of George Spratt, a young physician from Coatesville, Pennsylvania. Chanute, too, was tentatively planning a trip to the Wrights' camp.

Chanute's stated mission was simply to provide assistance to the Wrights—assistance Wilbur and Orville didn't need or want. According to some historians, Chanute was more likely trying to re-create the kind of community of experimenters among whom he had found his greatest aeronautical success in the Indiana dunes in 1896.

Whatever Chanute's motive, there was no gracious way for the Wrights to decline his offer. They would have company on the Outer Banks that year.

The Camp

The Wrights left home on July 7 and had an uneventful trip as far as Elizabeth City, where they were detained for several days by a major storm. Its exact severity is unknown, since the local wind-measuring instruments broke at either 93 or 107 miles per hour, depending on the account from the Wrights.

That year, for easier access to the big dunes, they decided to establish a more permanent camp at Kill Devil Hills, where they arrived on July 12 after spending a night in Kitty Hawk with the Tates. They soon began building their inaugural hangar, a 25-foot-long, 16-foot-wide, 6½-foot-high affair whose ends were hinged so they could be raised and used as awnings. Constructed of materials ordered in Elizabeth City, delivered by Bill Tate, and framed by another local man, Oliver O'Neal, that simple building, later joined by a larger sister, was one of the most famous symbols of the Wrights on the Outer Banks.

In 1901, the structure served the glider only, the Wrights and their guests continuing to sleep outdoors or under a tent. Over the next couple of years, it was gradually converted to personal space. In 1902, the Wrights extended the rear of the building to create a kitchen and a living room. They also built two bunks in the rafters so they could finally get out of the elements at night; when guests arrived, they added another four bunks. In 1903, they converted a used carbide can into a combination heater and stove, supposedly the best such device in the Kitty Hawk area. They also engaged Dan Tate, Bill's half-brother, to build a second structure, which served as their main hangar, workshop, and storage facility.

Each season after 1901 began with several days of repairs on the camp. Tar paper had to be reattached to the roof and leaks patched; the ends of the original building had to be raised because sand had

From left, Octave Chanute, Orville, Edward Huffaker, and Wilbur under
the awning of the original camp building. The tent where they slept is dimly
visible to the left, behind the water pump.
LIBRARY OF CONGRESS

blown out from underneath them; pilings had to be sunk; boards
had to be replaced; a foot of sand had to be removed from the floors;
old glider parts had to be unearthed or retrieved from where they'd
fallen; field mice had to be chased out. When the Wrights were
absent for more than a year, they returned to find little intact but
the exterior walls.

There were other threats to the structure as well. Bill Tate wrote
the Wrights in Dayton one winter asking whether he could have
their 1901 building, which he apparently intended to give to a neighbor. Adam Etheridge, a lifesaver at the Kill Devil Hills station, also
wrote, asking whether he could use the buildings. Vacationers at
Nags Head stopped by in later years to pick through whatever looked
interesting. The Kill Devil Hills lifesavers appropriated the Wrights'

water pump for their own use. Indeed, pieces of the buildings and the gliders they contained came into the possession of a good number of Outer Banks people. The Wrights eventually put Adam Etheridge on a yearly retainer to keep an eye on the camp and let them know how badly deteriorated it was.

Still, the camp held together through Orville's last glider trials in 1911. The buildings were ultimately blown down and carried off by scavengers.

In his taped interview with the National Park Service, Elmer Woodard, Jr., Bill Tate's grandson, told of a day in the late 1920s when he accompanied his grandfather and Orville Wright on their attempt to authenticate the site of the first powered flights. Having ridden down the beach in a Model T Ford fitted with balloon tires, the three met with a few of the first-flight witnesses at Kill Devil Hills.

According to Woodard, the plan was to spread out and try to locate debris from the old camp—preferably the buildings, since Orville was confident he could use them to determine the exact takeoff point. The men didn't expect to find much on the flat expanse of sand. The great dunes had migrated considerably by that date, so the whole area seemed unfamiliar. But to their surprise, someone stumbled across the corner of one of the old buildings. They then discovered that some of the below-ground timbers had left brown streaks in the sand as they rotted, and thus a perfect outline of the hangar.

That was apparently the ultimate fate of the camp buildings. From the marks in the sand, Orville used a compass and his extensive notes to locate the site of the famous flights, marked by the large boulders at Wright Brothers National Memorial today.

In fact, it is well established that in November 1928, when plans for the national memorial were being finalized, Bill Tate met with witnesses Willie Dough, Adam Etheridge, and Johnny Moore to authenticate the site of the flights. But Orville Wright is not generally reckoned to have been part of any such proceedings.

The camp buildings were reincarnated in the 1950s, when the National Park Service constructed replicas on the grounds of the national memorial. The replica of the original building is identifiable by its vertical boards; the boards of the later hangar run horizontally. Unlike the originals, which were abandoned for nine or ten months of the year at best and for years at a time at worst, the replica buildings have a full-time staff to help maintain them. Still, they take a pounding from the Outer Banks weather.

In 1901, the camp was in its infancy, the Wrights' tent pitched within a couple of feet of their building, but looking considerably less forlorn than it had tied to a tree near Kitty Hawk a year earlier.

The camp kitchen as it looked in 1902

Huffaker and Spratt

In retrospect, the Wrights should not have waited until 1902 to build their bunks in the rafters. With several days of wet weather following the storm of July 1901, conditions were ideal for the breeding of mosquitoes. Indoor shelter might have afforded them modest protection from the greatest predator of the Outer Banks.

English-speaking travelers to the New World began registering their complaints about mosquitoes in the late sixteenth century. The word supposedly entered the language courtesy of the writer M. Phillips in *The Principal Navigations Voyages and Discoveries of the English Nation*, published by Richard Hakluyt in 1589. As Phillips lamented, "We were also aftertimes greatly annoyed with a kinde flie. . . . The Spanyards called them Musketas."

In Georgia, it was colonial official William Stephens, who described one of the coastal islands there as "a Place so exceedingly pestered with Musketoes, by Reason of the adjacent Marshes, that no Person would ever be fond of taking his Abode there."

In South Carolina, it was famed explorer John Lawson, who noted as he headed north from Charles Town that "although it were Winter, yet we found such Swarms of Musketoes, and other troublesome Insects, that we got but little Rest that Night."

In North Carolina in more recent times, it was the Wright brothers. If eloquence is any gauge as to depth of misery, few travelers have been as badly troubled as Wilbur and Orville and their companions in the summer of 1901.

Orville wrote that the swarm of mosquitoes "came in a mighty cloud, almost darkening the sun. . . . The sand and grass and trees and hills and everything was fairly covered with them. They chewed us clear through our underwear and socks. Lumps began swelling up all over my body like hen's eggs." Arranging nets over their cots provided little relief, since "the tops of the canopies were covered with mosquitoes till there was hardly standing room for another one; the buzzing was like the buzzing of a mighty buzz saw."

According to Wilbur, the plague that season was the worst that the oldest local inhabitants had ever witnessed. He promptly wrote Octave Chanute, due to arrive later, that he should "by all means bring with you from the North eight yards of the finest meshed mosquito bar you can find."

Fellow experimenter Edward Huffaker found the conditions "all but unendurable," noting that "the mosquitoes are so slender that they slip through the meshes and after making a meal off of us are too large to get out again and so tend to accumulate."

The mosquitoes arrived about the same time Huffaker did, on July 18. That first night, the Wrights and Huffaker tried going to

Edward Huffaker
COURTESY OF STEVEN HENSLEY

bed at five o'clock on cots under the hangar's awnings, wrapping themselves completely in blankets except for their noses. But when the twenty-mile-an-hour wind abruptly died, they judged the summer heat worse than the mosquitoes and shed their blankets, at which time they changed their minds again and decided they preferred the heat. So it went until three in the morning, when they gave up and began preparing for their workday. When morning finally arrived, the pests' persistence caused them to cancel all plans to begin assembling the Wrights' glider.

Sleeping under netting was the next plan. Orville reported how the men initially "lay there on our backs smiling at the way we had got the best of them . . . but what was our astonishment when in a few minutes we heard a terrific slap and a cry from Mr. Huffaker announcing that the enemy had gained the outer works and he was engaged in a hand-to-hand conflict with them." After wandering through the sand for several hundred feet in search of a "place of safety," they were back to sleeping under blankets in the steamy heat.

By the time George Spratt arrived from Pennsylvania on July 25, the men had graduated to dragging old tree stumps to camp from distances of up to a quarter-mile away and setting them afire to drive out the mosquitoes with smoke. Unused to the rigors of Outer Banks camping, Spratt relocated to the open air when he began choking on the smoke, but soon returned with a report that the pests were worse. He spent his first miserable night moving back and forth between the fire and the mosquitoes.

Spratt probably wouldn't have believed it at the time, but the plague was already beginning to wane.

Mosquitoes weren't the only problem in setting up camp that season. The Wrights couldn't keep their tent pegs from pulling out of the wet sand. Then they lost their drill bit when they went searching for a water source, forcing them to drink the rainwater that ran off their tent's roof, generously flavored with the soap they'd used as a mildew retardant.

But the single biggest problem, in the Wrights' view, was Edward Huffaker. It wasn't for lack of talent or credentials. Huffaker was better known in the aeronautical community at that stage than were Wilbur and Orville Wright. Rather, it was a conflict of personality.

Like the Wrights the son of a minister, Huffaker was born in Seclusion Bend, Tennessee, near Nashville, in 1856. He spent most of his life in Chuckey City, located on the Nolichucky River in the mountainous eastern part of the state between Greeneville and Jonesborough. In 1888, after graduating from nearby Emory and Henry College in southwestern Virginia with that school's top prize in mathematics, Huffaker began graduate studies at the University of Virginia. Before receiving his master's in physics, he had already published a textbook on applied mathematics. He then received an offer of a Ph.D. scholarship from Johns Hopkins University. That he was uncertain about his direction in life is obvious in the fact that he declined the scholarship on the grounds that he was tired of academic life, only to turn around shortly thereafter and accept a job teaching at a private college in Mississippi. After a year of teaching, he returned to Chuckey City to work as a civil engineer. Among his credits was the resurveying of a tract in West Virginia to correct an error George Washington made during his days as a surveyor.

Huffaker's interest in flight dated from 1891. He liked to repair to the grassy hills around Chuckey City with a transit, a stopwatch, and a notebook to observe and record the performance of soaring birds. When he desired a closer look, he simply shot the birds out of the sky with a blast from his shotgun.

From his readings in journals, his observations of wing shape during flight, and his records of birds' wingspans, wing area, and weight began to grow a theory of flight. Having noted how wing curvature created differences in air pressure, generating lift, and having noted how birds' tails were used in controlling direction, he sought to apply the same basic principles to a flying machine.

In early 1892, Huffaker began building small-scale wooden gliders and sailing them from the East Tennessee hills, mostly on idle Sunday afternoons. By July, he was experiencing considerable success.

That same year, Huffaker initiated contact with the two principal figures in American aeronautics at that time.

As Wilbur Wright would do eight years later, Huffaker wrote Octave Chanute, offering his observations on the mechanics of soaring birds, a subject dear to Chanute's heart. Impressed, Chanute honored him with a visit in March 1893, at which time he witnessed the performance of Huffaker's flying models. He liked what he saw, even going so far as to offer the young Tennessean a chance to present a paper at a major conference on aeronautics in Chicago. That well-received paper, "On Soaring Flight," was later included among the materials sent to Wilbur Wright when he wrote the Smithsonian with his historic request for reading matter on the subject of flight.

Long before Edward Huffaker came along, men had been trying to take the performance of birds, boil it down to a few basic principles, and apply those principles toward systems of human flight.

One thing that was obvious by Huffaker's day was that there was little of practical value to be gleaned from small birds. The earliest aeronautical experimenters had gravitated toward dressing themselves up as birds and beating their arms in the wind, or building ornithopters—craft that moved by flapping their wings. All such attempts ended in disappointment for a simple reason: they underestimated the strength of small birds relative to their weight, as well as their enormous generation of energy. For a man to fly by donning feathers and flapping his arms, he would need fifty times his natural strength. Even using mechanical means, there was simply no way to duplicate small birds' ability to consume approximately their body weight in food every day and convert it to usable energy.

It seemed more fruitful to study soaring birds like hawks and vultures, which remain airborne for long periods while expending little energy. Of particular interest to Huffaker was the way that birds soaring in a spiral pattern could manage to gain altitude in what appeared to be a dead calm. His paper "On Soaring Flight" put forth the argument that under certain conditions, a bird soaring in a spiral could "disturb the equilibrium" so as to create "a feeble ascending current of warm air," a kind of "natural chimney" that would gather in strength, bearing the bird upward hundreds or thousands of feet even when there was no wind. In other words, birds had the power to create their own updraft. If what Huffaker said was true, the implications for human flight were great. To bolster his argument, he cited an experiment of his own in which he had taken strands of silk, waved a fan under them—thus "disturbing the equilibrium"—and watched them rise to great heights in calm air.

In truth, students of flight never learned much more from soaring birds than they did from small birds. For example, hawks and turkey vultures—two of the soaring birds most often studied—have wingspans of five and six feet, respectively, but weigh only four and five pounds. Such facts shone little light on how to sustain a minimum two hundred pounds of man and machine in the air. As Orville Wright once put it, "Nature has never succeeded in building a large creature which could fly. I believe the Pterodactyl [sic], which was the largest, weighed only in the neighborhood of thirty pounds, and evidently was but a poor flyer."

Further, students observing the same phenomenon often came to different conclusions. Where Edward Huffaker saw a turkey vulture creating its own updrafts when there was no wind, Wilbur Wright

saw air currents hidden from the naked eye. His own pronounce-
ment on the subject was short and final: "No bird soars in a calm."

Around the same time that he established contact with Octave
Chanute, Huffaker began writing Samuel Langley in an effort to
attract the great professor to his theories on bird flight. Langley twice
rebuffed him, but in Huffaker's third letter, he made the tantalizing
claim that his theories had recently been validated in model-glider
trials. He offered to forward a paper outlining his principles.
Langley took him up on it and liked what he read. A staunchly
upright man, Langley then requested a confidential letter from
Chanute on Huffaker's morals. When Chanute testified to Huffaker's
good character, Langley promptly hired the Tennessean.

Through an association lasting several years, the fastidious Langley
always had a respect for Huffaker's abilities, though he developed
some reservations about his personal habits, as would Wilbur and
Orville Wright several years later. Huffaker's opinion of Langley, a
notoriously difficult man to work for, was less flattering.

Soon after Huffaker's arrival in Washington, Langley wanted a demonstration of one of his flying models. They climbed to the roof of
the Smithsonian, Huffaker struggling with his glider on the narrow
stairs. When they reached the top, Huffaker made his choice of direction, tossed his craft over the parapet, and watched with Langley
as it made a graceful, gradual, impressive descent stretching six hundred feet. Langley promptly put him to work designing wings for
his Aerodromes.

Their personal relationship suffered its first blow one morning when
Langley walked past Huffaker's office and saw him sitting there without coat or tie, his feet up on the desk, and using a tin can
for a spittoon.

A more important factor in their relations was the pressure under
which Huffaker was forced to work. A perfectionist, Langley some-

times gave his engineers contrary instructions, or expected them to bear responsibility for things out of their control. These conditions took their toll. Arriving at the Smithsonian in 1894, Augustus Herring, who later accompanied Octave Chanute to the Indiana dunes and the Outer Banks, described Huffaker as "considerably worried— so much so that I believe he is on the verge of nervous prostration—he cannot multiply two numbers together without making a mistake."

Huffaker once wrote enviously of another Smithsonian employee who "cursed [Langley] first in English and then he tried cursing him in French, and then ended by cursing him in German. Unfortunately, I can only swear in English, and not very proficiently at that."

All the same, Huffaker hung on long enough to witness the successful flights of Langley's model Aerodromes on the Potomac in May 1896. He even lasted well into the development of Langley's man-carrying craft. His tenure ended in 1899, when his wife, Carrie Sue, staying with family in Tennessee after the birth of their second child, contracted typhoid and died. Following the tragedy, Edward Huffaker went home to Chuckey City.

Octave Chanute remained interested in Huffaker's work. He first commissioned the Tennessean to build a biplane model with movable wings, designed to produce automatic stability. That model was tested on the windy hills around Chuckey City. Satisfied with its performance, Chanute commissioned Huffaker to build a full-scale five-wing glider in the summer of 1900, even offering to bring Huffaker to Chicago for lessons in hang gliding as the craft neared completion.

When Chanute left Dayton in June 1901 after his first meeting with the Wright brothers, he headed directly to Chuckey City in his private railroad car to check on the progress of his glider. The arrangements were nearly set for the Wrights' second visit to the Outer Banks, with Chanute, it seemed, doing a fair portion of the planning.

Chanute was disappointed with what he found in Tennessee. Huffaker's greatest strengths were in the areas of theory and design, not building. Chanute, an engineer with an eye for solid construction, was concerned about the strength of portions of the glider's frame, which were made of paper tubing, and the strength of the wings, which could be folded for ease of transportation.

Usually a kind man, Chanute criticized Huffaker's work in letters to third parties the Tennessean hadn't even met yet.

"The mechanical details and connections of the gliding machine which Mr. Huffaker has been building for me are so weak," he wrote Wilbur Wright, "that I fear they will not stand long enough to test the efficiency of the ideas in its design. . . . If you were not about to experiment I should abandon the machine without testing, but perhaps it will stand long enough to try as a kite." He would send the craft to the Outer Banks, he told Wilbur, only "if you think you can extract instruction from its failure."

Chanute also wrote to George Spratt about the quality of Huffaker's glider. "Mr. Huffaker is to join [the Wrights] with a folding gliding machine which he has been building for me," Chanute wrote Spratt. "This latter will prove a failure, in my judgment."

It seems to have slipped Chanute's mind that the paper-tube frame and folding wings—the features for which he criticized Huffaker— were built according to his own specifications.

In his last-minute instructions to Huffaker, Chanute also offered an opinion that was soon to be proven badly in error: "I do not think you will need shelter for your machine."

The Wright brothers were thus prepared for Edward Huffaker to contribute little to their camp that season, but they probably wouldn't have liked him under any circumstances. Huffaker and the Wrights could hardly have been more opposite. Huffaker was a mountain man with a first-class education but little sophistication. The Wrights were city boys with modest educations but considerable savvy. The Wrights' do-it-yourself attitude extended to such mundane tasks as preparing meals and doing the dishes, which Huffaker wanted no part of. He was more inclined to give moral lectures to Wilbur and Orville—two men who have gone down in history as models of upright character.

Huffaker couldn't understand why the Wrights dressed daily in fresh celluloid collars in a place that was nearly deserted. The Wrights couldn't understand why Huffaker wore the same ripe shirt during most of his stay, or why he borrowed personal items without asking, or why he laid measuring instruments carelessly in the sand, or why he used their camera as a place to sit, or why he departed camp with property belonging to them.

In the years that followed, Huffaker never conceded that the Wrights were anything more than "bicycle mechanics"—his pet term for them. He felt the only thing they had over him was their skill in building, and he swore they had no idea why their machines flew. The Wrights resented that. They called the craft Huffaker had built for Chanute the "$1000 Beauty" and considered its signature feature to be its folly.

The Chanute-Huffaker glider never had a chance. Assembled, it looked frail. The Wrights' glider occupied the entire new hangar, so Huffaker's machine had to be stored outdoors. The Wrights' original man-carrying glider had survived such a fate in 1900, but Huffaker's could not. Its paper tubing melted away in a rainstorm, the craft never having been tested.

The Wrights took a parting shot at Huffaker. George Spratt left camp before Huffaker or the Wrights that year. After the season,

Wilbur wrote Spratt, "When it came time to pack up I made the unpleasant discovery that one of my blankets that had lived with me for years on terms of closest intimacy, even sharing my bed, had abandoned me for another, and had even departed without a word of warning or farewell. Although I regretted to part with it, yet I felt happy in the thought that its morals were safe, and it was in the company of one who made 'character building' rather than hard labor the great aim in life!"

Orville had photographed Huffaker's ruined machine, titling the shot "The Wreck of the $1000 Beauty." Wilbur sent a selection of photographs with his letter to Spratt. "I enclose a few prints," he noted. "That of the Huffaker machine you will please not show too promiscuously. I took it as a joke on Huffaker but afterward it struck me that the joke was rather on Mr. Chanute, as the whole loss was his. If you ever feel that you have not got much to show for your work and money expended, get out this picture and you will feel encouraged."

Edward Huffaker's reputation has suffered through the years, but in fairness, it should be noted that the opinions Octave Chanute and the Wright brothers held of him—and not his legitimate accomplishments—have gone down as his legacy. Despite his many strong points, Chanute was not always the best judge of glider design. And the Wrights saw Huffaker at his absolute worst during the 1901 season.

But if his mastery of such difficult concepts as ground effect and the travel of the center of pressure are taken into account, then Edward Huffaker was a man who made some important contributions to early aeronautics.

At least Huffaker brought solid credentials to the Outer Banks. The Wrights held out even less hope for George Spratt, their other young guest that season. Neither pilot nor technician, neither scientist nor designer, Spratt was a complete unknown in the aeronautical field. His only selling points were an active mind and a correspondence with Octave Chanute.

Spratt spent most of his life in and around Coatesville, Pennsylvania, near Philadelphia. His grandfather, a Baptist minister, was one of the founders of Bucknell University, and his father was a locally prominent physician and scientist. It was George Spratt's intention to follow his father into the healing arts, but upon his graduation from medical college in Philadelphia in 1894, he learned he had a heart condition. The life of a country doctor was a difficult one in those days, two of its principal features being irregular hours and long travel, often at night or in bad weather. It was too strenuous an occupation for Spratt. He ran an office practice for a time but had little luck getting established, most people preferring to be treated in their homes. Indeed, Spratt's health problems were to limit his activities throughout the remainder of his life.

In searching for an avocation, Spratt turned to the flight problem. His epiphany came one spring morning as he watched a large flock of geese heading north, a sight he had witnessed many times before. He suddenly saw the air as a kind of free highway for all manner of birds and insects—and perhaps man as well.

Years later, he told his hometown paper, the *Coatesville Record*, that his involvement in aeronautics grew partly out of a desire to create employment opportunities in the poor economic climate at the end of the century. If so, he may have been unique among early flight enthusiasts in envisioning an industry growing from such humble experiments as had been done up to that date.

Spratt began by surveying the literature on flight. He then took to flying kites and trying to balance tin pie plates in the wind, neither of which taught him much.

Next came careful field study of birds and insects. Spratt

thoroughly enjoyed observing birds, sometimes lying on his back in the fields for hours to study their flight. Afraid his neighbors would think him eccentric, he bought a fishing pole and began doing his bird-watching near water, hoping that by dangling a line and cultivating the look of a man out to catch his dinner, he could present himself as a more legitimate kind of outdoorsman. However, the fact that he never brought along any bait on his fishing excursions tended to give him away.

Spratt soon noted how well equipped birds were to deal with their native environments. He observed how species inhabiting thickets, where abrupt turns and landings on small branches were a matter of course, seemed to have the most prominent tail feathers, since they needed the greatest degree of control. By contrast, seabirds seemed to have nearly no tail feathers at all. Spratt began capturing birds and cutting off their tail feathers. Upon releasing the birds, he noted how little the loss of those feathers affected their performance.

Spratt also observed that birds have curved wings, and he postulated that insects, which have flat wings, achieved the same effect by moving their wings in a curved path.

He then began building small cardboard glider models, with little success. More notably, he designed and built an elementary wind tunnel and a pressure-recording device, using the two to test the effects of wind pressure on a variety of surfaces. The date Spratt began doing wind-tunnel work is uncertain, but it may have been before 1899. The wind tunnel was invented in 1871 by Englishmen Francis Herbert Wenham and John Browning. By Spratt's day, science-minded men were using a variety of means to test wind effects, with highly contradictory results.

When he felt he had knowledge worth offering the aeronautical community, Spratt, like so many others, wrote Octave Chanute. Despite Spratt's lack of engineering know-how, Chanute was intrigued

by his theoretical observations, even going so far as to pay him a
personal visit in Coatesville sometime in the latter part of 1900. At
that meeting, Chanute supposedly showed the Pennsylvanian a letter from Wilbur Wright. Chanute somehow came away with the
impression that Spratt's principal occupation was farming, though
that line of work is never mentioned in the extensive coverage of
Spratt in the local press and would probably have been too rigorous
for him.

When Chanute petitioned Wilbur Wright to welcome Spratt to
the Outer Banks in 1901, he did it under the guise of offering free
help. Trying to disabuse Chanute of the notion that he and Orville
needed any help at all, Wilbur agreed to accept Spratt only if "you
wish to get a line on his capacity and aptitude and give him a little
experience with a view to utilizing him in your work later." The

George Spratt (standing) with a glider he built and flew in 1908.
His son, George G. Spratt, is standing behind him. The car, in which
Spratt's wife is seated, was used to tow the glider into the air.
CHESTER COUNTY HISTORICAL SOCIETY

Wrights were sorry Spratt was coming at all, though Wilbur couldn't put it to Chanute in those terms.

In his later years, George Spratt grew fond of telling of his first meeting with the Wright brothers, a tale that may have been more fancy than fact. According to Spratt, the Wrights' 1900 glider had wings with a circular curve—that is, the highest point of the wings was halfway between the front and back edges. Spratt, on the other hand, favored wings with a parabolic curve—meaning that the highest point was located toward the front edge of the wings. He somehow conveyed that opinion to the Wrights, presumably through Chanute.

As the story goes, the Wrights then built their 1901 wings according to Spratt's design. With Spratt due to arrive in Kitty Hawk Bay on July 25, they made the trip north from their camp at Kill Devil Hills to meet him. Though Spratt had never laid eyes on Wilbur and Orville, he had no trouble identifying them—they were the ones on the shore yelling, "It won't work, Dr. Spratt, it won't work!" Normally a sober man, Spratt was moved to rise to his feet in the unsteady sailboat in which he was riding, shake a spirited fist at the overdressed brothers, and reply, "It will work! It must work! It can't help but work!"

Unfortunately for Spratt's story, the Wrights were likely using parabolically curved wings before they ever heard of the man from Pennsylvania; the simple drawings Wilbur included in his letter to Chanute immediately after the 1900 season seem to suggest so. And it remains to be seen why the Wrights would go to the trouble of building wings according to a principle they didn't believe in, on the secondhand recommendation of someone with no reputation in the aeronautical field. They certainly never gave George Spratt credit for introducing them to wings with a parabolic curve.

That is not to say they didn't like him. The Wrights were pleasantly surprised with Spratt. They found him to be intelligent, witty, diligent, and uncomplaining. His grasp of the flight problem was better than they'd expected. During idle hours, and thanks to his training in biology, he entertained everyone in camp with his ability to identify all the plant species they happened across on the Outer Banks.

Wilbur in particular sensed Spratt to be a kindred spirit. Spratt was prone to bouts of depression, an experience Wilbur had suffered during his own youth. Indeed, Wilbur sometimes tried to cheer up Spratt and bolster his confidence in the letters he wrote the Pennsylvanian.

And like both of the Wrights, Spratt was given to personal under-statement. He much preferred talking about the flight problem to talking about himself. His frequent interviews with the Coatesville-area media tell much about his views on bird flight and airplane wings and his various aeronautical projects, but they reveal precious little of the man himself. The Wrights would have envied him that.

Among the outsiders Octave Chanute invited to the Outer Banks to experiment with the Wrights, only George Spratt received an invitation to return.

Second Season

Actually, the Wrights were luckier than they realized to have Huffaker and Spratt. It was in 1901 that the brothers butted heads with some of the most intractable problems faced by early aero-nauts. Though Huffaker and Spratt had made little progress toward applying their ideas to practical ends—Spratt had never even seen a glider fly, much less built a full-scale craft of his own—they were at their best in tackling theoretical issues.

The Wrights had completed the design for their new glider back in Dayton in May. The machine was assembled and ready for trial on the Outer Banks by Friday, July 26. There were no shortcuts for lack of long-enough wing spars this year.

The 1901 Wright glider was the largest ever flown to that date. It had 315 square feet of wing and elevator surface, as compared with the 165 square feet of the 1900 machine. The wings measured 22 feet from tip to tip and 7 feet from front to back. They also had an aggressive curvature. The 1900 wings had boasted a camber of 1:23—meaning that, at their highest point, they were 1 inch high for every 23 inches from front to back. The new wings had a camber of 1:12, which was what Otto Lilienthal's tables recommended for maximum lift.

Wilbur still had visions of flying a glider as a manned kite. This year, he hoped to lie aboard the new craft as it was held on ropes by men on the ground. When the machine attained sufficient height, the ropes were to be cut loose, after which the craft would glide slowly back to earth. Wilbur would thus be able to accumulate a good deal of time in the air, and the Wrights and their helpers would be spared carrying the glider all the way back up the dunes after each flight. The increased wing surface and bolder curvature were intended partly to support the craft and its pilot in an average Outer Banks wind without forward movement through the air in a free glide.

The first trials were held on July 27. It was soon obvious that the plan of kiting the glider with Wilbur aboard would again come to nothing. The new craft simply didn't fly as well as the 1900 machine. During the initial attempts that Saturday, the glider showed a tendency to dive nose-first into the sand. Wilbur tried to compensate by positioning himself farther and farther toward the back, until he could barely stretch his arm to reach the elevator control. Even then, the glider would respond to the elevator only when it was in the full-up or full-down position. As a result, the craft nosed rapidly up and down, Wilbur unable to maintain anything resembling a level course.

That Saturday ended on a dangerous note. On one attempt toward the end of the seventeen free glides that day, the glider nosed up sharply until it slowed to stall speed. Wilbur scrambled forward on the wing to try to direct the craft downward so it could regain speed, but instead, the glider fell flat—or "pancaked"—into the sand from a height of about twenty feet. Luckily, neither pilot nor craft was injured.

The last glide of the day was even more ominous. The craft stalled nose-high again, and this time started falling backward toward the ground before Wilbur managed to bring the nose down. This was the same phenomenon that had killed Otto Lilienthal, the Wrights knew. It was time to end the manned trials until they could make a thorough inventory of the glider's shortcomings.

The lack of responsiveness in the elevator control was only the most obvious of several problems.

A major deficiency came to light in flying the glider as an unmanned kite in the succeeding days. The wings were only producing about a third of the lift they were supposed to. The craft, weighing between 75 and 100 pounds, had been designed to carry a 150-pound man in an 18-mile-per-hour wind. In practice, it wouldn't remain aloft, even unloaded, in winds of less than 23 or 24 miles per hour. The Wrights began to suspect that Lilienthal's air-pressure tables, which they had taken to be one of the few firm foundations in aeronautics, were seriously in error.

Edward Huffaker and George Spratt had more bad news for them. They suspected that the glider's tendency to dart suddenly toward the ground was the result of a reversal in the travel of the center of pressure, a phenomenon they had both encountered in their private studies.

In order for an airplane to fly, the craft's center of gravity must correspond to the wind's center of pressure. In the hang gliders of experimenters like Lilienthal and Chanute, the pilot was able to physically change the center of gravity by swinging his legs to compensate for changes in pressure. But with the pilot lying prone in a Wright glider, the center of gravity was fixed, meaning that the surfaces of the craft itself had to be adjusted in accordance with the center of pressure. In straight-course flight, that responsibility fell mainly on the elevator, which directed the nose of the glider up or down to correct for changes in wind.

Straight-course flight was proving less than simple, however. If a wing is stood on its edge and positioned perpendicular to the flow of wind, the pressure is centered at the wing's midpoint. If the wing is then tilted gradually toward the horizontal, the center of pressure travels steadily forward. Ultimately, when the wing reaches a horizontal position, the center of pressure is on the leading edge.

Or that's the way it is with a perfectly flat wing, at least. Experimenters using curved wings were discovering that at a certain angle above the horizontal, the center of pressure tended to reverse and travel rapidly to the rear of the wing, throwing the craft nose downward, with potentially disastrous results.

The Wrights used a simple test to verify that this was what was happening with their glider: they took a wing and flew it as a kite. In moderate winds, when the wing had to assume a relatively steep angle above the horizontal in order to be maintained in the air, it flew fine. But in higher winds, when the wing should have flown at only a slight angle above horizontal, it darted sharply toward the ground.

There were other problems with the 1901 glider as well. It had much greater head resistance than the 1900 craft. And it failed to pick up speed in downhill glides.

Once they had inventoried the craft's shortcomings, the Wrights set about addressing them.

They reduced the size of the elevator by almost half, hoping to reduce the lift at the front of the glider and make the craft more responsive to up-and-down commands. This was of limited success in itself.

They altered the front spars of the glider to reduce head resistance. This helped the craft gain speed in dives.

Most important, they reshaped the wings to give them a flatter curvature, reducing the camber from 1:12 to 1:19. This had far-reaching effects. It caused the center of pressure to travel steadily forward toward the leading edge of the wings at low angles above horizontal, so the craft would no longer be thrown into a dive. And in combination with the smaller elevator, the flatter wings made the glider as responsive to up-and-down control as the Wrights had hoped. Wilbur could again fly a straight course without fearing for his life.

There was little they could do at present about the lack of lift supplied by the wings. That would have to await another season.

The Wrights received one piece of good news during the early trials of 1901: their craft was safe under extreme conditions. In their original 1900 design, they had placed the elevator in front of the wings rather than behind them in the belief that it would be most responsive in that configuration. It had never entered their minds that their forward elevator would find its greatest usefulness as a safety feature. During a stall, it brought the nose of the craft up, so that the glider fell flat to the ground rather than entering an uncontrollable dive.

The sandy landing surface of the Outer Banks and the slow speeds and low altitudes at which the Wrights conducted their tests did not make gliding a safe activity. Many of their predecessors had died in circumstances no more dangerous. In fact, death and serious injury were as much responsible for the slow progress in aeronautics as was a lack of technical vision. Their forward elevator may have saved the Wrights' lives on a number of occasions.

Whatever satisfaction the Wrights derived from correcting a few of their glider's shortcomings didn't last long.

Octave Chanute arrived for his first visit to the Outer Banks on August 5. The paper-tube glider Huffaker had built for him was by

Orville with the 1901 glider

Dan Tate and Edward Huffaker launching the 1901 machine
LIBRARY OF CONGRESS

then well on its way to melting into the sand. The fact that the craft had never left the ground came as little surprise to him.

Still, Chanute's trip was not a complete loss, as he was very much interested in what the Wrights were doing. Their modified glider was ready for testing on August 8. Among the thirteen glides Wilbur made that day were seven that lasted at least twelve seconds, the longest stretching 389 feet.

The next day, the Wrights judged themselves ready to make their first attempt at using wing warping in a free glide. Banking the wings would allow Wilbur to compensate for side gusts. He also wanted to initiate a roll to turn the craft in flight.

His negative opinion of the Wrights in later years notwithstanding, Edward Huffaker was impressed with them at the time. As he noted that day in the diary he kept for Chanute, "A number of

Wilbur gliding
LIBRARY OF CONGRESS

excellent glides were made, Mr. Wilbur Wright showing good control of the machine in winds as high as 25 miles an hour. In two instances he made flights curving sharply to the left, still keeping the machine under good control—length of flight in each case 280 ft. Longest flight about 335 ft."

By contrast, the Wrights could not have been more disappointed.

Their wing-warping system had proven so successful in kite tests in 1900 that they took it for granted. When an airplane rolls to make a turn, its wings are presented at different angles to the wind. The craft turns away from the higher wing; if the right wing is banked high, the airplane turns left. In actual practice with their 1901 glider, however, the Wrights were discovering that this could not be depended upon. Sometimes, their craft even turned *toward*

LIBRARY OF CONGRESS

*The Wrights' craft looked more graceful
than Edward Huffaker's even in a state of ruin.
Above is the brothers' 1900 glider, below Huffaker's "$1000 Beauty."*

WRIGHT STATE UNIVERSITY

the higher wing. In the last glide on August 9, the craft ran hard into the ground during a failed turn, Wilbur suffering a bruised nose and a black eye. If Chanute and Huffaker remained impressed after such a performance, it was only because of their incomplete understanding of the flight problem.

The Wrights had reached their limit that year. The technical hurdles confronting them seemed insurmountable. They turned to kiting the glider with sandbags aboard, only to see their wing-warping problems continue. Wilbur tried a few more free glides, but his distances decreased.

Meanwhile, Chanute, Spratt, and Huffaker departed camp separately in mid-August.

In 1900, the Wrights had arranged their Outer Banks trip so as not to interfere with their bicycle business. By 1901, they had grown so enamored of flying that they left their business in the hands of a friend during peak season so they could get to North Carolina at the ideal time of year for experimenting. Now, they were ready to leave the coast with six or eight weeks of good weather remaining. They broke camp on August 22 simply because they had no reason to stay.

In describing their dark mood, Wilbur once wrote, "We doubted that we would ever resume our experiments. . . . At this time I made the prediction that men would sometime fly, but that it would not be within our lifetime."

It was the closest they ever came to quitting.

Meanwhile

Between the Wrights' first two seasons on the North Carolina coast, another major experimenter—and a future correspondent and friend of Orville's—was setting up shop just across Roanoke Sound from the site of their flights. Thanks to this man's efforts, the opening years of the twentieth century would have been the greatest era of invention in Outer Banks history even if it weren't for the Wright brothers.

Reginald Fessenden was born in 1866. Growing up in the provinces of Ontario and Quebec in Canada, he dreamed vaguely of radio as other boys dreamed of flying machines. The telegraph and the telephone were developed before he entered active experimentation. Those, however, required a vast network of lines connecting every point of transmission and every potential receiver. The idea that an electronic signal could be broadcast omnidirectionally through the air and received by anyone with suitable equipment was considered a pipe dream.

In his early twenties, Fessenden settled in the New York area and went to work for Thomas Edison's laboratories, the greatest in the world. His first major assignment for Edison was to come up with a new coating for electrical wires. In those days, poorly insulated wiring buried within plaster walls was starting fires at a rate that threatened to kill a promising new industry. Edison wanted a coating that would not be overheated by electrical current, that would not be affected by oils and acids, and that would be as flexible as India rubber. Fessenden's laboratory work on the subject involved some basic atomic research well ahead of its time. When he finally delivered what his mentor asked, he earned a place among Edison's top scientists.

Ironically, Fessenden next went to work in a New Jersey laboratory controlled by George Westinghouse, where his major assignment was to design a light bulb that would circumvent Thomas Edison's patent for that device. Successful again, he came up with a bulb that was superior to Edison's—one that earned Westinghouse the lighting contract for the World's Columbian Exposition in Chicago in 1893, a major coup. The Westinghouse lights pioneered by Fessenden were one of the marvels of the exposition, which was attended by tens of thousands of visitors, among them Wilbur and Orville Wright on their first major journey away from home. The event created the first popular market for home lighting.

The ease and offhandedness with which Fessenden came up with some of his inventions is remarkable. One day, finding that the piles of paper on his desk were becoming unmanageable, he invented microphotography. Another time, frustrated that he had to leave his office to call for workers scattered far and wide over the research complex, he invented the pager. The holder of more than five hundred patents over the course of his career, he invented such things as the electric gyrocompass and silicon steel. He held an American patent on what his supporters say was a workable television system in 1919, but lacked the funds to develop it. It wasn't until seven years later that television came into being in England.

But radio—or "wireless telephony," as he called it—was always his passion. Laid off by Westinghouse in 1892, he took university jobs in Indiana and Pennsylvania, where he finally found the freedom to design his own experiments.

During most of his work in radio, Fessenden labored in the shadow of Nobel Prize winner Guglielmo Marconi. Unlike the cash-poor Fessenden, Marconi came from a family wealthy enough to support his research efforts. He was also a far more charismatic public personality and a better businessman. Ultimately, however, his theory of wave transmission was inferior to Fessenden's. Marconi understood electrical waves to be transmitted in short, sharp blasts of energy. He was sending Morse code across the English Channel while Fessenden was still unable to transmit across his laboratory. But once Fessenden arrived at his theory of continuous-wave transmission—

in which electrical signals are seen as traveling outward from their source in a continuous flow, like ripples from a stone dropped into a pond—he was on his way to leaving his Italian rival behind.

Toward the end of 1899, Fessenden's work came to the attention of the United States Weather Bureau, at that time a division of the Department of Agriculture. A wireless system would be an aid to rapid weather forecasting and would allow easy communication with outlying areas where laying cable was costly. Fessenden conducted a demonstration for representatives of the Weather Bureau. His system of sending and receiving Morse code impressed them so much that they promptly hired him away from his university job.

Fessenden's first experiments during his tenure with the Weather Bureau took place on Cobb Island, Maryland, a five-hundred-acre island forty-five miles south of Washington, located opposite Colonial Beach, Virginia. In October 1900, he transmitted such clear Morse messages on Cobb Island that even his employers were startled. Two months later, he transmitted the first intelligible human speech by wireless.

With results like those, the Weather Bureau was ready to fund a larger operation. Its chosen site was coastal North Carolina.

A telegraph line was already in place on the Outer Banks, but its performance was not entirely satisfactory. The line stretching down the barrier islands was often knocked out of commission by severe weather and required close maintenance. The cable that stretched under the sound to the mainland was little better, subject as it was to underwater currents, shifting shoals, and saltwater corrosion. In fact, the system was most prone to breaking down exactly when accurate weather information and lifesaving services were needed most: during heavy weather. With the volume of shipping traffic plying the Gulf Stream and the area's long tradition as a graveyard for unlucky vessels, there was a great deal at stake. A radio mast might blow down in a hurricane, of course, but failing that, wireless transmissions were unaffected by wind and sand, slicing through bad weather as easily as good.

Fessenden set his North Carolina operation in motion in January 1901. His main facility was located at Weir Point on the northwestern shore of Roanoke Island, with outlying stations to the south at Cape Hatteras and to the north at Cape Henry, Virginia.

Unlike the Wrights, Fessenden took up full-time residence on the coast. He and his staff—those not stationed at Cape Hatteras and Cape Henry—lived in eight or ten rooms on the second floor of a Manteo hotel. His experiments were well under way by the time the Wrights arrived for their second season and were joined by the likes of Edward Huffaker and George Spratt.

The following year, 1902, was to prove an eventful one both on the shore of Roanoke Island and in the dunes at Kill Devil Hills.

CHAPTER 3

1902

Wireless telephone communication is a
fact. Instruments invented by Professor
R. A. Fessenden have been installed in
homes along the coasts, near Cape Hatteras
and Roanoke island and for a distance of 14
miles the ticks from the wireless telephone
instruments can be heard over the telephone.

Elizabeth City North Carolinian,
July 10, 1902

The Wright Bros., two young bicycle
manufacturers of Dayton, Ohio; Prof.
O. Chaneut [sic], a noted scientist and
aerialist of Chicago, and Dr. Spratt, a
Philadelphian who has delved deep in the
mysteries of aeronautics are encamped at Kitty
Hawk, in lower Currituck county. On the
bleak sand banks they have erected a machine
shop and in their secluded quarters are
thinking, planning, and perfecting in hopes of
some day startling science and the world with
a presentation, to mankind, of transportation
through space.

Elizabeth City Tar Heel,
October 3, 1902

Radio

Whether the Wright Brothers and Reginald Fessenden ever met on the Outer Banks is a subject for speculation.

Among students of Fessenden's career, it is an article of faith that they did. Fessenden's supporters suggest they met in Manteo—date unknown—and say Fessenden was an occasional visitor to the Wrights' camp at Kill Devil Hills. Canadian author Thomas Carpenter describes the Wrights as "two men [Fessenden] befriended" and tells how Fessenden "listened in fascination as Wilbur and Orville Wright described their experiments with aviation at Kitty Hawk." Fessenden's wife, Helen, paints it as if the two camps were one in spirit across Roanoke Sound, writing, "It was a companionable thought that in this element, the air, two men not so many miles away from us were achieving mastery in one form while we at

Manteo were achieving mastery in another." But proof of any association has yet to be discovered.

Among students of the Wrights, who are far more numerous, the subject is a matter of indifference. No biography of the brothers so much as mentions Fessenden. In the two-volume set of the Wrights' published letters, there is a 1907 letter from Orville to Fessenden, along with an error-filled footnote that identifies Fessenden as an American and has him conducting his advanced radio experiments on Roanoke Island at the age of fifteen, rather than thirty-five. Reginald Fessenden is a small fish in the Wright brothers' pond.

The answer may lie in what appears to be an introductory letter Fessenden wrote to the Wrights in April 1907. "When you were in North Carolina I was at Manteo, working at wireless telegraphy, and became interested in your work," it begins, before going on to its main purpose of offering advice on acquiring patents. Indeed,

Reginald Fessenden

with the flight camp lying only about six miles from Manteo, it's likely that the Wrights and Fessenden were at least aware of each other's experiments, even if they weren't acquainted during their residence.

The new year showed great promise for the radio workers. By early April 1902, Fessenden was winging musical notes around the Outer Banks as easily as Morse code, and sending clear signals among his stations on only three watts of power. He boasted that he could transmit "across the Pacific Ocean if desired."

But Fessenden was not without his problems. The basic difficulty was that, unlike men who built flying machines from inexpensive materials, radio pioneers needed towers and sophisticated electronics in multiple locations, at an expense that was well beyond the private means of anyone poorer than Guglielmo Marconi. As a result, they had to align themselves with companies, government agencies, or wealthy individuals, who often had different ideas about the means and goals of the operation.

Fessenden was also a poor businessman. Despite his many patents, he lived near poverty until his later years. In fact, what little money he had was generally consumed by patent fees. He was far from alone among the inventors of his generation who made great advances in technology and many millions of dollars for others, but who received little recognition or profit themselves.

The operation on Roanoke Island began to fall apart about the time Fessenden was predicting transmission across the Pacific.

Fessenden had been hired in 1900 with the understanding that he would retain patent ownership of all the devices he invented during his employment, though the Weather Bureau would be free to use the devices themselves. However, once Willis Moore, the head of the Weather Bureau, visited the Roanoke Island facilities in 1901 and began to comprehend the potential of Fessenden's radio system, he started trying to insinuate himself into the inventive process.

A former printer from Pennsylvania, Moore had been in charge of the Weather Bureau since 1895. He was the same man who in December 1899 sent Wilbur Wright the packet of weather information that informed him of the existence of Kitty Hawk.

In early 1902, Moore summoned Fessenden to Washington and demanded to be listed as co-owner of all the patents Fessenden had received since coming to work for the Weather Bureau. Moore made it clear that should Fessenden decline, Marconi's radio system would be used for all future Weather Bureau operations.

The experiments on Roanoke Island were by then important enough to merit attention at the highest level. Back in Manteo, Fessenden wrote President Teddy Roosevelt complaining of staff cuts and of Moore's designs on his patents. Roosevelt reviewed the letter

Willis Moore
LIBRARY OF CONGRESS

and passed it to the vice president. It later found its way into the hands of Willis Moore, who responded by stepping up the staff cuts. Eventually, Fessenden was left with just two operators, one of whom was trained only in telegraphy and the other of whom was suffering from a bad leg infection. His experiments ground to a halt.

On July 30, 1902, Moore recommended to Secretary of Agriculture James Wilson that Fessenden be fired for insubordination. The end of his employment with the Weather Bureau in sight, Fessenden tendered his resignation on September 1.

Biographer Ormond Raby has him leaving Roanoke Island for good in August. According to Raby, the last thing Fessenden did before departing North Carolina was pay a farewell visit to the Wrights' camp. Actually, Raby has Fessenden loading up his wagon, making a final visit to his radio facilities, and then rolling directly into Kill Devil Hills, a remarkable feat considering that Roanoke Sound lies between Roanoke Island and that portion of the Outer Banks. The Wrights left Dayton for North Carolina on August 25 that year, so it is possible that they arrived shortly before Fessenden's departure, but no reasonable exit route from Manteo would have led Fessenden through Kill Devil Hills. Such a farewell visit appears to be a fantasy.

His days with the Weather Bureau a bad memory, Fessenden received a further insult two years later, when Guglielmo Marconi established the first commercial wireless station in the Western Hemisphere near Cape Point on Hatteras Island, not far from Fessenden's southernmost facility on the Outer Banks.

Though his fame never approached Marconi's, Fessenden may have been the ultimate winner. In January 1906, during his tenure with the National Electric Signaling Company, he made the first two-way wireless transmission of Morse code across the Atlantic, between Brant Rock, Massachusetts, and Scotland. This put him well ahead of his rival, who was still having difficulty sending one-way after more than five years of trying.

That November, as one of Fessenden's operators was making a wireless voice transmission from Brant Rock to Plymouth, eleven miles away, the message was picked up unexpectedly by the Scotland station—the first voice transmission across the ocean.

On Christmas Eve, Fessenden made the first radio broadcast in history, a program of music and prayer picked up mainly by a fleet of banana boats belonging to the United Fruit Company, a major purchaser of his wireless sets. For the men crowding the wireless rooms of boats as far away as the Caribbean, it must have been memorable.

Today, Reginald Fessenden is widely credited with the discovery of amplitude modulation, the principle behind AM radio.

He and Orville Wright cultivated a friendly, if sporadic, correspondence beginning in 1907. Fessenden sent the Wrights photographs of his wireless facilities and told them how they could receive transmissions aboard their airplanes by pasting tinfoil to the wings, rather than by employing dangling wires, as was being discussed in Europe at the time.

During Orville's first public flights, which took place at Fort Myer, Virginia, in 1908, Fessenden was in the crowd of onlookers. He also offered Orville free use of his company's shop in nearby Washington, going so far as to instruct his staff that "Mr. Wright's work will take precedence of all my own work except that marked 'urgent,' and where Mr. Wright states that he is in a hurry, it will take precedence also of this and you will work overtime and engage additional men, if necessary." Orville was not to be charged for any services rendered.

When Orville suffered a bad crash during his Virginia trials, Fessenden wrote with his sympathies. Always free with his money when he had some, he went so far as to offer a loan.

In 1911, Fessenden's attention turned to developing an airplane motor. He wrote Orville on December 22 of that year to ask him to evaluate his drawings and determine whether the Wrights might be interested in buying the motor. This venture came to nothing.

As for Willis Moore, the man who ranks as a footnote to the Wright brothers' career and a villain of the first magnitude in Reginald Fessenden's, his tenure with the Weather Bureau came to an ignominious end. Moore was hounded by allegations of misuse of government funds beginning in 1904. His Weather Bureau dispensed pay raises sparingly and harsh reprimands liberally, and was fond of transferring employees to distant locations on short notice.

Moore became the subject of public scorn in 1909 when, in the time-honored weatherman's tradition, he personally issued a forecast of "clear and colder" for William Howard Taft's inauguration, only to have a snowstorm blanket the festivities.

When a government investigation descended on his office in 1913, a wheelbarrow bearing incriminating documents was supposedly disappearing out the back door as officers entered the front. He tendered his resignation shortly afterwards, only to have President Woodrow Wilson fire him before it took effect.

Off-Season

Experts agree that the Wright brothers' best work was not done on the Outer Banks. In fact, their best work wasn't done in Virginia or France or at any of the other sites of their great flights. It didn't involve engines, propellers, or gliders. It took place in their bicycle shop in the winter between the 1901 and 1902 seasons and involved materials no more grand than a wooden box, a fan, some cut-up hacksaw blades and bicycle spokes, and six-inch pieces of sheet metal shaped with tin shears.

One of the greatest services Octave Chanute ever performed was bringing Wilbur Wright out of his depression following the 1901 season. Understanding less about the flight problem than the Wrights but being more intimately acquainted with the failure of a variety of other experimenters, Chanute remained highly impressed with the brothers' accomplishments. In August 1901, he invited Wilbur to speak the following month in Chicago before the Western Society of Engineers, one of the most prestigious engineering organizations in the country. A speech on the subject of flight would be educational for the members and would also bring Wilbur the wide exposure he deserved.

Wilbur prepared a draft of a speech, only to have Orville criticize it for asserting that the Wrights had been led astray by the inaccurate data of other experimenters. That judgment should be reserved until the brothers could prove their predecessors wrong, Orville felt. Wilbur deleted the negative references and resolved to do just what Orville suggested: build a body of accurate aeronautical data.

Wilbur's presentation that September included a slide show featuring his craft in flight. He defined the basic elements necessary for powered flight and touched on some of the high points reached by previous experimenters. He discussed his own tests on the Outer Banks, a sampling of the engineering problems he'd encountered, and the conclusions he'd reached thus far. Bill Tate would have been pleased to hear himself credited by name before such an august body. And given the state of his reputation, Edward Huffaker would have been happy to hear himself described as simply "an experienced aeronautical investigator," with no commentary on his character flaws. Slightly revised and widely reprinted under the title "Some Aeronautical Experiments," the speech exerted a major influence on the aeronauts of the day.

When Wilbur arrived back home, the Wrights set about designing their own laboratory experiments to assess the lift and drag of wing surfaces. First, they tested the accuracy of Otto Lilienthal's tables, which all serious students of flight took as their starting point. Their method was to mount two opposing surfaces, one a miniature wing and the other a flat plane, on the rim of a bicycle tire in such a way that the lift of the wing should have matched the resistance of the plate. They then mounted the rim—lying flat and free to turn— above the handlebars of one of their bicycles and pedaled up and down the street. They discovered that, instead of remaining stationary as it should have, the rim rotated toward the flat plate, meaning that its resistance was greater than the wing's lift. In other words, the wing was generating less lift than Lilienthal's tables said it would. This test, simple as it was, served to prove that all of aeronautics rested on a flimsy foundation.

They then built a couple of wind tunnels, the second of which was a six-foot-long wooden box with a viewing window on the upper side. A fan directed a constant twenty-seven-mile-per-hour wind through the box. One homemade balance made of hacksaw blades and wire measured the lift of their miniature wing surfaces and another measured the ratio of lift to drag.

The Wrights generally shunned empirical—trial and error—testing. Men like Samuel Langley and Octave Chanute had the means to build and test a variety of designs to see which performed the best. By contrast, the Wrights, operating on a modest budget and on time stolen from their bicycle business, needed a reasonable assurance of success in advance. Having the time and money for only one machine per season, they had to know their gliders would fly before they ever built them.

In their wind-tunnel tests, they enjoyed a luxury they didn't have when experimenting with full-scale craft. Cutting sheet metal into six-inch miniature wings was cheap. They could fashion as many configurations as they liked. Over the course of several weeks, they determined the wing curvature that was most efficient at a variety of angles to the wind. They determined exactly where the highest point of a wing should be, how wide a wing should be from front to back in relation to its span, how far apart the upper and lower wings of a biplane should be, whether the upper and lower wings should have the same curvature, and what the shape of the leading edge of a wing should be.

Though other experimenters had performed wind-tunnel tests on wing sections, no one had successfully quantified such things before. Some were hampered by a lack of mechanical ability. George Spratt, for example, spent more time in trying to carve a few simple wing sections than the Wrights did in making dozens of sections and performing hundreds of tests on them. Others were at a loss as to how to take accurate measurements, the task being to suspend a wing section in an enclosed space so that it could move freely, then devise a means of calculating the effects of the wind blowing over it. Still others were doomed by inconsistent experimental methods, or by a poor understanding of the full range of variables that needed to be tested.

It was an enormous and complicated task, but one the Wrights completed with great speed.

Critics like Edward Huffaker may have been motivated by sour grapes, but they were more right than they realized when they said that Wilbur and Orville had little idea why their machines flew. Airplanes had been flying for years before it was explained precisely how a curved wing surface generates lift. Wright biographer Tom Crouch makes the case that the brothers were engineers, not scientists. Scientists seek to understand why phenomena occur, while engineers seek to solve practical problems. Sometimes, engineering precedes science—a new machine can be made to work before anyone understands why it works.

All the information the Wrights accumulated that winter still didn't tell them how to build a light, powerful motor, how to craft an efficient propeller, and how to design a control system to turn an airplane in flight. Nonetheless, unlike anyone before them, they now knew how to make wings that could fly.

Augustus Herring

Between the 1901 and 1902 seasons, Wilbur considered moving the gliding experiments from the Outer Banks. He broached the subject in a letter to Chanute in late May: "If we could depend on proper winds, we would probably spend July and August at Kitty Hawk. . . . But we are dubious about the winds and weather after our experience of last year. . . . It is a pity that the hills near Chicago are not smooth bare slopes."

In addition to the fickle winds and weather of the Outer Banks, there was also the great travel distance, the uncomfortable conditions, the difficulty of obtaining supplies, and the mosquitoes. In many regards, it would have been easier to experiment elsewhere.

Judging from his response on May 30, Chanute was pleased that the site of his aeronautical triumph of 1896—and a site much nearer his home—was under consideration: "If you are to have leisure before July 1, I would be very glad to go with you to the hills near Chicago, to have you judge of the safety of carrying on your experiments there."

Wilbur dropped one final hint in his letter to Chanute dated June 2: "We could arrange to come up to the Lake Michigan sand hills and spend a little time spying out the most suitable locations."

After that, the matter was laid to rest. Wilbur never made any such scouting trip. How serious he was about not returning to the Outer Banks is uncertain. On July 9, he wrote Chanute about expanding the camp building at Kill Devil Hills, hardly a sign he wanted to go elsewhere.

As in 1901, Chanute was playing a greater role in organizing their camp than the Wrights would have liked. Wilbur and Orville worked best alone. Chanute, on the other hand, was still fond of the idea of a group of experimenters gathering to test a variety of craft. Chanute had extended so many offers of money and equipment, had given such steady encouragement, had been so free with aeronautical information, and was such a valuable sounding board on engineering matters that the Wrights couldn't flatly refuse him. All they could do was try to contain his enthusiasm and limit the growth of their camp.

Chanute planned to fill the Wrights' hangar with gliders.

First, he contracted with Charles Lamson to build a folding-wing craft. Lamson was a Maine native who in 1895 had become the first man to fly a Lilienthal glider in the United States. After that, he had built a man-carrying kite of his own. He had since moved to California and gone into the jewelry business. Chanute's offer of a construction contract was his attempt to bring Lamson back into the aeronautical fold.

Next, he offered the Wrights a contract to build new versions of his original triplane and *Katydid* designs of 1896. The brothers had no interest in tinkering with Chanute's failed designs of six years ago, but out of courtesy, they agreed to accept his proposal and then subcontract the actual building of the gliders to someone else. That way, they would only be responsible for overseeing the project, not for the finished gliders themselves.

Before this came to pass, Chanute was contacted by an old associate, Augustus Herring, his principal pilot from the Indiana dunes experiments. Finding his fortunes at an ebb, Herring appealed to Chanute to help him get back into the mainstream of aeronautics. Knowing something of Chanute's current loyalties, Herring even teased him with the boast that, given a fair opportunity, he could "beat Mr. Wright." Intrigued by Herring's brashness, Chanute asked Wilbur if he would be willing to back out of the proposed construction contract so that it could be given to Herring. Wilbur was happy to oblige.

The prospect of opening their camp to gliders they knew were inferior was burden enough for the Wrights. Hosting Augustus Herring was something else altogether. His current misfortune notwithstanding, Herring was probably the most accomplished glider pilot

Augustus Herring in the Indiana dunes
NATIONAL AIR AND SPACE MUSEUM

alive. He had flown craft of several different designs and even made a couple of respectable attempts at powered flight. Chanute wrote Wilbur that he wanted either Herring or William Avery, his other main pilot from the Indiana dunes, to come to their camp to participate in the tests. Knowing something of Herring, Wilbur stated his strong preference for Avery. He got Herring.

Augustus Herring was born in 1867 at either Covington or Sommerville, Georgia. He came from a distinguished family. His maternal great-grandfather was the man for whom Conyers, Georgia, was named, and his father was a wealthy cotton broker. His family moved to New York when he was sixteen.

Though he received a first-class education at boarding schools in Switzerland and Germany, Herring was not a gifted student. He entered the Stevens Institute of Technology in Hoboken, New Jersey, in 1884 to study mechanical engineering but had difficulty with his coursework in mathematics, analytical chemistry, and drafting. His passion for aeronautics, which had begun when he was thirteen, did him more harm than good at Stevens. After agreeing to write his undergraduate thesis on marine engines, he began lobbying to submit one called "The Heavier than Air Flying Machine as a Mechanical Engineering Problem." It being the age of Darius Green, the faculty would have none of that. Herring left school in the second half of his fourth year without graduating.

During his college days, Herring's mind was occupied more with building gliders than with his studies. In 1887, he constructed a small-scale craft. The following year, he built one of man-carrying size. It failed in testing.

His father died around this time, leaving Herring with an inheritance that allowed him to pursue his hobby seriously. According to researcher Eugene Husting, Herring's career began to gather momentum when he purchased a monoplane glider from Otto Lilienthal.

He then built two gliders of a similar type, of such a degree of sophistication that they were held together by hollow bolts to save weight. He tested those craft in 1894 in an open area of the West Bronx.

Like Edward Huffaker, Herring was an associate of both Octave Chanute and Samuel Langley. Unlike Huffaker, it was Herring who was sought out by his elders.

Chanute was impressed with Herring's observations of birds, his ability to express wind effects in engineering terms, even his facility with languages, picked up during his boarding-school days. For a time, he apparently relied on Herring for translations of German aeronautical material. Most important, Chanute, despite his considerable study of the subject, had never flown, and Herring had. He wanted to learn everything Herring could tell him. In late 1894, Chanute engaged him to build a series of model gliders.

The following May, just as Chanute was about to start work on a man-carrying craft, Herring was hired by Langley to head the aerodynamics experiments at the Smithsonian. From the days of his "whirling table" experiments, Langley mistakenly believed that flat wings generated more lift than curved, and it is Herring who is credited with convincing him otherwise. Herring also designed the high-temperature burner for the steam engines that powered Langley's small-scale Aerodromes.

Herring was back in Chanute's employ by 1896, having split from the Smithsonian. Over his entire career, Herring never got along with any of his associates for long. He thought Samuel Langley was difficult. He thought Octave Chanute was senile. He thought the Wright brothers were pilferers.

A number of young men made glides during the Indiana dunes experiments, among them three "professional" aeronauts, Chanute's son Charles, and several newspaper reporters who wandered into camp and were invited to try their hand. A natural pilot, Herring was easily the finest of the group, with numerous glides stretching into the hundreds of feet. His two best efforts reportedly stretched 359 feet. Some accounts claim he made as many as 1,200 flights.

Meanwhile, he managed to alienate everyone in camp. One of the craft being tested was an ungainly contraption nicknamed the *Albatross*, designed by Paul Butusov, a Russian. Herring considered the craft dangerous and refused to work on it. In fact, he was disinclined to exert any effort toward testing ideas that didn't originate with himself. In an experiment grounded in joint participation and mutual encouragement, the effect was divisive.

Later, he and Chanute argued over who was the moving force behind the biplane craft tested that season, the best glider in the world before the Wrights. Chanute gave Herring credit only for designing the tail section, while Herring claimed the general design of the entire craft was his.

They finally parted company over the issue of powered flight. Herring believed that the breakthrough was finally at hand, that his and Chanute's biplane design could be modified for a motor and propellers. Chanute was pleased with the glider trials, but not so pleased that he couldn't recognize that powered flight was still a remote goal. Herring left camp to begin work on a powered machine while Chanute's experiments were ongoing.

Around this time, Herring exhausted his inheritance. On the other hand, he found himself a patron: Matthias Arnot, a young banker from Elmira, New York. Arnot put Herring on a modest salary and bankrolled his major construction expenses.

Herring got married during this period to Lillian Mullen, one of five daughters of a New York banker. The couple took up residence in St. Joseph, Michigan, a town chosen partly for its fine machine facilities and its stretch of beach on the Lake Michigan shore, ideal

for testing a powered craft. Herring opened a motorcycle shop and
began publishing a magazine called *Gas*, which sung the praises
of light gasoline engines suitable for bicycles and—quite optimistically—airplanes.

In 1897, Herring and Arnot went to the Indiana dunes to test a
new biplane glider that would be the basis for their powered craft.
The results were outstanding, with early glides of two and three
hundred feet and best efforts reportedly stretching six hundred feet.
On hand to witness some of the trials, Chanute took photographs
of the craft in flight. Since his photographs of the 1896 biplane—a
nearly identical craft—were of poor quality, Chanute later used his
shots of Herring's glider in lectures and publications without asking
Herring's permission or even identifying the substitution. This deep-
ened the rift between the two.

Augustus Herring's methods differed dramatically from those of
the other aeronautical experimenters of his age. In an effort to avoid
publicity, Samuel Langley retreated behind high fences to conduct
his tests. Octave Chanute moved his camp from one location to
another in the Indiana dunes to make it less accessible to reporters.
Wilbur and Orville Wright traveled to a place reached only by boat.
But Augustus Herring courted publicity. He had already contacted
Barnum and Bailey about the possibility of exhibition gliding. During his 1897 tests, he made sure the press was aware of what he was
doing, turning reporters' attention to his advantage with considerable sophistication. Many members of the aeronautical community
resented him for it.

Back in St. Joseph, Herring set to work on a powered version of
the biplane, contracting the building of the frame to a local boatyard
while he took responsibility for the engine. The wings of the new
craft were eighteen feet from tip to tip and fifty-four inches from
front to back. Unable to design a gasoline engine that met his

requirements for lightness and power, Herring settled upon a small compressed-air motor. It would turn two five-foot propellers, one a tractor and the other a pusher—one was mounted in front of the wings and the other behind the wings, in other words. The completed craft weighed only eighty-eight pounds.

On October 3, 1898, Herring spoke to a reporter about his vision of the future of aviation. Though he did not expect airplanes to ever carry more than two people, he predicted speeds of seventy-five miles per hour and flights of up to four hundred miles. He also predicted that air travel would one day be the cheapest form of transportation, with costs as low as a quarter-cent per mile.

Eight days later, Herring proved just how distant those dreams were. Retrieving his craft from where it was stored in a dance pavilion on the Lake Michigan shore, he rolled it out onto Silver Beach, near St. Joseph, and, with Arnot as a witness, made a powered hop of fifty feet against a wind of twenty or twenty-five miles per hour, his feet barely clearing the ground. As with the Wright brothers' powered flights of 1903, the distance covered is more impressive than it seems. Against such a stiff wind, his hop of 50 feet over the ground was equivalent to a distance of about 260 feet through the air.

Encouraged, Herring wanted to orchestrate another attempt in front of a more substantial group of witnesses. Octave Chanute, at the top of Herring's list, was summoned by telegram. Chanute came promptly but left when the wind failed to pick up. He thought little of Herring at that point and even less of the immediate prospects for powered flight.

Herring's second hop took place on October 22 in front of witnesses variously identified as Arnot, a couple of reporters, a hot-dog vendor on the beach, and several boys watching surreptitiously from behind some bushes. This time, in his eight or ten seconds in the air, he covered about 75 feet over the ground against a wind of about twenty-six miles per hour, for the equivalent of about 350 feet through the air. Arnot had a camera, but he was too preoccupied to snap a picture until the very end. He caught Herring just at the point of landing.

Compared with most newsmen of the period covering the subject of flight, the reporter for the *Benton Harbor Evening News* who witnessed Herring's experiment that day had a remarkably balanced view. While characterizing Herring's effort as "the first time in the world's history that a true flying machine . . . has ever carried its operator in successful flight," he correctly reported that the craft was suited only for "short flights" and "experimental purposes," and he described its progress through the air as "remarkably slow."

Experts are agreed that Augustus Herring did not achieve powered flight, which is defined as sustained, controlled movement through the air free of ground effect, with the point of takeoff no higher than the point of landing. Anything short of that is considered a "powered leap" or an "airborne condition," less rigorously defined as merely moving through the air upon wings that generate lift. That is how Herring's efforts of October 1898 are categorized. He is justly credited with being the first American to achieve a "powered leap" or an "airborne condition"—no small feat.

To his credit, he never claimed otherwise, saying only that his efforts had proven powered flight "solvable." In fact, with his compressed-air motor capable of delivering just three to five horsepower for a maximum of thirty seconds, he had never considered his 1898 craft more than a kind of intermediate stage between a glider and a powered flyer.

Herring's trials proved powered hang gliders to be a technological dead end. The pilot's only means of steering and correcting for gusts of wind was swinging his legs to one side or the other, a technique that could only work with craft of small size—imagine a pilot trying to change the course of a modern airliner by shifting his weight. By contrast, the Wrights' system—in which the pilot operated the craft from an internal position and controlled its movement by means of levers that varied the angle of the wing and elevator surfaces—could be used in craft of much larger size.

Augustus Herring's subsequent attempt at developing an engine powerful enough for sustained flight was anticlimactic, ending in 1899 when a fire destroyed the boatyard where all his equipment was stored. By some estimates, he had gone through twenty-five thousand dollars in his quest for powered flight.

Having taken his best shot at flight, Herring turned his attention full-time to a project he had been developing simultaneously with his powered hang glider. The Wright brothers knew something about two-wheel ground transportation, but Herring went them one better, constructing what were perhaps the first motorcycles offered commercially in the United States, using the trade name "Mobikes." He also built and sold lightweight bolt-on gasoline engines for bicycles.

For their day, Herring's Mobikes were excellent machines. Sold in both conventional and motorcycle-built-for-two versions, they weighed between seventy-five and ninety-five pounds, carried $1^1/_3$-horsepower motors, and sold for $250 to $275. They rode on puncture-proof tires, ran fifty or sixty miles between fuelings, handled moderately difficult grades with ease, and operated dependably on the poor roads of the era. Herring sold about two hundred of them. Though his Mobike operation was destroyed in the same fire that claimed his aeronautical project, he rebuilt and resumed production, with a long-range view to manufacturing a line of automobiles. That plan was never realized.

Herring's interest in flight was rekindled when he read "Some Aeronautical Experiments," the published version of Wilbur Wright's paper delivered before the Western Society of Engineers.

When he received Herring's letter about getting back into aeronautics, Octave Chanute was past his anger with the younger
man. He was also not the type to turn away someone in financial difficulty.

In granting Chanute's request that they allow Herring to experiment with them in 1902, the Wright brothers were welcoming a
man who had more extensive associations in the field than they did,
who had more glides to his credit, and who had attempted powered
flight. Herring had even exceeded them in two-wheel transportation, having received a fair amount of praise for his Mobikes in
national publications like *The Horseless Age*.

On the other hand, they were opening their camp to a man who
had a reputation for jealous self-interest even in his best days, who
had exhausted his best ideas on flight, and who had little left to
bring to the subject but contentiousness.

Third Season

After a year's respite from bad voyages, the Wrights had a trying
time making their way across Albemarle Sound again in 1902.

They left Dayton at 9:00 A.M. on Monday, August 25, and arrived
in Elizabeth City at 5:45 P.M. on August 26. Finding a two-masted
schooner, the *Lou Willis*, tied at the dock and scheduled to depart
for Kitty Hawk before dawn, they hurried back to the rail depot to
retrieve their crates just before the storage facility closed at 6:00,
bought a barrel of gasoline as the Standard Oil warehouse was closing for the evening, and entreated a shopkeeper to reopen his store
to sell them a small oven.

Things slowed down considerably after that. They waited nine hours
for the *Lou Willis* to cast off, at 3:45 A.M. Wednesday, and then endured a cruelly slow voyage that didn't see them to Kitty Hawk

until thirty-six hours later, at an average speed of about a mile per hour.

It wasn't the captain's fault. The Wrights couldn't have been in better hands than those of Franklin Midgett of Kitty Hawk. Part of the most famous family of lifesavers on the Outer Banks, Midgett had only recently left the lifesaving service to start a boat line. However, there was nothing he could do about the dead calm, and the wind that later blew from the east, and the water so unusually shallow that they ran aground briefly.

In a collection of letter excerpts called "Our Life in Camp at Kitty Hawk" that he compiled for *U.S. Air Services* magazine in 1943, Orville captured the difficulties of this trip and the worse time awaiting the Wrights setting up camp at Kill Devil Hills.

Having made only ten miles by four o'clock Wednesday afternoon, Captain Midgett gave up for the day and anchored. With a lady passenger on board and the *Lou Willis's* cabin only about six feet square, the woman-shy Wrights decided to spend the night on the open deck, Orville trying to sleep lying atop a lumber pile.

Upon awakening, they found the *Lou Willis's* galley little more appetizing than Israel Perry's aboard the *Curlicue*. "After the mate had drawn us each a bucket of water with which to wash off the wrinkles from our faces the next morning," Orville noted, "he proceeded to wash the dishes from the night before in cold water, without soap, in the same bucket; and then carrying it below, he made up the dough for bread in it, I suspected. However, as I had had hardly anything to eat for a couple of days, I didn't follow it below deck to see just what it was used for there, for I found the more I saw the less I ate."

The *Lou Willis* sailed again at four-thirty Thursday morning and arrived at Kitty Hawk at four that afternoon. Before disembarking, the Wrights helped get a barrel of sugar out of the hold through an opening "several inches smaller than the barrel itself," in Wilbur's estimation. From Kitty Hawk, Dan Tate ferried them in his spritsail boat to a site opposite the camp at Kill Devil Hills, after which they went by horse cart over the dunes, having to get out and push part of the way.

If they were looking toward their camp as an oasis after a trying journey, they must have been disappointed. Anxious to put their wind-tunnel findings to a practical test, they spent eleven days just getting their facilities in order—driving a deeper well, raising the ends of the building where the sand had blown away, laying foundation posts for better support, constructing a combination kitchen and dining-room addition, "upholstering" their table and dining-room chairs with burlap, adding bunks in the rafters, weatherproofing the exterior of the building, tar-papering the roof.

They also had to contend with the wildlife, large and small, that was overrunning the camp.

According to Orville, the brothers were driven to distraction by the local mouse population, a problem they tried to solve by means considerably less ingenious than what they applied to the flight problem. They baited homemade traps with bits of cornbread, chased mice with sticks, and blazed away at them indoors with guns. "The mark of the bullet is in the corner right back of where [the mouse] stood," Orville wrote. In chasing a mouse that kept escaping through cracks between the floorboards, the Wrights even tried stationing "one [man] above and one below the floor," one with a stick and the other with a gun—which sounds patently dangerous for the man bearing the stick.

Orville wrote of one particular mouse that liked to knock pieces of cornbread onto the tin oven to wake him up, then "come onto my bed and promenade on my head, to tell me to get up and put another piece on the shelf."

Outside, there were hogs that had to be driven from camp. The weapons of choice here were tent pegs, which the Wrights apparently threw at the interlopers. In the case of one hog that overturned the brothers' chicken coop and then "laid himself down on its former site to sun himself," Orville, a noted marksman with gun or tent peg, placed the first peg "with terrific force squarely in the pit of his stomach, the second the full length of his side, and the third on the back of his head." In his estimation, it was "a victory equal to Dewey's at Manila."

They were another eleven days in assembling their new glider— laying the frame for the upper wing, adding the ribs to the frame, covering the wing with cloth, kiting it to test the angle at which it flew, building the lower wing, cannibalizing the uprights from their 1901 glider for use in the new machine, wiring and hinging the wings in tandem, building and covering the elevator, adding a vertical tail. It was September 19 before they finally tested the completed craft, making about twenty-five glides, none of them entirely free.

Bill Tate had moved north from Kitty Hawk to Martins Point to oversee a large tract of land and a lumber operation for an absentee owner, so he was no longer a fixture in camp as he had been the previous two seasons. Instead, the Wrights retained his half-brother, Dan Tate—the father of Tom Tate, the boy who rode aboard the 1900 glider—as a paid employee. Dan was their principal helper— bringing them supplies, working on the camp building, running with one wing of the glider during launches, even warning them of approaching weather—until their professional guests began arriving. On days when Dan didn't come to camp, they could do no more than kite their glider.

On September 20, they made about fifty glides, only two of them free.

After spending three years reading about flight, theorizing with his elder brother, making calculations, writing letters, taking photographs, conducting wind-tunnel tests, building gliders, and keeping flight and instrument records, Orville finally got his chance at gliding on September 23. That morning, he rode the craft with Wilbur and Dan Tate running at the wingtips. After dinner, he made his first free glides, one of them covering a respectable 160 feet. However, he still had a ways to go to catch his brother. Wilbur could now keep the wings level in flight and bring the glider to a virtual standstill in the air.

Just how much Orville had to learn came to light during a flight later that afternoon, when he grew so preoccupied with the

Dan Tate (near) and Wilbur flying the 1902 glider as a kite

wing-warping mechanism that he forgot about the elevator control. Wilbur's and Dan Tate's yells from the ground came too late. The craft nosed up at a forty-five-degree angle, stalled, and fell to the sand from a height of twenty-five or thirty feet. Orville was unhurt, but the glider required several days of repairs, the wing coverings having to be removed and the broken ribs spliced. They didn't fly again until September 29.

Having left home thirty-six days earlier, the Wrights got in only three days of free gliding before their company began to arrive. First in camp was their elder brother Lorin. Katharine, their sister, had informed them that Lorin might be making the trip to the Outer Banks, but there was some confusion as to his date of departure.

Wilbur and Orville were in the dunes preparing for their first glide of the day on September 30 when they saw two men, both heavily burdened, struggling across the sand on foot. Taking them to be George Spratt and someone helping to carry his bags, they left their glider and hurried back to camp to greet them. Instead of Spratt, they found Lorin, who had traveled halfway across the continent for no better reason than to watch his brothers' experiments and to help however he could. Wilbur and Orville built him a bed before the day ended.

The two oldest children in the Wright family were restless souls who headed west in their early adulthood. Reuchlin, the eldest, settled in Missouri and Kansas and remained distant from the family. Lorin, four and a half years older than Wilbur, moved to Kansas before eventually returning to Dayton, where he lived less than a block from the family home. A familiar part of his younger brothers' lives, he worked with them briefly in their printing business and was no doubt familiar with their bicycle business and their aeronautical ambitions. A married man with four children by 1902, he worked as a bookkeeper and took odd jobs on the side to pay the bills. He later kept books for Wilbur and Orville after they became famous.

On the Outer Banks, Lorin went fishing, ran errands with Dan Tate, and took photographs of the glider in flight. Though he assisted at launches and witnessed numerous discussions of aeronautics, he didn't contribute toward the building of the Wrights' gliders or the theory behind them. Neither did he fly.

Lorin Wright with one of his daughters
LIBRARY OF CONGRESS

George Spratt arrived the following day. Up until at least September 16, there had been considerable doubt that he was coming at all.

Spratt had been having a bad time since he last saw the Wrights. Back home in Pennsylvania in late 1901, he had built a device designed to measure some of the forces acting on a wing surface. By late January, he was apparently having difficulty with his experiments. Wilbur wrote him a letter on the art of fashioning model wings from sheet metal, even sending Spratt four of the miniature wings he and Orville had tested in their wind tunnel. However, sheet-metal surfaces didn't suit Spratt's new measuring device, and he had to resort to the far more tedious process of carving wooden wings. Octave Chanute also tried to help, writing Samuel Langley to ask that some grant money be sent the Pennsylvanian's way, a request Langley turned down. Recognizing his middling laboratory skills and his limited financial means, Spratt grew depressed with being a marginal member of the aeronautical community.

He was more than that to the Wrights. Just how badly Wilbur wanted him in camp is revealed in his letters.

On January 23, he wrote Spratt a brief motivational lecture: "I see from your remark about the 'blues' that you still retain the habit of letting the opinions and doings of others influence you too much. We thought we had partly cured you of this at Kitty Hawk. It is well for a man to be able to see the merits of others and the weaknesses of himself, but if carried too far it is as bad, or even worse, than seeing only his *own merits* and *others'* weaknesses. In the present case there was no occasion for your 'blueness' except in your own imagination."

When Langley vetoed a grant for Spratt, Wilbur tried to cheer his friend by attributing it to Langley's jealousy of Chanute, or to Langley's bad experience with a previous Smithsonian employee Chanute had recommended—Edward Huffaker.

Finally, in September, Wilbur tried to entice Spratt with a rosy description of conditions at the 1902 camp—the absence of mosquitoes, the new kitchen, the indoor beds, the improved well.

It worked. Spratt proved himself a popular and valuable member of the camp again that season.

Lorin Wright and George Spratt witnessed what were perhaps the greatest glides in history a couple of days after their arrival. On October 2, Wilbur made three glides over five hundred feet.

There were some highly encouraging aspects of the new glider's performance. Thanks to the lessons the Wrights had learned during their wind-tunnel tests, their wings were generating far greater lift than in previous years. Any object in flight, whether bird or man-made craft, must have its wings angled above the horizontal to maintain a glide. Gliding efficiency is measured by the degree of angle above the horizontal: the smaller the angle necessary to maintain a glide, the more efficient the craft. By that standard, the Wrights were now gliding better than the birds.

Wilbur gliding
LIBRARY OF CONGRESS

But there were problems with the craft, too. After the 1901 season, the Wrights had surmised that differential drag was responsible for their glider's tendency to slip sideways in turns. When an airplane is banked during a turn, it is paramount that the upper and lower wings move at the same speed. But the Wrights found that when they warped their wings, the upper wing had more of its surface exposed to the wind than did the lower wing; the lower wing continued to move at the same speed as before warping, but the upper wing began to slow, throwing the craft into a spin.

In 1902 for the first time, the Wrights were flying a glider equipped with a tail. Since the tail's two fixed vertical vanes would be presented at an angle to the wind during turns, they would serve to increase the drag on the lower, or faster, wing until it was equal to that of the upper wing, so the two would continue to move at the same speed.

That was the theory, at least. In actual practice, the twin six-foot vanes only exacerbated the problem, sometimes throwing the glider into such severe spins that it seemed to bore into the sand upon impact; the Wrights called this phenomenon "well-digging."

Following supper on October 2, the three Wrights and Spratt discussed the problem before retiring to their bunks in the rafters. After the others were asleep, Orville, awake from drinking too much coffee, reasoned that making the vertical rudder movable and placing it under the pilot's control would allow him to correct for differential drag in any wind. Used in combination, wing warping and a movable vertical rudder would at last make balanced turns possible.

Before he broached the subject with Wilbur the following morning, Orville supposedly gave a quick wink at Lorin, expecting Wilbur to dismiss his theory out of hand, as he seemed to do on principle. This time, however, Wilbur immediately saw the merit in his younger brother's idea. He even proposed taking it a step farther. With the pilot having to work the elevator with a hand lever and the wing-warping mechanism with a hip cradle, controlling the glider was already complicated enough. He suggested tying the vertical rudder in with the wing-warping mechanism so they worked in tandem.

From the start of the Wrights' experiments, Orville had contributed excellent glider-building skills and an intelligent counterpoint to Wilbur's ideas on flight. Now, he was also taking his turn as a pilot. His breakthrough on the vertical rudder may have marked his coming of age as Wilbur's equal in aeronautical design as well.

Once the movable rudder was added, the 1902 machine became the first glider in history that could be controlled in three axes of motion. From there, all that was left was adding a motor and propellers to achieve powered flight.

Octave Chanute and Augustus Herring were there to witness the fruits of these developments. They arrived around noon on Sunday, October 5, unlike the Wrights taking the easier boat route via Manteo, rather than direct from Elizabeth City. One of Chanute's gliders had already been in camp nearly two weeks, having been shipped aboard the *Lou Willis* and carried through the sand by Wilbur and Dan Tate.

Chanute's return to the Outer Banks said something about his commitment to aeronautics and his high regard for the Wrights, of course, but it was also a testament to his fortitude.

Today, Chanute is remembered as a kind of aeronautical man about town, someone whose wealth and professional standing allowed him to influence nearly everyone trying to fly, though his own understanding of the flight problem was limited. Actually, Chanute saw his share of troubles during his lifetime. He was a worrier and a workaholic. In 1875, while working for the Erie Railroad and trying to design an elevated railway system for New York City, he "had what would be called a 'nervous breakdown'," according to the editor of his travel diaries. His doctor insisted Chanute leave the country for an extended walking tour of Europe, away from all personal and professional responsibilities. In his diary, the troubled Chanute wrote of his "state of depression," his "shattered health," his need of recovering "the mental tone and balance necessary for future success and the earning of a living" to support his wife and five children.

Toward the end of the century, Chanute's principal business was a Chicago-based company whose purpose was to preserve railroad ties by injecting them with a creosote mixture. Long used to keep railroad ties, telephone and telegraph poles, and a variety of underground timber from rotting, the process was designed by Chanute himself. In the 1890s, he tried to get out of the business, leaving it in the hands of his son Charles and another man, only to be drawn back into the daily operation of the company at a time when he was ready to retire and devote himself to the flight problem.

At the time of his 1902 visit to the Wrights' camp, he was still recovering from the death in April of Annie Riddell James Chanute, his wife of forty-five years.

Camping and working with gliders on the Outer Banks were young men's pastimes. Orville Wright was thirty-one in 1902. George Spratt was thirty-three. Wilbur Wright and Augustus Herring were thirty-five. Lorin Wright was thirty-nine. Dan Tate, usually the senior man in camp, was forty-one.

Octave Chanute, however, was seventy. Conditions on the Outer Banks were doubly hard on him. A wealthy, famous, elderly gentleman, he left the comforts of home for the privilege of risking difficult travel across the coastal waters, enduring climatic extremes, living in cramped quarters, eating bad food, and going to the bathroom in the woods.

With the arrival of Chanute and Herring, the Wrights had their

liveliest camp to date. Discussions of aeronautics lasted well into the
evening. Sometimes, Orville broke out his mandolin and played for
the men. It must have been a strange sound to hear from a make-
shift wooden building on a lonely expanse of sand, but then again,
it's unlikely that anyone happened near enough to witness it.

Perhaps the music aided digestion. Camp fare was neither better
nor more bountiful than in the past. In one of his letters, Wilbur
described how Orville, having a hankering for wild fowl, went to
the beach and shot three "sea chickens" one day. "That will make
one mouthful for me, and a half mouthful for him," Wilbur noted.
"After a bullet has gone through one of them there is just a little
meat left around the edges. Our meat, you see, is costing us about
60 cents per pound in cartridges, so you understand what epicures
we are in our eating." The muffins they baked were said to "re-
semble the shell of a terrapin in hardness."

Even with the poor food and the six bunks crowded into the
rafters, conditions in camp were much improved over the previous
year. The Wrights now had a dependable water source and reasonably good facilities for cooking and dining. The improvements even
extended to transportation. The Wrights had brought along a balloon-tire bicycle that traveled easily across the sand, making social
visits and errands a far more pleasant prospect than in the past.

Augustus Herring may have seen matters differently. Out with
Wilbur on an errand to fetch some blankets his first day in camp, he
was caught in a downpour and soaked to the skin. That was perhaps
the high point of his stay. Whether motivated by hunger or a love
for all God's creatures, he took to worrying about the chicken the
Wrights kept outside the camp building, predicting that it would be
stolen while they slept. One night, he woke everyone at two in the
morning with an announcement that the chicken had indeed been
stolen by a fox, though how he came to that knowledge from his

position in the rafters is anyone's guess. Morning found the chicken to be present and in good working order.

Herring had bigger things to worry about than poultry. He assembled his "multiwing" glider on October 6, the day after his arrival, and was ready to test it that evening. On his second glide, which covered only twenty feet, he landed on the right wing and broke the main cross-span between the upper and lower surfaces. He tried again two days later but could not get airborne at all. The same fate befell him on Friday, October 10. On October 11, the Wrights tried to help him fly the multiwing as a manned kite, but it wouldn't take to the air even when they ran along with it.

Between these tests, Herring made a variety of field measurements of his and the Wrights' glider, all of which told him little about why the multiwing was failing. In his diary, Orville attributed it to structural weakness, noting that winds too light even to sustain the craft in flight distorted the shape of its wings. The Wrights' wind-tunnel tests had led them to believe that the performance of Chanute's 1896 biplane glider had been exaggerated, and what they saw of Herring's multiwing, a similar craft, confirmed their opinion.

A frustrated Chanute laid the blame on Herring's construction, writing Samuel Langley on October 21 that Herring was a "bungler." Chanute's criticism was less than fair, since he had personally inspected the craft while it was being built and had written Wilbur back in July that Herring was "putting excellent workmanship on the machine."

On Monday, October 13, Orville, Herring, and Spratt assembled and tested Chanute's other glider, the craft designed by Charles Lamson, the California jeweler. It had arrived the previous Wednesday aboard the *Lou Willis*. Flown only that one day, the Lamson glider performed little better than the multiwing, Herring attaining a best glide of forty-five or fifty feet.

The Chanute-Herring multiwing craft of 1902 during a test on the Outer Banks
WRIGHT   STATE   UNIVERSITY

In case the point needed to be driven home, the performance of the Wrights' modified glider let Herring know just how far behind he was.

The brothers completed work on their movable tail rudder—a single vane five feet high and fourteen inches from front to back—on Monday, October 6, and tested it that Wednesday and Friday. It appears Herring and Chanute witnessed no glides of monumental length either day. However, what they saw was of far greater importance. Orville was still having a beginner's trouble with the controls, but Wilbur quickly mastered the rudder and wing-warping combination. For the first time in history, a glider was capable of executing turns. The control system of the Wrights' 1902 craft also allowed them to make corrections for gusts of wind from any quarter. That Friday, Lorin Wright took history's first photograph of a glider turning.

Herring and Chanute left camp on October 14, a day after Lorin's departure. Chanute's understanding of what he had seen on the Outer Banks that season defies analysis. He had witnessed the utter failure of the two gliders built under his sponsorship, but he somehow held out hope that the Wrights would spend valuable time continuing to test them in his absence. He still believed that building inherently stable craft was the means to achieving flight, which suggests he had a poor grasp of the Wrights' accomplishments. Yet upon leaving North Carolina, he headed to Washington to sing the Wrights' praises to Samuel Langley.

Herring also set course for the nation's capital to seek an audience with Langley, traveling separately from Chanute. According to Wright biographer Fred Howard, his intent was to exchange what he knew of the brothers' "secrets" for a job at the Smithsonian. Wanting no part of Herring, Langley declined to meet with him.

That is not to say Langley was uninterested in the Wrights. His interest piqued by Chanute's visit, he wrote Chanute on October 17 that he was considering sending someone to the Outer Banks to witness the Wrights' experiments, or even going himself. Two days later, he cabled Wilbur at the Weather Bureau office in Kitty Hawk asking permission to visit the brothers' camp. He followed that with a letter to Wilbur. Langley was still interested in December, writing Chanute with a request for information on the Wrights' control system and even inviting the brothers to Washington, telling Chanute he would pay their travel expenses if they would discuss their experiments with him.

Wilbur turned down Langley's request to visit the Outer Banks on the grounds that it would fall too close to the end of the season. He was perhaps being less than completely honest. From the time Langley's telegram arrived on October 19, it was eight days before Dan Tate quit the Wrights' employment to take charge of a fishing crew, which left the brothers without the manpower to launch their glider and brought their trials to a close. Even then, as Wilbur wrote Chanute, the brothers "should have liked to have prolonged our stay a few weeks longer." A visit from Langley and whatever contingent he might have brought from Washington presumably would have allowed them that opportunity.

Having been on the Outer Banks about two months, the Wrights were perhaps weary of camp conditions. Or they may have had enough of entertaining visitors. More likely, they were disinclined to share their hard-gotten aeronautical advances with the man who was deeper into the pursuit of powered flight than anyone alive.

George Spratt remained in camp for six days after the departure of Chanute and Herring. He saw little gliding during that time, the days being spent mostly in leisure activities like bird-watching, botanizing, and gathering seashells and crabs. On October 16, Orville reported going to the beach and killing starfish with gasoline. Like the shells and crabs, the starfish were presumably intended as souvenirs for the family back in Dayton.

The main reason the Wrights experimented little those days was the weather, fickle as always. For example, the night of October 14, with fifty-mile-per-hour winds, was followed by a day so calm that they couldn't even get their glider into the air.

First-time visitors to the Kitty Hawk area are often surprised at the strength of the wind. The northward-flowing Gulf Stream tends to stall pressure systems over the Outer Banks. Isolated from the mainland, with no mountains and few forests, the Outer Banks suffer the full effect of ocean winds. Along the entire coast of the continental United States, only Florida is hit harder by hurricanes. The winds on the Outer Banks can blow at a variety of intensities from a variety of quarters—often within the span of a single day. Or the air can be completely calm.

Or conditions can be perfect for gliding. George Spratt should have delayed his departure for the mainland. The same day he left, October 20, the Wrights enjoyed the finest day of gliding they'd ever had, at the beginning of their best-ever week. That day, they recorded five glides over five hundred feet, including Orville's first glide of that length. They remained in the air over twenty seconds on all of those efforts. Their average glides were extending well over three hundred feet now.

As always, the Wrights did their best work in private. On October 24, a steamer plying Albemarle Sound noticed their activities and veered closer to shore for a better look, but beyond that isolated incident, only Dan Tate was on hand to witness the flights.

In a two-day span, the Wrights made over 250 glides. For anyone who has ever tried to handle a standard umbrella—with perhaps 15 square feet of surface area—in a stiff breeze, carrying a glider with

Dan Tate chasing the 1902 glider
LIBRARY OF CONGRESS

305 square feet of wing area uphill through sand might seem like a labor out of Greek mythology. While gliding on the Outer Banks was at times a strenuous undertaking, it wasn't as difficult as it first appears. As Orville once explained to Amos Root, a man who in 1904 witnessed the first circular flight of a powered airplane, the Wrights always glided against the wind. Then, on their return up the dunes, they had only to angle the wings slightly so that the wind pushed them up the slope.

On the ninth glide of the day on October 23, Wilbur sailed 622½ feet in twenty-six seconds, setting American records for both distance and time aloft. After three more glides, all over 500 feet, Orville nearly equaled his brother's best distance, traveling 615½ feet.

Orville proudly wrote his sister that day, "We have gained considerable proficiency in the handling of the machine now, so that we are able to take it out in any kind of weather. . . . We now hold all the records! The largest machine . . . the longest distance glide (American), the longest time in the air, the smallest angle of descent, and the highest wind!!!"

The Wrights were at the brink of powered flight. They had mastered two of the three conditions necessary, having designed wings capable of sustaining a craft in flight and a control system that allowed them to maintain balance and execute turns.

After making some short glides on October 24, they broke camp on October 28 and walked to Kitty Hawk through "a cold drizzling storm blowing over 30 miles per hour," in Wilbur's description. Their trip across Albemarle Sound was as frustrating as the one two months earlier—another thirty-six-hour affair. After starting out aboard the *Lou Willis*, they had to transfer to a boat called the *Ray* when Captain Franklin Midgett refused to complete the journey because of high winds.

The Wrights had already done calculations on a powered machine:

the size of the wings, the weight of the airframe, the weight of the engine, the horsepower necessary to get the craft off the ground and keep it there. All they needed now was to acquire a motor and do some reading on the subject of propellers.

The 1902 machine executing a turn
LIBRARY OF CONGRESS

CHAPTER 4

1903

Our section [Kitty Hawk] got its full share of the heavy hurricane of a few days ago, the wind reaching a velocity of 80 miles per hour at which time it blew the anemometer off the weather station and from that time the record was lost. . . .

The surfmen who were obliged to do double duty on account of thick weather claim it is the most severe storm they have experienced for many years. These brave fellows are poorly paid for the hardships they endure and the risks involved in the performance of their duty is great. . . . These men during the past hurricane night and day faced the storm in the discharge of their duties while the salt spray brought tears to their eyes and the flying sand and pebbles bit like bird shot, still they did not complain. We believe that to the faithful there will sooner or later come a reward.

Elizabeth City Economist,
October 16, 1903

Off-Season

Wilbur Wright did an odd thing that winter. Back in Dayton, he contacted an organization called the Redpath Lyceum Bureau about the possibility of becoming a touring lecturer on the subject of flight. The bureau responded that if Wilbur could pay his own expenses, hire a lantern operator, and inject a little humor into his presentation, some bookings might be arranged.

As with Wilbur's short-lived interest in moving his glider experiments to the Chicago area following the 1901 season, it is unclear how serious his intentions were. The Wrights were in the process of preparing their first patent application, and showing slides of their work to crowds of strangers could hardly have been in their interest. With powered flight within his reach, close to the solution of one of history's great engineering problems, it was unlike Wilbur to want to leave the shop and go off lecturing.

Maybe he figured he had some time on his hands. The Wrights had always taken the addition of an engine to be the easiest part of solving the flight problem. There were plenty of companies in the business of making gasoline engines. They had only to have a motor built to their specifications. And as for a means of converting their engine's power into forward thrust, they could take their cue from the literature on marine propellers. Once they knew the theory behind marine-propeller design, they could adapt it to the special case of moving through air.

They were badly mistaken on both counts. Wilbur wrote ten or more reputable manufacturers in New York, Pennsylvania, Massachusetts, and Ohio saying he needed an engine that would deliver eight or nine horsepower, weigh no more than twenty pounds per horsepower, and run free of vibration. None of the manufacturers could deliver such an engine. As for the theory behind marine-propeller design, there was none. Propeller designs had always been arrived at through empirical means. There was no particular strategy for determining in advance what made for the greatest efficiency.

The Wrights would have to build an engine and propellers from scratch. What had looked like a winter of taking advantage of the labor of others was turning into a series of engineering hurdles as challenging as any they'd ever faced.

Luckily, they had help in the person of shopkeeper, machinist, friend, and fledgling engine builder Charlie Taylor. The Wrights had hired Taylor as an assistant in their bicycle shop in 1901 for the sum of eighteen dollars a week, or thirty cents an hour. He was a bargain of the first magnitude.

It's unlikely that customers of the shop ever mistook Taylor for a member of the Wright clan. Katharine Wright could barely stand him at times, finding him insolent. A man who apparently took pride in his vices, Taylor smoked as many as twenty-five cigars a day and enlivened the shop with blue language. That is not to say he was bad for business. It was Taylor who, beginning in 1901, allowed the Wrights the freedom to escape to the Outer Banks without having to worry about affairs back home.

The Wrights and Taylor had minimal experience with engines. Wilbur and Orville had built a one-cylinder motor to power the machinery in their bicycle shop. Taylor had worked on engines but never constructed one.

For a piece of machinery that, over the entire course of its working life, performed its intended function for a total of 101 seconds, the engine of the Wright Flyer has received a good deal of scrutiny. At least one complete book and dozens of papers and articles have been written about it.

The Wrights didn't make comprehensive drawings of their engine. Rather, they just scratched out a representation of the next component to be built on whatever scrap of paper was at hand. Orville or Taylor then tacked the paper to the wall over the workbench and set about making the part. The machinery on hand to aid in the work was as basic as might be expected for such a bare-bones operation: a drill press and a lathe.

To save weight, they used an engine block made of aluminum, cast at a local foundry. Taylor bored the engine's four cylinders on the lathe. He made the pistons himself, too.

As always, the Wrights were concerned with aerodynamics. The radiator, built in a vertical configuration, was to be mounted separate from the engine on the central forward upright of the airplane.

The long, thin gas tank was attached behind a strut near the upper wing. Its capacity was only four-tenths of a gallon.

The engine was undeniably crude, with no spark plugs, carburetor, or fuel pump. Gas was delivered via a rubber speaking-tube hose. The fuel-delivery system was gravity-fed, the gas flowing downward from the tank directly into the cylinders. Like the fuel line, the radiator was made of speaking-tube hose, though in this case the tubing was metal. The speed of the engine could not be adjusted in flight; it ran wide-open. The motor smoked, gave off noxious fumes, overheated quickly, spat oil and raw gasoline on the pilot, and made a noise to wake the dead.

Nonetheless, it was a remarkable achievement under the circumstances. Begun in late December, the engine was completely built by mid-February. On the second day it was tested, February 13, the bearings froze, shattering the crankcase. The Wrights arranged with the foundry to have another one cast, but it was a full two months before it was finally delivered. Taylor had the engine rebuilt by May.

Its performance was better than expected. The Wrights figured they needed an absolute minimum of eight or nine horsepower to get their airplane off the ground. In testing, their rebuilt engine delivered a surprising sixteen horsepower immediately after cranking, which quickly dropped to a fairly steady twelve horsepower.

Charlie Taylor deserves a large share of the credit for the engine of the Wright Flyer, but the brothers faced their struggles with propeller design alone.

They needed to know whether two propellers were preferable to one. They needed to know whether it was better to mount a propeller in front of or behind a wing. They needed to know how long and how wide their propellers should be, and what curvature they should have. They needed to know how fast they should turn for maximum efficiency.

The Wrights didn't have the time or the means to test a variety of propeller designs. With no tools other than pencil and paper, they had to take a complex practical problem, express it in mathematics, and come up with an unequivocal answer: the best propellers for their particular engine and airframe should be so long, so wide, have such a curvature, and rotate at such a speed. The Wrights gave themselves one chance. They would build only a single set of propellers.

Orville described the basic problem years later:

> It is hard to find even a point from which to make a start; for nothing about a propeller, or the medium in which it acts, stands still for a moment. The thrust depends upon the speed and the angle at which the blade strikes the air; the angle at which the blade strikes the air depends upon the speed at which the propeller is turning, the speed the machine is travelling forward, and the speed at which the air is slipping backward; the slip of the air backward depends upon the thrust exerted by the propeller, and the amount of air acted upon. When any of these changes, it changes all the rest, as they are all interdependent upon one another.

Before the Wrights, aeronautical propellers were generally understood along the lines of a screw boring into a hard surface—pushed forward through the air while spinning, they generated lift. By contrast, the Wrights conceived of propellers as rotary wings, or wings moving in a spiral course—spun on their axes, they generated thrust. Much as a wing rises because the pressure on its lower side is greater than that on its upper side, a propeller moves forward because the pressure behind the blade is greater than that in front of the blade.

Once the Wrights conceived of propellers as rotary wings, they understood that their wind-tunnel data on wing sections could be applied directly to propeller design. The airfoil shape that generated the greatest lift at different angles of attack would also generate the greatest thrust under a variety of conditions.

No sooner did they solve one aspect of the problem than other difficulties presented themselves. For example, it stands to reason that the faster propellers turn, the more thrust they will produce. But that is not exactly the case. There comes a point at which propellers lose their "bite" on the air and fail to generate thrust. Keeping an airplane in the air requires that thrust be maintained. The Wrights calculated the speed at which their propellers would deliver maximum thrust and geared them accordingly, so that for every twenty-three rotations of the engine shaft, the propellers rotated eight times.

What they finally arrived at, after filling five notebooks with calculations, were two narrow, slowly rotating propellers nearly eight and a half feet long. They would be mounted behind the wings and spin in opposite directions, so as to eliminate the effects of torque.

One of the best testaments to the Wrights' engineering genius is the fact that, on the Outer Banks the following fall, their propellers delivered thrust within 1 percent of what they'd calculated on paper.

Five years after the first powered flights, other aviators were still discovering that, while their engines had more horsepower than the Wrights', they still had less thrust at their disposal. The reason was the inefficiency of their propellers. The Wrights' engine may have had a homemade feel to it, but their propellers were beyond state of the art.

The brothers kept Octave Chanute apprised of their work, and he followed their progress closely. He also threw a scare into them a couple of times. Knowing the approximate size and weight of their airplane, and knowing that they were planning to power it with an engine producing only eight or nine horsepower, he gave the reasonable opinion that they were cutting their calculations too close. It was advisable to have a surplus of power, yet the Wrights' engine might be inadequate to get them into the air even if it performed exactly as designed. Chanute further told them that they could anticipate a 25- to 30-percent loss of power between the engine and the propellers. They had only figured on a 10- to 15-percent loss. If Chanute was correct, they would never get off the ground.

Once they found in Dayton that their engine delivered roughly twelve horsepower, rather than eight or nine, and once they learned on the Outer Banks that the loss of power in transmission was only 5 to 10 percent, not 25 to 30, they knew they could fly.

Those Who Witnessed

Long before the 1903 season, the Wrights were well known around the Kitty Hawk area. They had visited in the homes and shops of a number of local people, a good many of whom had in turn come to see their camp. Members of the Tate family—everyone from Bill and Addie to Dan and young Tom—had played an active role in stitching their wing cloth, launching their gliders, or even riding aboard them. But the Wrights had never required more than minimal help with their actual experiments. Having one extra person around camp to man a wing during launching was all they needed.

That changed in 1903. The 1901 glider had weighed a little under 100 pounds. The 1902 machine had boasted 305 square feet of wing area and a 32-foot wingspan. Craft of such size were easily maneuvered by two men. By contrast, the 1903 Flyer—informally dubbed the "whopper flying machine"—checked in with slightly over 500 square feet of wing area, had a 40-foot wingspan, and weighed nearly 675 pounds. Now, the Wrights needed all the help they could get.

Their first attempt at powered flight, on December 14, 1903, was a case in point. For launching, the Flyer sat atop a small carriage that ran along a sixty-foot monorail. Built in four fifteen-foot sections, the rail was jokingly christened the "junction railroad." Faced with moving the Flyer across a flat stretch of sand and part way up the side of the dune from which they planned to launch, the Wrights and their helpers that day apparently laid the junction railroad outside the hangar, pushed the Flyer sixty feet along the track, dug up the last fifteen-foot section, placed it in front of the Flyer, moved another fifteen feet, dug up the last rail, placed it in front of the Flyer, moved another fifteen feet, and so on. It was a laborious quarter-mile.

December 17, the date of their historic flights, was no easier in that regard. The Wrights and their helpers laid the junction railroad on a flat stretch of sand and left it there, apparently manhandling the Flyer back to the starting point after each flight.

All of a sudden, manpower was at a premium.

With a goal of making the first powered heavier-than-air flights in history, they also wanted witnesses—as many as they could get. They extended a general invitation to people in the area to come and witness their flights, as well as a couple of personal invitations. However, since their activities were heavily dependent on the weather and could not be scheduled far in advance, and since their means of announcing an attempt at flight was no more sophisticated than a flag tacked to the side of one of their camp buildings, it was unlikely that their plans would reach the attention of more than a few.

For all practical purposes, their witnesses were to be limited to whatever camp guests were on hand and the men of the Kill Devil Hills Lifesaving Station.

The Wrights had been developing a friendship with the Outer Banks lifesavers ever since their first visit to North Carolina. Their photographs from 1900 included shots of the Kitty Hawk station and of its crew formally posed and drilling on the ocean. In 1902, they got four men of the Kill Devil Hills crew to pose in the doorway of their station wearing white hats and jackets. The Wrights sometimes visited the stations during idle hours or took shelter there when their camp was in disrepair.

Their relationship with the lifesavers was never closer than in 1903. Orville's journal from that year contains numerous references to his and Wilbur's trips to the Kill Devil Hills station. On other occasions, one or another of the lifesavers traveled to the Wrights' camp to deliver parcels.

Jesse Ward, the station keeper, ferried George Spratt across Roanoke Sound to Manteo when he was on his way back north in 1903.

Surfman John Daniels brought the Wrights word when Octave Chanute left home and headed east in hopes of witnessing the 1903 experiments; surfman Adam Etheridge brought news of Chanute's imminent arrival on the coast; and Captain Ward apparently escorted the elderly gentleman into camp personally. After Chanute's visit, surfman Willie Dough sailed him back to Manteo.

In short, the lifesavers were a part of the daily lives of the Wrights and their associates and a major aid to the running of the camp throughout the 1903 season.

Anyone familiar with the story of the Outer Banks lifesavers will not be surprised to learn of that level of service. Many of the old stations have been moved, restored, or converted for use as private

Taken sometime around 1903, this photograph shows three of the Kill Devil Hills lifesavers who witnessed the famous flights and a fourth who was present at the failed trial of December 14, 1903. The first and second men are keeper Jesse Ward and Tom Beacham. The fourth and fifth are John Daniels and Willie Dough. The man in the middle is unidentified.

homes, restaurants, museums, and offices. They are about as beloved among history-minded visitors to the Outer Banks as the great lighthouses, Fort Raleigh, and the national memorial to the Wright brothers.

The water along the Outer Banks has seen heavy commercial traffic since the early days of the United States. Historian David Stick reports that in the 1830s, visitors to Nags Head could climb Jockey's Ridge and see as many as half a dozen vessels on the horizon at one time. Conservative estimates of the number of ships lost in the area known as the Graveyard of the Atlantic place the total upwards of six hundred. More likely, wrecks number in the thousands. A single major storm could sink six or eight vessels off the Outer Banks.

The United States Lifesaving Service began operations in 1847 with stations on the New Jersey coast. Seven years later, it expanded to Long Island and the Great Lakes. In 1874, in an effort to cut shipping losses, Congress allocated funds for the building of seven lifesaving stations on the Outer Banks. Those original stations, twelve to fifteen miles apart, were at Jones Hill (Currituck Beach), Caffeys

A crew and its surfboat

NORTH CAROLINA STATE ARCHIVES

Inlet, Kitty Hawk, Nags Head, Bodie Island (Oregon Inlet), Chicamacomico, and Little Kinnakeet, from north to south.

Just how necessary lifesaving service was came to light three years later. In late November 1877, the steamer USS *Huron* sank off Nags Head, 103 persons drowning. Tragically, this took place just a week before the lifesavers—then employed seasonally—were scheduled to begin winter duty.

In late January 1878, the steamer *Metropolis* went down off the northern Outer Banks, 85 people perishing. This wreck occurred off Poyner Hill, between the Currituck Beach and Caffeys Inlet stations. The lifesavers could not reach the scene in time.

Partly due to two such losses occurring within a two-month span, another eleven stations were funded, the Kill Devil Hills station among them. The plan was to have stations spaced roughly seven miles apart, which would allow quick response anywhere along the Outer Banks.

Though only four years had passed since the first stations were built, the design was already evolving. The differences between the first and second generations can be seen in the 1874 Kitty Hawk station, now a restaurant, and the 1878 Kill Devil Hills station, now a real-estate office in Corolla, on the northern Outer Banks. The 1874 stations were barnlike and had open-air lookouts, while the 1878 versions were more elaborate two-story affairs, generally with enclosed lookout towers and distinctive gingerbread trim.

More important, the competency with which the stations were run was also evolving.

By most standards, the stations were a failure initially. Keepers were paid two hundred dollars annually. Surfmen received forty dollars a month for their three or four months of resident service, along with a three-dollar stipend for each time they were called to a wreck during the off-season. This was good pay for the time and place, good enough to tempt local politicians to appoint their relatives and associates to the stations with little regard for their fitness for duty. Investigations into North Carolina and Virginia stations between 1875 and 1877 led to the dismissal of nearly 20 percent of their employees, including four keepers. Among these lifesavers were several teachers and a blacksmith—men with no knowledge of their particular duties, or of sea rescue in general. The investigators found insubordination and nepotism. At one station, five of the seven employees were dismissed as incompetent.

Hiring practices were well on their way to being overhauled by the time the second wave of Outer Banks stations was built.

A further problem was the staffing schedule. Unless a vessel happened to wreck during December, January, February, or perhaps March, it was out of luck unless the keeper and the six surfmen could be rounded up immediately from far and wide.

Staffing was expanded to eight months of the year in the 1880s, and an eighth man was added to the crews. Year-round staffing came after the outbreak of World War I.

From those haphazard beginnings grew a disciplined, professional service. The lifesavers were not the supermen they are sometimes romanticized to have been, but simply local fishermen. Some of them were illiterate. In fact, the ability to read and write was sometimes the deciding factor in the selection of station keepers.

Lifesavers were held to a high standard. District supervisors supposedly wore white gloves during unannounced inspections. At some stations, the men were not allowed to play cards during idle hours. One keeper made his men sit down to meals in the same alignment in which they hauled their surfboat to the beach and manned it during rescue operations, with punishment doled out to anyone who deviated. At another station, a surfman supposedly lost his job for no other reason than his inability to see a bird atop a telephone pole some distance down the beach. He wept upon being fired.

As the service grew in sophistication, so did the stations themselves. They were built for one specific purpose—sea rescue—not as outposts dedicated to civic betterment. Nonetheless, communities tended to grow around them. The lifesaving stations generally had their own stables, coal yard, and separate cookhouse. They eventually had a communications room containing telephone and telegraph equipment. They generally had the best facilities for gathering rainwater in the area, with large tanks to catch water running off each side of the roof, and off the cookhouse roof, too. During dry conditions, local people sometimes came to the lifesaving stations for water. People also came for shelter during heavy weather. They gathered to watch the weekly surfboat drills on the beach. Children came to watch the lifesavers can figs or make ice cream.

Activity at the lifesaving stations was similar to that at modern fire stations, with long stretches of routine drills punctuated by periods of dangerous activity under extreme conditions. One day of the week was devoted to beach-apparatus drills and another to surfboat drills. Another day was spent in groundskeeping and building maintenance, another in resuscitation drills, and another in signal drills, during which the lifesavers were trained in communications with ships offshore.

That was during the easy times. It was an unfortunate fact of life that the lifesavers were most likely to be called upon to perform rescue operations in the worst weather.

During heavy storms and at night, tower lookouts were of limited value. Beach patrols were especially important at those times. One heading north and one south, the surfmen walked roughly three and a half miles down the beach to where a small halfway house stood between each pair of stations. There, they waited for the life-saver patrolling from the neighboring station. The two men exchanged small badges they had been issued before their patrol, walked the three and a half miles back to their home stations, and turned in the badges as proof of having done their duty.

Nighttime patrols were a difficult task. The men sometimes walked backwards to keep the rain and blowing sand out of their faces. Some stepped on birds huddled on the beach. A few even stumbled across human bodies washed up on the sand. Some contracted pneumonia.

Naturally enough, the preference was always for staying out of the water during rescue operations. The two best-known implements of rescue for ships wrecked close to shore were the Lyle gun and the breeches buoy. The Lyle gun—a small bronze cannon with a range of five hundred yards—was brought to a point on the beach oppo-site the wreck, from where it fired a line to the ship. A three-inch hawser bearing a breeches buoy—a life ring with pant legs—was later drawn out to the ship. The stranded sailors stepped into the breeches buoy like a pair of trousers and were pulled to shore one at a time.

When wrecks occurred beyond the range of the Lyle gun, rescues were made the old-fashioned way. In early days, the lifesavers had to drag the surfboats through the sand to the water themselves; the draft horses later kept at the lifesaving stations for that purpose were renowned for their size and strength. In heavy weather, the lifesav-ers sometimes had to launch their boat several times before they could get beyond the breakers. After rowing to the wreck, they had to pull swimmers from the water, rescue them from on deck or even in the masts, or escort lifeboats through the surf.

What was probably the signature rescue of the Outer Banks

Members of a lifesaving crew with a Lyle gun

NORTH CAROLINA STATE ARCHIVES

*Members of the Kill Devil Hills crew
in the door of their station*

LIBRARY OF CONGRESS

stations took place during World War I from the Chicamacomico station, on Hatteras Island. On August 16, 1918, the British tanker *Mirlo*, bearing fifty-two men and a cargo of gasoline, was heading north to Norfolk when it hit a mine laid by a German submarine. Leroy Midgett, stationed in the tower of the Chicamacomico station, saw the explosion and immediately notified the keeper, John Allen Midgett.

The lifesavers had motorized surfboats by those days, but it still took the Chicamacomico men three launches to reach the open sea. Approaching what was left of the *Mirlo*, they found three lifeboats afloat and learned that a fourth had overturned near the wreck. Navigating a maze of burning oil amid exploding barrels of gasoline, Captain Midgett and his men made their way to the capsized lifeboat to save its former occupants. They then transferred sailors from the other three lifeboats to their surfboat for the dangerous run into the beach. To get all the men ashore, they had to land and launch several times. The rescue took six hours, but only ten men of the *Mirlo* were lost, a remarkable feat.

Ironically, the sailors of the *Mirlo*, once hysterically grateful at seeing their rescuers, turned salty during their brief residence at the station, reportedly complaining about the accommodations and spitting tobacco juice on the floor.

The British and American governments later bestowed numerous honors on the Chicamacomico lifesavers.

The Kitty Hawk and Kill Devil Hills stations were not among the busiest on the Outer Banks. Generally speaking, the farther south—the closer to Cape Hatteras and the infamous Diamond Shoals—the busier the station. The surf is also rougher farther south on the Outer Banks, as the water remains relatively deep near shore. The shoals lying close to shore off the Kitty Hawk–Kill Devil Hills area tend to break up the waves before they hit the beach.

Latter-day men of the Kill Devil Hills station did participate in what was perhaps the most improbable pair of rescues in the history of the Outer Banks lifesavers. This took place after the Lifesaving Service and the Revenue Cutter Service were combined under the banner of the Coast Guard.

In December 1927, the Greek tank steamer *Kyzikes*, formerly the *Paraguay*, was battered by a storm and began taking on water two hundred miles off the coast. Its crew radioed for help. Six different ships responded to the call but either failed to locate the *Kyzikes*, lost it in the dark, or were damaged themselves. Finally, with its radio out, four of its crew washed overboard, its engines dead, and its lights inoperable, the *Kyzikes* ran aground and broke apart a mile north of the Kill Devil Hills station shortly before dawn. A group of sailors made their way to the bow and flashed a distress signal. They were relieved to see a bright light answer promptly. But after additional messages were exchanged, it came to be understood that it was members of the ship's own crew answering, and from only ten or fifteen feet away; the stern of the ship had broken off cleanly and swung around almost alongside the bow. A gangplank was promptly run between the bow and the stern, and the crew was reunited.

Shortly after dawn, a couple of men on shore, one a member of the Kill Devil Hills crew, spotted the *Kyzikes*. The lifesavers assembled on the beach, fired a line to the ship, and eventually rescued twenty-four sailors.

Less than two years later, in September 1929, the Swedish steamer *Carl Gerhard* lost its way while traveling down the coast from Nova Scotia to Florida. For five days, the sky was so overcast that the captain could neither take star sightings at night nor see the sun during the day. Neither could he locate any lighthouses on the coast. Finally, just before dawn one morning, the *Carl Gerhard* bumped a sand bar and then slammed into a partially submerged obstruction—the remains of the *Kyzikes*, a mile north of Kill Devil Hills. Four crews were quickly summoned, including the men of the Kill Devil Hills station. A line was fired to the ship. Twenty-five living beings rode the breeches buoy to shore that day: twenty-one men, a woman, two dogs, and a cat. The *Kyzikes* and the *Carl Gerhard* still lie together today.

The lifesavers of the Kill Devil Hills station in 1903, as listed in the official payroll records, were Jesse E. Ward, keeper, Robert L. Westcott, William T. "Tom" Beacham, Adam D. Etheridge, John T. Daniels, Willie S. Dough, Benjamin D. Pugh, and Otto C. Ward, substitute. Adam Etheridge had previously been with the Caffeys Inlet station and Bob Westcott with the Oregon Inlet station. Willie Dough was a former fisherman and farmer. John Daniels, a former day laborer, had been a lifesaver for less than two years. He and Adam Etheridge were close friends, being married to half-sisters.

Men sometimes worked at one station one year and another the

next, or worked as a lifesaver one year and at some other occupation the following year. This led to a certain informality in the be-
stowing of the lifesaver designation and to some confusion in the
official records. For example, Benjamin W. "Uncle Benny" O'Neal,
one of the witnesses at Wilbur Wright's failed attempt at powered
flight on December 14, 1903, is generally described as a Kill Devil
Hills lifesaver, though he does not appear in the 1903 records as
such. Likewise, S. J. Payne, said to have witnessed the famous flights
through a spyglass from the Kitty Hawk station four miles away, is
invariably described as the captain of that station, though it appears
that title was officially held by Avery B. L. Tillett.

Given their service to the Wright brothers and their legacy of
heroism on the Outer Banks, it seems fitting that it was a group of
lifesavers—accompanied by a teenage boy and a man from Manteo
hobnobbing at the station—who were summoned to witness North
Carolina's most famous event. Most of the men at the Kill Devil
Hills station were privileged to see either Wilbur's failed attempt on
December 14 or the brothers' successful flights of December 17,
whether in person or from afar.

To say that the witnesses to the first powered flights were low-key
about their involvement with the Wright brothers would be an un-
derstatement. Their attitude was epitomized by Bob Westcott, the
No. 1 surfman at the Kill Devil Hills Lifesaving Station. On watch
at the station on the morning of December 17, 1903, Westcott alternately discharged his duty, scanning the sea for passing ships, and
turned his spyglass on the activity at the Wrights' camp. From a
distance of nearly a mile, he could easily identify the men at the
site, and he saw all four of the flights.

Westcott's involvement was apparently common knowledge at the
station, yet no one bothered mentioning it publicly. It was twenty-

five years before it came to light in a court case that he had witnessed one of the great events of the century. Even Orville Wright,
who kept close track of such things, didn't know to count Westcott
among the witnesses until many years after the fact.

So it was with the other witnesses. Little was ever heard publicly
from Willie Dough, Adam Etheridge, and Manteo lumber merchant
W. C. Brinkley. John Daniels gave a few interviews in later years,
but he certainly didn't go courting attention. Muskrat trapper Johnny
Moore, seventeen years old at the time of the flights, was a figure of
note at a few latter-day functions honoring the Wrights mainly because of his reticence. Asked about his memories of the Wrights or
his opinion of the state of aviation, he'd issue a gruff comment, be
described by the newspapermen present as "bored," "noncommit-
tal," "unimpressed," or "Coolidge-like," and head back home.

These, then, were the men present on the famous day.

Those Who Didn't

Others were less modest than the first-flight witnesses. News of
the flights was initially met with skepticism or indifference, but over
the years, as the importance of the Wrights' accomplishment came
to be understood, a cast of would-be and could-have-been witnesses
started to grow.

Four of the men who contributed most to the Wright brothers'
efforts were not on hand to witness their triumph.

Now living at Martins Point, fifteen miles away by horseback, Bill
Tate was no longer seen frequently around Kill Devil Hills. Still, the
Wrights valued his company. They told him they intended to make an
attempt at powered flight on December 17 and invited him to make
the trip.

Upon rising that morning, Tate looked outside. The wind was gusting and the temperature was around the freezing mark. He doubted the Wrights would fly under such conditions and decided to stay home. Reconsidering, he later mounted up and headed south. By his own account, he made it as far as the Kitty Hawk post office when a man—identified in some sources as one of the lifesavers and in others as Johnny Moore—came running up the beach shouting, "They have done it! They have done it! Damned if they ain't flew!"

Bill Tate had missed the event. Over the years, he came to regard it as "the greatest regret of my life." No one was more responsible for the Wrights' presence on the Outer Banks than Tate.

The brothers' relationship with Dan Tate deteriorated through the 1903 season. Dan, a fisherman, had become a fixture in camp over the past couple of years, running errands, helping in the construction and maintenance of the hangars, and assisting at glider launches. Now, he was apparently having misgivings about his role. According to Orville, about two weeks after the Wrights arrived, Dan showed up in camp one morning, announced that the price of fish had gone up, and asked whether the brothers would require his help again that year, and for how long. If so, he wanted his salary increased, and he wanted to be paid weekly.

The Wrights agreed to up the incentive to seven dollars a week—nearly double the local rate—but that being the case, they wanted to formalize the conditions of Dan's employment. They stipulated that he be in camp by eight o'clock every morning and that he work a ten-hour day, with an hour of that time allowed for travel to and from home. The Wrights would also provide him dinner.

This arrangement only worsened matters. All of a sudden, the Wrights found Dan's carpentry skills lacking. As Orville put it, "Whenever we set him at any work about the building, he would do so much damage with his awkwardness that we found it more profitable to let him sit around." Having determined it was best for Dan to be sitting around, they came to consider him "spoiled" when he did so.

The Wrights needed to have someone on hand whenever the weather turned suitable for flying, and they were willing to pay Dan for a good deal of idle time in return for that assurance. In exchange, they expected his uncomplaining help with menial tasks and with flying.

Dan's perspective was different. The Wrights' elder, and a man accustomed to wresting a living from the sea, he suddenly found he was qualified to do nothing better than a maid's chores—and his employers weren't even satisfied with the way he did those. Clearly frustrated, he began griping when the Wrights asked him to do the dishes. He also complained when they requested his help out in the dunes.

They parted company over a minor squabble on Wednesday, October 28. The weather had turned cold, and Wilbur instructed Dan to go to the beach and gather some driftwood for the camp stove. Dan, chafing at more busywork, countered that gathering driftwood wasn't worth the trouble, since cut wood was available for only three dollars a cord from one of the Baum family. When the Wrights asked that he do as he was told, Dan "took his hat and left for home," according to Orville. He didn't come back.

Dan Tate was never again close to the Wrights. Though no one beside the Wrights themselves knew the feeling of running beside a wing and launching a glider better than Dan, he missed out on the powered machine.

As did George Spratt. In ill health between the 1902 and 1903 seasons, Spratt recovered well enough to make his third visit to the Outer Banks, arriving on October 23. He was just in time to endure some miserable weather and to witness the Wrights having trouble with their engine. Spratt judged them ill-prepared for powered flight. He even thought they were courting disaster.

Spratt stayed only two weeks. By the time the Wrights' propeller shafts were damaged in a test on November 5, he had seen enough. In fact, he was on his way to the boat within two hours of the mishap, taking the damaged shafts with him, to be expressed from Norfolk back to the bicycle shop in Dayton, where Charlie Taylor would set them straight.

Spratt did contribute indirectly to the powered flights before his departure, by building portions of the junction railroad. The Wrights missed his presence. No one was more welcome in camp.

It was pure coincidence that Spratt, in Manteo at the beginning of his trip home, bumped into Octave Chanute, who was on the final leg of his journey to witness the Wrights' experiments. Spratt gave his opinion that the brothers' chances were poor.

Chanute's reaction is puzzling. After visiting Kill Devil Hills, he felt obliged to write Spratt and tell him how promising he felt the Wrights' work was. And upon learning of the flights of December 17, he sent Spratt an I-told-you-so letter. To the Wrights, however, he was far less encouraging. It was Chanute's position, after all, that the brothers' engine was underpowered and that they were cutting their calculations too close.

Given the rough climate and the Wrights' slow progress, Chanute stayed on the Outer Banks only a week and missed the flights.

Chanute was also the conduit by which another outsider nearly came to the Wrights' camp in 1903. In December 1902, Patrick Alexander, a balloon pilot, a parachute jumper, and a figure inhabiting the fringes of British government, had traveled across the ocean, finagled a letter of introduction from Chanute, and knocked unannounced on the Wrights' door in Dayton the day before Christmas.

That he charmed the Wrights is proven by the fact that they told him he would be welcome on the Outer Banks, though they barely knew him. In fact, the only thing that kept Alexander from witnessing the brothers at work at Kill Devil Hills in 1903 was missing a travel connection with Chanute in Washington. Alexander later carried so much information about the Wrights back to the British government that the brothers came to believe he was a spy.

A couple of North Carolinians may have come even closer to witnessing the historic flights.

Mrs. Lillie Swindell, whose first husband was Kill Devil Hills lifesaver Adam Etheridge, told in her later years how, during the late-morning hours on December 17, 1903, she had been standing at her kitchen window in Kitty Hawk, where she had a distant but plain view of the Wrights' camp. Though the flights took place right in front of her, she didn't bother to watch for lack of interest.

And Ora L. Jones, a seventeen-year-old, six-dollar-a-week reporter for the *Asheville Citizen*, later claimed he was sent all the way across the state to cover the Wrights' trials.

Jones had gained favor with his supervisor for a humorous piece ridiculing Samuel Langley's efforts at powered flight. "The feature I wrote on this prompted my editor to send me . . . to Kitty Hawk, where he said two other cranks were trying to fly," he told the Asheville paper in 1964. "He thrilled me by handing me $50 expense money and saying he wanted me to go down there and write some really funny stuff."

How a newspaper editor in a North Carolina mountain town came by his knowledge of the Wrights is anyone's guess.

"Naturally I expected the Wright brothers to be impressed and appreciative when I told them I had traveled 500 miles just to 'write

them up,'" Jones remembered. "On the contrary they made it pain-
fully clear that they wanted no publicity. They ordered me to get
away from Kill Devil Hill and stay away."

Jones claimed he watched some of the Wrights' preparations
through a spyglass borrowed from the lifesavers but was huddled by
a stove in a boardinghouse a mile from Kill Devil Hills at the time
of the flights. He supposedly learned of the brothers' success on his
way back to Asheville.

Certain aspects of his account—how mosquitoes plagued the Outer
Banks in mid-December; how he planned to return to Elizabeth
City, across Albemarle Sound, by horse and buggy; how he found
lodging so close to uninhabited Kill Devil Hills—make his story
suspect. It is also worth noting that his paper carried no news of the
Wrights at least through mid-January. But if his account contains
any truth at all, if six decades of memory simply obscured some of
the details, then Ora L. Jones was easily the closest reporter to the
scene of the flights.

One of the strangest claims of involvement with the Wright brothers
came to light in the early 1960s. Frank B. Wood, a Florida octoge-
narian, and a balloonist, parachutist, and automobile and bicycle racer
in his younger days, told a UPI reporter how he had been in Philadelphia in late 1903 when he ran into a friend and fellow thrill
seeker, the great Barney Oldfield. According to Wood, Oldfield happened to be on his way to the Outer Banks to ask the Wrights to
build him a special-order bicycle, and he invited Wood and perhaps
a third man along.

They started out by automobile and completed their journey by
horse and buggy, train, and ferry. Arriving at the Wrights' camp on
December 14, they helped launch the failed attempt at powered
flight that day. In fact, Wood described three trials on December 14,

the first stretching about 44 feet, the second about 60 feet, and the third about 166 feet.

Though they departed before the historic flights three days later, it was Oldfield, according to Wood, who made them possible, by instructing the Wrights how to lengthen their elevator lever so the plane would "get more air."

Wood's story was given credence by a second UPI report and an account by the *Raleigh News and Observer*. Unfortunately, it holds little water. The Wrights made only one attempt at powered flight on December 14. They documented the witnesses to that trial both on paper and on film, and Frank B. Wood and Barney Oldfield were not among them. Barney Oldfield, a brash, cigar-chomping twenty-five-year-old, was the number-one driver on Henry Ford's racing team. Just six months earlier, he had become the first man to drive an automobile at the speed of a mile a minute. The presence of such a personage on the Outer Banks would have been worthy of note.

And as for Wood's assertion that Oldfield stood behind the Wrights' success, a long line of claimants had already formed. Edward Huffaker believed the brothers had learned some of their most important lessons from him. George Spratt ultimately broke with the Wrights over their unwillingness to admit that one of his ideas led them to powered flight. In weak moments, Octave Chanute let Wilbur and Orville be characterized as pupils whose success was dependent on his instruction.

When all such claims are totaled up, there is little left for the Wrights beyond taking the blame for their crashes.

At least one man besides Bill Tate received a personal invitation from the Wrights to witness their powered flights. Unlike Tate, this man didn't hesitate on account of the weather. He had something better to do. In fact, he was the central local figure in what appeared to be the greatest news story ever to hit the Outer Banks, an event that at the time rendered the activity at Kill Devil Hills insignificant. The 1903 season saw the introduction of one of the most memorable and controversial of the peripheral figures in the Wright brothers' story: Alpheus "Alf" Drinkwater, a telegrapher by trade.

On December 2, 1903, the navy tug *Peoria* was en route, depending on the account, from New York, Newport, or New London to either Annapolis or Norfolk. Regardless, it got caught in a bad storm and overshot its destination by a wide margin. In the rough seas, the *Peoria* lost control of the two vessels it was charged with towing, the submarines *Moccasin* and *Adder*.

The original United States Submarine Service, a fleet of seven vessels, had been organized earlier that year, and the news that two of its ships were adrift and unmanned in the rough Atlantic was of major national concern.

Boatswain Patrick Deery of the *Adder*, a forty-three-year-old Brooklynite, was riding with his crew mates aboard the *Peoria*. Answering the call for a volunteer to try to save his ship, he tied a rope around his waist, jumped into the frigid Atlantic, and swam a hundred yards to the *Adder*. He attached a line and then swam back to the *Peoria*. After a couple of stiff drinks to warm him up, he volunteered to go after the *Moccasin*, but the *Peoria* was already heavily burdened in the high seas and unable to maneuver into position to save the second drifting vessel.

So it was that the *Moccasin* fell into Alf Drinkwater's lap at Currituck Beach, thirty miles north of Kill Devil Hills.

Submarines were little recognized among the general public at the time. The telegraph operator at False Cape, Virginia, first identified a "submerged barge" drifting toward shore, then amended his description to a half-sunk pontoon with a kerosene barrel on top. It

The A-4, *formerly the* Moccasin, *in Manila Bay around 1912*

was Drinkwater who correctly identified the *Moccasin* and informed the navy when it washed up opposite the Currituck Beach Lighthouse at eleven-thirty on the evening of December 3.

The *Moccasin* was twenty-eight-year-old Alf Drinkwater's big break. Drinkwater claimed to be the grandson of an Englishman shipwrecked on the Outer Banks in 1830. His father was the keeper of the Oregon Inlet Lifesaving Station, and an uncle of his was the keeper of the station at Cape Hatteras. With such a heritage, it was natural that he should aspire to a lifesaving career himself. But at a frail-looking 120 pounds, he was judged by his father to be unfit for the life of a surfman.

That judgment may have been premature.

When his father transferred to the lifesaving station at Virginia Beach, Virginia, Alf Drinkwater supposedly picked up the art of telegraphy by hanging around the railroad station there. In 1900, he was hired as a telegrapher at the lifesaving station at Currituck Beach, beginning a lengthy career that saw duty with the Signal Service, the Weather Bureau, the Lifesaving Service, the Coast Guard, Western Union, and the Associated Press.

In his later years, Drinkwater was fond of saying that he had witnessed more shipwrecks than any man alive, the basis for his claim being that whenever lifesavers were mustered to fire a line or launch a surfboat, a telegrapher was required to go with them, climb the nearest telegraph pole, and cut in his key so additional help could be summoned if needed. He said there wasn't a pole in 125 miles of coast that he hadn't climbed for the purpose of making repairs, stringing wire, or preparing emergency communications.

The grounding of the *Moccasin* was tailor-made to forge a young man's reputation. Sixty-seven feet long and powered by a 160-horsepower engine, the *Moccasin* was part of the first generation of practical submarines. Capable of a little over seven knots submerged, and sporting a single torpedo tube in its bow, it also marked a new era of war machinery. Fanfare surrounding the *Moccasin* was such that, earlier that year, President Teddy Roosevelt's daughter, Alice, had gone aboard for a submerged test in Narragansett Bay, to great public controversy. Now, with the vessel aground on the Outer Banks, President Roosevelt supposedly wanted a report on the progress of salvage operations every three hours.

The reading public was anxious for news, too, and Alf Drinkwater was just the man to supply it. He set up his telegraph on an orange crate and cut into the line to Norfolk. As salvage operations dragged on, he found an old beach-cart cover, made it into a tent, and slept nights on the sand beside the *Moccasin*.

The navy tried dragging the submarine back to the water, as many as six tugs maneuvering close to shore and pulling with cables. But after three weeks, the *Moccasin*'s hull was still seven feet deep in sand. The navy finally engaged the services of a private engineering firm and even brought down the vessel's New Jersey-based builder, who assured the salvage engineers that the *Moccasin* would hold together even if it were dragged overland all the way to Norfolk. Employing a set of hawsers and two winches, the salvage men dragged the vessel inch by inch over the sand. It took a week, but by early January, the *Moccasin* was back in the water.

In the meantime, residents from up and down the Outer Banks came to witness the spectacle.

Alf Drinkwater was thoroughly frozen and pretty well exhausted after more than a month of roughing it on the beach. He was supposedly the only professional news source on the scene, and his

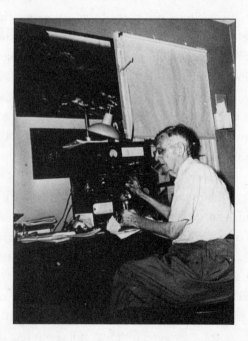

Alf Drinkwater in later years

OUTER BANKS HISTORY CENTER

accounts of the salvage operation appeared on the front pages of papers from the *Washington Post* and the *New York Times* on down, though they didn't carry a byline in those days. His work was judged so good that he was given a 20-percent pay raise, from $600 to $720 annually. He also received a couple of commendations from an admiral.

Forgotten in all this excitement was a short trip south Drinkwater had made several weeks earlier. In the Kitty Hawk area to effect some line repair in late November, he had run across Wilbur and Orville Wright and inquired about the progress of their experiments. The Wrights told him of their powered machine and invited him to come watch the trials. But by mid-December, Drinkwater wouldn't have thought of budging from Currituck Beach even if he'd known the exact date of the flights.

Still, thirty miles to the north, baby-sitting a beached submarine, Alf Drinkwater carved himself a piece of the Wright brothers' story. For years, Drinkwater was credited by many North Carolina sources with transmitting the first news of the powered flights, but that was clearly false. That honor belonged to Joe Dosher at the Weather Bureau office in Kitty Hawk. As it developed, Drinkwater's story was that, near the time of the flights, there was a break in the telegraph line south of Currituck Beach. News of the flights was telephoned from down the coast, and he then telegraphed it on to Norfolk.

The scene painted by Drinkwater is possible, if unlikely in the extreme. Most experts—including Orville Wright—have discounted it entirely, though Drinkwater still has his supporters.

Whatever the truth behind his first-flight story, Drinkwater bet on the wrong horse when he stayed at Currituck Beach rather than traveling to Kill Devil Hills.

The *Moccasin*, redesignated the *A-4*, was later lashed to the deck of a transport vessel—along with its old friend *Adder*, now the *A-2*—and carried halfway around the world to serve on patrol and escort duty in the Philippines during World War I. That service completed, the *Moccasin* was made a target ship and was blasted into oblivion sometime around 1922.

The Wright Flyer now hangs in a prominent place in the National Air and Space Museum, part of the Smithsonian, our national museum.

Fourth Season

When visitors to Wright Brothers National Memorial stroll from the visitor center past the replica camp buildings to the boulders commemorating the events of December 17, 1903, many are surprised at the shortness of the first powered flights. Most high-school quarterbacks can throw a football as far as the first flight. And as for the Flyer's speed relative to the ground, top runners can cover the distances of the four flights twice as fast on foot. Through its entire career, the world's most famous airplane flew barely more than a quarter-mile.

Except for its resolution, the 1903 season was as plagued by trouble as the 1901 season. Having been saddled with the formidable tasks of building an engine from scratch, arriving at a theoretical basis for propeller design, and designing and building the components of what was by far the largest craft of their career, the Wrights weren't prepared to start for North Carolina until early fall. They spent a fair portion of their time on the Outer Banks either housebound during storms or huddled around a stove during wintry weather. Though

they had dedicated the season to achieving powered flight, most of
their days out on the sand saw them flying their 1902 glider. A long
way from anywhere, and with minimal tools, they found themselves
in need of the kind of workshop they had back in Dayton to get
the Flyer in working order. When they finally succeeded, they were
probably within a few days of packing up and heading home for
Christmas without having achieved their goal. Whether they
would have returned to the Outer Banks the following year is a
matter for speculation.

The Wrights shipped their camp supplies, tools, and airplane parts
from Dayton between September 9 and September 18 and departed themselves September 23, three days behind Wilbur's ten-
tative schedule. They would get only farther in arrears as the
weeks passed.

Arriving in Elizabeth City on September 24, they learned that
the freight depot of the Norfolk and Southern Railroad had burned
eight days earlier—about the time their first shipment from Dayton
would have passed through the same building. In fact, when they
saw tomato, soup, sardine, salmon, and lard cans resembling their
own lying on the wharf, they had reason to fear the worst.

From Elizabeth City, the Wrights took the boat *Ocracoke* to
Roanoke Island, arriving in Manteo about one-thirty in the morning on Friday, September 25. In seven passages to and from the
Outer Banks, this was their first time through Roanoke Island. In
Manteo, they boarded a gasoline launch for the trip to Kill Devil
Hills. They reached camp early Friday afternoon. Their concerns
about the Elizabeth City fire were quickly soothed, as they found
their provisions and tools waiting for them, along with lumber for a
second camp building. Their airplane parts, having been shipped
later, were never at risk from the fire.

Wilbur had predicted to Octave Chanute that the brothers would spend about a week constructing a hangar big enough for the new machine, then several weeks in assembling the Flyer itself, with powered trials to take place sometime around October 25. The plan was to take the 1902 machine out for gliding practice when the winds were favorable and to work on the powered machine on rainy and calm days.

Orville judged the conditions that late September to be extremely favorable for gliding, an assessment borne out on Monday, September 28. That day, the Wrights made between sixty and a hundred flights. Gliding success is measured by distance relative to the ground. But men had also long dreamed of the kind of flight practiced by eagles—of *soaring*, in which success is measured by time aloft. Now, for the first time, the Wrights were on the verge of doing just that. Under the right wind conditions, they were able to remain virtually stationary relative to the ground. Wilbur had one flight that lasted over thirty seconds. Another flight lasted over twenty-six seconds but covered only fifty-two feet—a forward speed of only two feet per second. The flights that day averaged twenty seconds. That was longer than all but one of the Wrights' four powered flights two months later.

During the week they were building their new hangar—with the help of Dan Tate, before his fall from grace—the Wrights flew two more days, October 3 and October 5. The wind was not high enough for soaring on either occasion. On October 3, Wilbur made a flight lasting forty-three seconds and covering 450 feet. Several other glides broke thirty seconds. They also tried quartering—flying not into the wind, but with the wind at roughly a forty-five-degree angle behind them. This lent their glides great speed.

The parts of their new machine arrived in camp October 8. Coincidentally, Samuel Langley's first attempt at powered flight had taken place just the previous day.

The Flyer outside the 1903 hangar

LIBRARY OF CONGRESS

The fact that the two most concentrated pushes for powered flight in United States history were culminating at virtually the same time, and only 150 miles apart, begs the question of whether there was a race between the Wright brothers and Samuel Langley.

The two projects could hardly have been more different. Langley was a famous man brave enough to risk an outstanding career in science for the dream of flight. He was a public official, and his project was dependent on government funds—plenty of them. The burden of expectations was entirely on him.

By comparison, the Wrights' operation was so humble, and was centered in such an out-of-the-way place, that it almost entirely escaped notice. Since the Wrights built their flying machines with their own funds, the only pressure on them was self-imposed. They

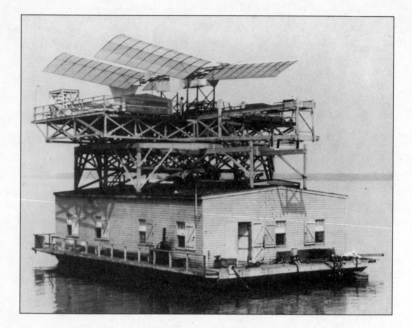

The Great Aerodrome being prepared for launch

NATIONAL AIR AND SPACE MUSEUM

were free to quit whenever they chose, with no loss to anyone but themselves.

As to the issue of competition between the two camps, Langley had shown considerable interest in visiting the Wrights on the Outer Banks in 1902, but as far as he knew, they hadn't cast their sights beyond gliders. The Wrights had asked Octave Chanute not to spread the word about their plans for powered flight, and he had obliged. If there was any feeling of rivalry, it was on the Wrights' side.

The brothers learned of Langley's first attempt through a newspaper clipping sent them by a neighbor in Dayton. They received their first detailed information when Chanute visited them on the Outer Banks in early November. He brought several pictures of Langley's

Great Aerodrome. More important, he told the Wrights a couple of sobering details: the craft weighed about 750 pounds and had a fifty-horsepower motor. That was about the same weight as the brothers' machine, but with four times the power. Roughly three and a half years in the making, Langley's lightweight engine was the best of its kind in the world. Of course, that is not to say the Great Aerodrome itself was airworthy. Years later, with the luxury of closer examination, Orville said the Wrights would never have worried about Langley's craft if they'd known how flimsy it was.

No one felt the burden of poor construction more acutely than Charles Manly, Langley's pilot and chief engine builder. The Wrights' machines had proven sturdy beyond all demands placed on them. With safety the foremost concern, the brothers had aimed toward developing complete control over their craft. They traveled halfway across the country to conduct their tests at extremely low altitudes over a forgiving surface of sand. By contrast, Charles Manly would have little control over the Great Aerodrome's orientation in flight. His cockpit, located between and below the front wings, would be the first thing to hit the water when the craft completed its flight and settled onto the Potomac, and he would likely have to extricate himself from a submerged position. If the craft happened to reach land, the prospects were worse yet.

Launched on October 7, the Great Aerodrome dropped like a stone, its front wings collapsing before it even cleared the houseboat from which it was launched. Its rear wings and rudder were also broken. Manly's easy swim to safety was the most successful happening that day. Two months later, when he was dunked again, he nearly drowned.

Meanwhile, the Wrights were unpacking the pieces of their new machine when a severe storm arrived. Dark clouds gathered Thursday, October 8. The Wrights spent a sleepless night in the rafters of their thin shelter amid winds Wilbur estimated at fifty miles per hour.

Though they could hear water sloshing on the floor below, their biggest worry was the new hangar, the walls of which were not yet completely braced.

Dan Tate was apparently devoted enough to the cause of aeronautics to make the trip to camp in thirty-mile-per-hour winds the following morning. He returned home when the storm grew more severe in late morning or early afternoon. The winds topped out at seventy-five miles per hour, the official figure recorded by the Weather Bureau.

Dan was not the only man out and about. Wilbur's letter to his sister describing the blow—complete with drawings in the margin— is one of the most entertaining things he ever wrote.

Having braced their new hangar on Friday, the Wrights were back in their 1901 building when they heard its tarpaper tear loose. It seemed the entire roof would soon follow. As Wilbur described it,

> Orville put on my heavy overcoat, and grabbing the ladder sallied forth from the south end of the building. At first it appeared that he was going down to repair some of the rents in the Big Hill which was being badly torn to pieces, for he began by walking backwards about 50 feet. After a while I saw him come back past the side opening in our partially raised awning door. . . . Thereupon I sallied out to help him and after a tussle with the wind found him at the north end ready to set up the ladder. He quickly mounted to the edge of the roof when the wind caught under his coat and folded it back over his head. As the hammer and nails were in his pocket and up over his head he was unable to get his hands on them or to pull his coattails down, so he was compelled to descend again. The next time he put the nails in his mouth and took the hammer in his hand and I followed him up the ladder hanging on to his coattails. He swatted around a good little while trying to get a few nails in, and I

became almost impatient for I had only my common coat on and was getting well soaked. He explained afterward that the wind kept blowing the hammer around so that three licks out of four hit the roof or his fingers instead of the nail. Finally the job was done and we rushed for cover. He took off the overcoat and felt his other coat and found it nice and dry, but after half an hour or so, finding that he was feeling wetter and wetter, he began a second investigation and found the inside of his coat sopping wet, while the outside was nice and dry. He had forgotten when he first felt of his coat, that it, as well as the overcoat, were practically inside out while he was working on the roof.

The Wrights went so far as to try a few glides the following afternoon, but the folly of this was quickly apparent. On Orville's second flight, a gust of wind lifted him so rapidly that, in struggling to descend, he hit Wilbur on the head with the corner of the left wing. The glider was slightly damaged by the wind. The door of the 1901 building was broken.

The next day, with winds still at forty or fifty miles per hour, they wisely stayed indoors.

Wilbur gave the blow's obituary this way: "The storm continued through Saturday and Sunday, but by Monday it had reared up so much that it finally fell over on its back and lay quiet."

With their buildings and flying machines largely intact, the Wrights were not the hardest hit on that portion of the coast. According to Dan Tate, five vessels washed ashore between the camp and Cape Henry, Virginia. One of them was visible from the highest dune at Kill Devil Hills.

For a time, progress on the powered machine went smoothly. The Wrights unpacked the last of its parts on the worst day of the storm, then began assembling the three sections of the upper wing and installing wires and hinges on October 12. By the time they stretched the cloth two days later, they realized their new wings were to be "far ahead of anything we have built before," as Wilbur wrote Chanute. In previous years, the spars running from tip to tip had created a noticeable hump on the underside of the wings about two-thirds of the way back. Now, the Wrights had thinner spars that allowed the wings to taper smoothly from front to back, resulting in improved aerodynamic efficiency.

They started on the lower wing October 15. Unlike their gliders, the 1903 craft was asymmetrical, owing to the fact that its lower wing had to accommodate both a pilot and a motor. The right wings were four inches longer than the left, so providing additional lift for the motor, which was to be mounted slightly right of center. The pilot was to lie to its left.

Wilbur was now predicting a powered trial around November 1.

Next came the twin surfaces of the elevator, the tail surfaces, the skids to be mounted beneath the craft, the braces, the wires and pulleys between the upper and lower wings, the frame for the elevator and the uprights between its upper and lower sections, and the frame for the tail. As in the original design for the 1902 glider, the Flyer had a tail composed of twin vertical vanes, though these were now fully integrated with the wing-warping system. By November 2, the Wrights were ready to assemble, mount, and test the engine.

During this period, they continued practicing with the 1902 glider. On October 19, they made several glides in the 500-foot range, the longest glide, by Orville, stretching 603 feet. With favorable winds on October 21, Orville soared for just over a minute; the Wrights stayed aloft for over forty-five seconds numerous times that day. They were also flying at heights of 40 to 60 feet, their greatest ever. Their best day came on October 26. In twenty attempts, they soared for more than a minute six times, covering distances of 450 to 500 feet.

Given that the Wrights were late in arriving on the Outer Banks that year, and that they had already endured one fierce storm, and that their intention was to achieve powered flight, their continued interest in gliding is difficult to understand. The weather was not likely to get any better as they approached November, yet at times, they seem to have been in no particular hurry to assemble and test the Flyer.

For example, on October 21—the date of Orville's first flight over a minute—the Wrights were out gliding at eight o'clock in the morning. They moved to a different hill in midmorning, then returned to camp when the wind died. They worked on the Flyer until twelve-thirty, but by one o'clock, they were back on the dunes gliding, where they remained until dinner.

Likewise, parts of a couple of other days were organized around capturing flights of the 1902 machine on film, though they already had pictures from the previous year. And when George Spratt and Octave Chanute arrived in camp, the Wrights felt no compulsion to rush the Flyer to readiness, but made sure they took their guests out to witness glides.

Perhaps this only reflects their priorities ever since they'd begun building flying machines. Samuel Langley's motor was much better conceived than the Great Aerodrome's general construction and its control system. For the Wrights, a motor and propellers were still secondary to control and balance. Their three and a half seasons of sporadic practice notwithstanding, they were still new to gliding, and there was much left to be learned.

The Wrights' prospects began a downturn around the time George Spratt arrived.

On the night of October 24, the wind picked up to forty-five miles per hour and the temperature fell. The next day, the Wrights and Spratt fashioned a carbide can into a stove, apparently covered parts of the 1901 building's walls with carpets to keep out the wind, and spent a good deal of time sitting on the floor to avoid the smoke. The stove had its drawbacks, as Orville wrote his sister: "Everything about the building was sooted up so thoroughly that for several days we couldn't sit down to eat without a whole lot of black soot dropping down in our plates."

The homemade stove soon took on a fair bit of sophistication, as the Wrights added iron legs, dampers, and a stovepipe. However, it also caused some unexpected damage: it dried out the wing fabric and wood of the 1902 glider, which, unlike the Flyer, did not rate storage in a separate building. The Wrights flew the glider only four more days, the last time on November 12, when they practiced launching it off the track built for the powered machine. Finding the cloth and trussing loose that day, they pronounced the glider dangerous and promptly retired it.

The problems with the powered machine were becoming frustrating in the extreme. During the first test of the motor and propellers, on November 5, the engine ran so rough that it damaged the propeller shafts. With no equipment on hand to repair the damage, and with no machinist they knew and trusted closer than Charlie Taylor back at the bicycle shop, they had no choice but to ship the shafts to Dayton and wait for their return. George Spratt carried them to Norfolk on the first part of his journey home to Pennsylvania.

Dan Tate had quit camp for good. Octave Chanute came, got a taste of the weather, and left in a week. The Wrights' new machine was inoperable without its propeller shafts, and their old glider was dilapidated. Alone for the first time in a month, they performed a variety of tests and minor duties—running the motor, planing the junction railroad, assessing the strength of their elevator, making calculations on their propellers, assessing the strength of the wings—but by their own assessment, they were essentially loafing. On November 15, Orville recorded that he was holed up in camp studying German and French, the immediate purpose being to translate an article from a German newspaper concerning one of the brothers' flying machines. Even that turned out to be a test of patience, with no German dictionary on hand.

They were also getting hungry. The provisions the Wrights had brought from Dayton were long used up. Expecting a shipment to arrive via Captain Midgett and the *Lou Willis* on November 19, they finished off nearly all of what they had on hand early that day. When the boat didn't show, they were down to crackers and condensed milk for supper that night and rice cakes and coffee for breakfast the following morning.

The propeller shafts arrived November 20, after a fifteen-day wait.

A couple of days in late November, it was too cold to work. One morning, the Wrights awoke to find the ponds around camp and the water they kept in their wash basin frozen. They also encountered snow flurries. The previous year, they had devised a system to classify cold conditions: there were 1-, 2-, 3-, and 4-blanket nights. "We now have 5 blanket nights, & 5 blankets & 2 quilts," Wilbur wrote his father and sister on November 23. "Next come 5 blankets, 2 quilts & fire; then 5, 2, fire, & hot-water jug. This is as far as we have got so far. Next comes the addition of sleeping without undressing, then shoes & hats, and finally overcoats. We intend to be comfortable while we are here."

Meanwhile, the engine tests proceeded quickly. The same day the propeller shafts arrived, the Wrights installed them and tried the

motor. The engine vibrated so badly that the sprockets on the propeller shafts kept loosening up, a problem the Wrights solved in typically simple fashion: by applying a liberal dose of tire cement. Tested
again, the engine ran reasonably well, and the propellers produced a
thrust the Wrights judged adequate to get them into the air. After
fixing one more minor problem—a couple of broken hubs on the
carriage designed to bear the Flyer down the junction railroad—
they were ready to fly.

November 25 was to be the day, but rain set in just as they were
ready to take the machine out for a trial. The next two days were
cold enough to keep the brothers indoors.

Disaster struck again on November 28, when they discovered that
one of the propeller shafts was cracked. Orville caught the first boat
off the Outer Banks and returned home to help Charlie Taylor make
shafts of heavier steel.

Unlike his brother, Wilbur had no avowed interest in German and
French. He didn't even play the mandolin. It must have been a lonely
two weeks in camp, with few or no visitors and little to do but
chop wood and write letters.

Orville returned December 11. En route from Dayton, he read a
newspaper account of Samuel Langley's second trial, which had taken
place December 8.

Predictions of Langley's demise had been premature—if only by a
couple of months. Back in mid-October, after the professor's first
failure, Wilbur had written Octave Chanute, a touch cavalierly, "I
see that Langley has had his fling, and failed. It seems to be our turn
to throw now." On December 2, less than a week before the
professor's second trial, Wilbur wrote George Spratt, "It is now too
late for Langley to begin over again."

Perhaps Langley should have taken the hint. His second effort was

an even more abject failure than the first. This time, the Great Aerodrome flipped upside down on launching and fell straight into the
Potomac. Charles Manly discovered himself underwater with his coat
caught on a piece of metal. He came up beneath some ice on the
river, and one of Langley's workers jumped in to try to help him. Once
Manly was out of the water, the clothes had to be cut from his body.

Charles Manly was done with flying. So was Samuel Langley. That
left the Wrights with the only major push toward heavier-than-air
flight in the country.

The Wrights found it ironic that Langley blamed his houseboat-
mounted catapult system for the failure. It cost twenty thousand
dollars, or about twenty times what the brothers had spent on all
their aeronautical efforts to date. And that didn't begin to count the
cost of the Great Aerodrome itself, and that of its small-scale predecessors, and that of Langley's engine-development program.

The Wrights' junction railroad cost four dollars in materials, and
it worked perfectly.

With Orville back in camp, the Wrights moved quickly. The day
after his return, they installed the new propeller shafts and made
preparations for a trial, only to find there was inadequate wind for
starting from level ground and not enough daylight to wrestle
the Flyer into the dunes. Instead, they practiced starting the craft
on the junction railroad, breaking part of the tail frame in
the process.

The wind was favorable on December 13, but that was a Sunday,
a day of rest.

After repairing the tail frame on the morning of December 14,
they were ready. Around one-thirty, they hung out their prearranged
signal, which was promptly spotted at the Kill Devil Hills Lifesaving
Station. Before long, Bob Westcott, John Daniels, Tom Beacham,

Willie Dough, and Uncle Benny O'Neal were on hand to help move the Flyer part way up a dune. A couple of boys—one of them John Beacham, son of Tom Beacham—and a dog accompanied them. The boys and the dog stayed long enough to have their image recorded for posterity—as part of the Wrights' photograph of the preparations for flight that day—but they didn't witness much of anything, fleeing over the sand at the awful noise when the brothers started the motor.

The honor of piloting the powered machine was decided by coin flip: Wilbur would go first.

It is doubtful that the Wrights would have viewed the trial that day as a success even if Wilbur had flown better than he did. Starting with a downhill run meant that they were violating one of their

The crowd—men, boys, and dog—assembled for the December 14 trial

own criteria for powered flight: that the machine's landing point had to be at least as high as its takeoff point. Orville also found it necessary to enlist a couple of the lifesavers to help with the launch. This was another contingency the Wrights had sought to avoid, lest there be any claim that their machine was assisted into the air.

The Flyer started down the track before Orville was ready. He grabbed hold of an upright and began running with the machine, but it outpaced him within 35 or 40 feet and lifted shortly afterwards. Wilbur made the mistake of directing the craft upward just past the end of the track, when it barely had enough speed to be airborne. It reached a height of 15 feet about 60 feet out, then began to lose speed and dip toward the ground. The left wing struck first. The skids dug into the sand, and some braces and struts for the elevator broke on impact. The craft had covered 105 feet in three and a half seconds.

The Wrights never considered calling the attempt that day a powered flight, since in addition to being started down an incline, it was short and poorly controlled. Nonetheless, they now had complete confidence in their ability to fly, as reflected in the telegram Wilbur sent his father the following day: "Misjudgment at start reduced flight . . . power and control ample rudder only injured success assured keep quiet."

Though sworn to silence for the moment, the Wrights back in Ohio were ready to issue the news as soon as they received word of the first successful flight. Lorin would notify the local papers and the Associated Press. Bishop Milton Wright had copies of a description of the Flyer and a sketch of Wilbur and Orville. To Katharine fell the responsibility of notifying Octave Chanute.

Wilbur and Orville spent the next day and a half repairing the elevator. They were ready again by noon on December 16, but around the time they were setting up the junction railroad—on level ground this time—the wind died. They waited for several hours, the Flyer poised on the track. Finally, they had to wrestle it back to the hangar for the night.

On the morning of December 17, the weather was cold enough to freeze puddles around camp, and the wind was blowing between twenty and twenty-five miles per hour—dangerous conditions for flying a prototype aircraft even these days. The Wrights aimed to be home by Christmas, however, and they had to take advantage of what opportunities they had left. They tacked up their flag to summon the lifesavers.

To the north, a couple of invited guests were about to miss the action, Alf Drinkwater camping beside the *Moccasin* and Bill Tate getting a late start south on his horse.

To the west, in Dayton and Chicago, the Wright family and Octave Chanute were awaiting news from the Outer Banks.

Beyond these small circles, it was to be an event unknown and unexpected anywhere in the world.

The contingent of helpers arrived on foot: Willie Dough, Adam Etheridge, six-foot-one, 240-pound strongman John Daniels, W. C. Brinkley, and Johnny Moore. Lumber merchant Brinkley had been conducting some business on the beach the previous day when he heard of the proposed flights, upon which he had decided to stay over with the lifesavers and watch. Young Johnny Moore lived in a shack in Nags Head Woods. His mother, a widow, was the local fortuneteller, most of her business coming from the summer vacationers at Nags Head. Moore is generally thought to have accompanied the surfmen and Brinkley, though some North Carolina newspaper accounts contend he happened by on his way home from a fishing trip, or that he made the three-mile trip from his home, strolled into camp, and introduced himself, at which point the brothers invited him to stay and help.

At the Kill Devil Hills Lifesaving Station, Bob Westcott was watching through a spyglass. Four miles away, at the Kitty Hawk station, S. J. Payne was doing the same.

The Flyer was mounted on the track about a hundred feet west of camp, heading south to north. The Wrights each cranked a propeller and let the motor run. "Wilbur and Orville walked off from us and stood close together on the beach, talking low to each other for some time," remembered John Daniels. "After a while they shook hands, and we couldn't help notice how they held on to each other's hand, sort o' like they hated to let go; like two folks parting who weren't sure they'd ever see each other again."

It was an uncharacteristic bit of drama from the Wrights.

Witnessing such a gesture, the spectators might have supposed Orville was about to depart on a long journey. Their mood equaled the Wrights' in sobriety. According to Daniels, "Wilbur came over to us and told us not to look sad, but to laugh and hollo and clap our hands and try to cheer Orville up when he started.

"We tried to shout and hollo, but it was mighty weak shouting, with no heart in it."

The coin flip from the failed attempt on December 14 carried over: it was now Orville's turn. He got aboard the lower wing and tested the controls.

The Wrights' aspirations didn't end with coaxing the Flyer into the air; they wanted as much flight data as they could gather. The machine was ingeniously rigged with an anemometer, a stopwatch, and an engine counter, so as to calculate "the distance through the air, the speed, the power consumed, and the number of turns of the screws," as Wilbur put it.

A visual record was just as important. Orville had set up the camera behind and to the right of the Flyer and centered the frame on a point just beyond the end of the track, so as to capture the flight at an angle from the rear. Wilbur then selected John Daniels—who had never before taken a photograph—and coached him on how and when to snap the shutter. At 10:35, when Orville slipped the line holding the Flyer and headed down the track, Daniels was in position under the black cloth at the back of the camera.

What he caught was one of the classic shots in the history of photography—and also one of the most-analyzed shots. Every aspect of this photograph has been carefully scrutinized: the angle of the elevator, the footprints in the sand, the carriage on which the Flyer rode down the rail, the small bench on which its right wing rested before launch, the coil box and cables that sparked the motor, a C-clamp, a shovel, a can containing a hammer and nails. The blur pattern created by the propellers—which rotated at a known speed—has even been used to calculate the shutter speed of the Wright brothers' camera: $1/60$ of a second.

It was supposedly the only photograph John Daniels ever took.

The Flyer lifted about forty-five feet down the track. Orville had difficulty with the elevator almost immediately; improperly balanced, it turned too far in either direction, so that it alternately sent the craft upward quickly, then made it dart toward the sand when Orville tried to make an adjustment. Twelve seconds and 120 feet out, one of these downward movements brought the craft to the sand, cracking a skid.

The witnesses may not have known the textbook definition of powered flight, but they recognized success when they saw it. They hurried forward with Wilbur to congratulate Orville. It was the first time in history that a heavier-than-air craft had taken off from level

John Daniels's classic photograph of the first flight

ground, moved forward under its own power, and landed at a point as high as that from which it began.

The men then retired inside the 1901 building to get warm. Johnny Moore was the butt of some humor when he marveled at the Wrights' stock of eggs and was naive enough to believe that the one scrawny hen that resided in camp laid six to eight a day.

After the cracked skid was repaired and the Flyer was carried back to the starting rail, it was Wilbur's turn at the controls. At 11:20, with the wind slightly calmed, he covered 175 feet in about fifteen seconds.

Twenty minutes later, Orville flew 200 feet in fifteen seconds.

At noon came the flight that settled the issue once and for all. With Wilbur aboard, the Flyer started off on an undulating course, as before, but straightened out after 300 or 400 feet. Around 800 feet, it began pitching again and finally darted to the ground after 852 feet and fifty-nine seconds. The elevator frame was broken in landing.

As with Augustus Herring's hang-glider leaps on the shore of Lake Michigan, this feat is more impressive when the headwind is taken into account: Wilbur's 852 feet over the ground translate to more than half a mile through the air. He said in later years that with more experience, he could have taken off from a standstill under the conditions present that December 17.

Wilbur and Orville removed the damaged elevator. The men then carried the Flyer back to camp and set it in the sand just west of the buildings. That the Wrights were ecstatic about their accomplishment that day is shown in the fact that they discussed flying the four miles to the Weather Bureau office in Kitty Hawk—an utter pipe dream given the high wind, the low altitude at which they operated, and the unreliability of the elevator.

They never got a chance to try. A gust of wind hit the Flyer and started to flip it. Orville grabbed hold of a strut. John Daniels did, too, but he made the mistake of holding onto the craft from the inside, so he was knocked down and tangled up with the motor and the propeller chains.

"I can't tell to save my life how it happened," Daniels remembered, "but I found myself caught in them wires and the machine blowing across the beach heading for the ocean, landing first on one end and then on the other, rolling over and over, and me getting more tangled up in it all the time. I tell you, I was plumb scared. When the thing did stop for half a second I nearly broke up every wire and upright getting out of it."

Daniels, miraculously uninjured, summed up his experience: "I ate sand for a whole week after that."

The Flyer was ruined for good.

CHAPTER 5

1908

Often as the machine buzzed along above the sand plains, herds of wild hogs and cattle were frightened from their grazing grounds and scurried away for the jungle, where they would remain for hours looking timidly out from their hiding places. Flocks of gulls and crows, screaming and chattering, darted and circled about the machine as if resentful of this unwelcome trespasser in their own and exclusive realm. There was something about the scene that appealed to one's poetic instincts—the desolation, the solitude, the dreary expanse of sand and ocean and in the centre of this melancholy picture two solitary men performing one of the world's greatest wonders.

Byron Newton
in the June 1908 issue of
Aeronautics magazine

Aftermath

Following the fourth powered flight of December 17, 1903, and the wreck of the Flyer, the witnesses dispersed and the Wrights retired inside to enjoy their dinner. Early that afternoon, they set out on foot the four miles to the Weather Bureau office in Kitty Hawk and Joe Dosher's telegraph machine.

This is the message they sent home to their father: "Success four flights Thursday morning all against twenty-one mile wind started from level with engine power alone average speed through air thirty-one miles longest fifty-seven seconds inform press home Christmas."

The telegram bore Orville's name as the sender, somehow mistranscribed en route to Dayton as *Orevelle.* The stated figure of fifty-seven seconds for the longest flight was also in error; the correct time was two seconds longer. The twenty-one-mile-per-hour wind speed was intended to express the minimum wind over the course of the entire four flights.

That simple telegram and the news of the flights grew into a confused mess over the years. Alf Drinkwater, camped beside the *Moccasin* at Currituck Beach, was only the first of many to stake a claim to the story as it flashed north to Norfolk and then west to Ohio.

Drinkwater maintained that, with the telegraph line out of commission, Joe Dosher telephoned the Currituck Beach Lifesaving Station with a batch of messages to be sent northward. The Wrights' big news supposedly arrived among transmissions from vacationing duck hunters telling the folks back inland when they'd be heading home. The messages were then presumably delivered to Drinkwater at his telegraph on the beach. According to Drinkwater, word from Dosher came through about eight o'clock that night, and the Wrights' message read, simply, "Flights successful. Will be home for Christmas."

His claim appears doubtful. The Wrights arrived at the Weather Bureau office around three o'clock, not eight, and Joe Dosher was in the process of telegraphing—not telephoning—their message as they left the premises. He made contact with Norfolk almost immediately. In fact, he supposedly received a reply quickly enough to call the Wrights back into the office. The operator on the other end, sensing something important, wanted permission to share the story with the local press. The Wrights wanted the news to come out of Dayton, so they declined.

On the Norfolk end, the chain of events is even more muddled, with four principal figures involved.

Charles C. Grant was on duty at the Weather Bureau office in Norfolk on December 17, sitting in for the regular man, Jim J. Gray. Grant later claimed that the first message about the flights came in at eleven in the morning, not three in the afternoon, and that it was from lifesavers Willie Dough and John Daniels, not the Wright brothers themselves. It supposedly read, "Wrights made a short flight this morning and will try again this afternoon."

This also appears doubtful. The first flight took place just after ten-thirty, and it is unlikely that Dough and Daniels could have conveyed the message to Kitty Hawk by eleven o'clock. Besides, their help was needed in carrying the Flyer back from where it landed. It is well documented that Daniels was caught in the wreck of the Flyer after the fourth flight, and aside from Grant's claim, it has never been suggested that Daniels or Dough left the Wrights' camp and returned between the first and fourth flights.

The more likely scenario is that Charles Grant received the news from the Wrights via Joe Dosher at three o'clock, then wired back asking permission to pass it along to the press. Though instructed to keep mum, he apparently took a broad interpretation of the Wrights' directive—intended only for their family in Ohio—to "inform press." When Edward O. Dean of the *Norfolk Virginian-Pilot* called on the Weather Bureau office during the regular course of his beat late that afternoon, Charles Grant told him of the flights.

Edward Dean was a young reporter from South Carolina who was hoping that a temporary stint in Norfolk would prove a means to a journalistic career in New York. He knew a hot tip when he heard one, but he also understood that his knowledge of the coast was inadequate to guide him in handling an important story. He therefore took his information to the *Virginian-Pilot*'s precocious city editor, Keville Glennan.

Keville Glennan was the son of an early owner of the *Norfolk Virginian*, one of the papers that merged to become the *Virginian-Pilot*. Though only twenty-three, he was already a veteran. He received his introduction to newspaper work at age eleven, his first beat being the Norfolk docks, where he chased down produce prices and news of shipping through the Dismal Swamp Canal.

While the report of the powered flights was unexpected, it was Glennan's contention that he already knew of the Wright brothers' activities. In early 1902, he had supposedly gone by horseback to cover a shipwreck off Cape Henry. Huddled behind a dune with a group of lifesavers in frigid conditions, Glennan had voiced a complaint about his plight, only to have one of the surfmen jokingly tell him that it wouldn't be long before he could travel through the air to the site of wrecks, that there were two Ohio men farther down the coast experimenting with flying machines. Glennan claimed that between then and December 1903, he had established a small network of contacts to keep him apprised of the Wrights' activities and had also boned up on the literature pertaining to flight, including the stories of Samuel Langley.

If it is true that Glennan went to such lengths to compile information on the Wrights and flight in general, then it is a legitimate question why his paper generally disparaged the cause of aeronautics and contained virtually no coverage of the brothers until after the powered flights.

Edward Dean had a hot tip but no knowledge of aeonautics or the Wright brothers. His editor, Keville Glennan, supposedly had some background on the subject but no specifics on the Flyer or the flights themselves. The two men were in the process of discussing how they could play the limited facts at their disposal into a story when a third newsman, a man who claimed to have the complete details, walked into the room.

Like Glennan, Harry P. Moore claimed knowledge of the Wrights. He contended that he had known of their activities since their first trip to the Outer Banks in 1900, and that he had even visited their camp and witnessed some of their glides without revealing his newspaper connection.

Younger than both Glennan and Dean, Moore, too, had big-time aspirations. Some accounts describe him as the mail-room supervisor at the *Virginian-Pilot*, though Glennan said Moore alternated between taking want ads and working in the circulation department. He also wrote as a stringer for newspapers outside the Norfolk area. It was Moore's aspiration to become a full-time reporter, and the story of the flights was ideally suited to advance his career.

It was to Harry Moore that the phantom eleven o'clock telegram from Willie Dough and John Daniels was supposedly addressed. Moore claimed that after he received it, he spent part of the afternoon trying to verify the story with Daniels and another of his contacts among the lifesavers.

Whatever his sources, Moore did in fact have independent knowledge of the flights when he met with Keville Glennan and Edward Dean at the *Virginian-Pilot* around five or six o'clock.

Glennan's main concern was that his newspaper not be scooped by its Norfolk rival, the *Landmark*. He quickly took measures to prevent that from happening. First, young Dean was sent back to the Weather Bureau office "to guard that source until it closed at 8:30," as Glennan put it. What Dean could have or would have done to prevent further dissemination of the news is anyone's guess.

It has often been written that the Associated Press declined to pick up the story of the flights, or that the AP distributed the story far and wide, only to have it run in just a handful of papers.

But according to Glennan, the *Virginian-Pilot*'s charter required that it offer any news story centered within thirty miles of Norfolk to the AP. Conveniently enough, Kill Devil Hills was outside that range.

Afraid that the story would be distributed by the AP and picked up by the *Landmark* in roundabout fashion, Glennan decided to keep it off the wire. However, Harry Moore was not technically a reporter for the *Virginian-Pilot*, so he was free to sell the story to whomever he chose. As a compromise, Glennan drew up a select list of out-of-town papers, and Moore agreed to confine his efforts to those.

From all these machinations came the first story of powered flight. One of the great scoops of the century, it is believed to have been a collaborative effort between Harry Moore, who supplied what passed for facts, and Keville Glennan, who did most of the writing. Edward Dean later characterized Glennan as "a master of descriptive writing"—no irony intended.

The headline ran all the way across the front page on December 18, with descending subheadlines beneath it, in the manner of the day: "FLYING MACHINE SOARS THREE MILES IN TEETH OF HIGH WIND OVER SAND HILLS AND WAVES AT KITTY HAWK ON CAROLINA COAST. No Balloon Attached to Aid It. Three Years of Hard, Secret Work by Two Ohio Brothers Crowned With Success. Accomplished What Langley Failed At. With Man as Passenger, Huge Machine Flew Like Bird Under Perfect Control. Box Kite Principle With Two Propellers."

The article read, in part,

> The problem of aerial navigation without the use of a balloon has been solved at last.
>
> Over the sand hills of the North Carolina coast yesterday, near Kitty Hawk, two Ohio men proved that they could soar through the air in a flying machine of their own construction, with power to steer it and speed it on its way. . . .
>
> [There] are two six-bladed propellers, one arranged just below the center of the frame, so gauged as to exert an upward

force when in motion, and the other extends horizontally to the rear from the center of the car, furnishing the forward impetus. . . .

Wilber [sic] Wright, the chief inventor of the machine, sat in the operator's car and when all was ready his brother unfastened the catch which held the invention at the top of the slope.

The big box began to move slowly at first, acquiring velocity as it went, and when half way down the hundred feet the engine was started.

The propeller in the rear immediately began to revolve at a high rate of speed, and when the end of the incline was reached the machine shot out into space without a perceptible fall.

By this time the elevating propeller was also in motion, and, keeping its altitude, the machine slowly began to go higher and higher until it finally soared sixty feet above the ground.

Maintaining this height by the action of the under wheel, the navigator increased the revolutions of the rear propeller, and the forward speed of the huge affair increased until a velocity of eight miles an hour was attained.

"It is a success," declared Orville Wright to the crowd on the beach after the first mile had been covered.

But the inventor waited. Not until he had accomplished three miles, putting the machine through all sorts of maneuvers en route, was he satisfied.

Then he selected a suitable place to land, and, gracefully circling drew his invention slowly to the earth, where it settled, like some big bird, in the chosen spot.

"Eureka," he cried, as did the alchemist of old.

Wilbur might have been pleased to see himself given a head of hair—"raven hued and straight," according to the *Virginian-Pilot*. He might not have been so thrilled with his "swarthy complexion" and his "nose of extreme length and sharpness." Orville was "not quite so large as Wilber [sic] but is of magnificent physique."

The punch line to the entire episode is that no one cared about the story. It came only a week and a half after Samuel Langley's second failure, and the credibility of flying-machine builders stood at an all-time low.

The Wrights may have had Bob Westcott and S. J. Payne watching their flights through spyglasses, but Langley had a whole gaggle of owl-stuffers and scientists watching his disaster from the Smithsonian tower. People in the wider world also awaited news of the great professor's activities. The story of his failure played on front pages across the country, to Langley's everlasting humiliation.

"Langley's Dream Develops the Qualities of a Duck," the *Raleigh News and Observer* headlined its version of the Associated Press story. "It Breaks Completely in Two, but Without Even An Expiring Quack, Drops a Wreck into the Icy Potomac."

The *Charlotte Observer*, generally sympathetic to the cause of aeronautics, went with the withering headline, "As Bad As Darius Green. Langley Airship Total Wreck."

"It would serve no useful purpose to say anything which would increase the disappointment and mortification of Prof. Langley at the instant and complete collapse of his airship," the *New York Times* noted in an editorial, then went on to air its opinion anyway: "The fact has established itself that Prof. Langley is not a mechanician, and that his mathematics are better adapted to calculations of astronomical interest than to determining the strength of materials in mechanical constructions."

The *Wilmington* (N.C.) *Messenger* went so far as to question the manhood of a sixty-eight-year-old: "We notice that the professor does not have sufficient faith in his work to risk his life in the machine when the attempts to fly it are made. He either goes to Washington City or places himself at some safe distance when the attempts are made."

"In the past," the *Washington Post* commented, "we have paid our respects to the humorous aspects of the Langley flying machine, its repeated and disastrous failures, the absurd atmosphere of secrecy in which it was enveloped, and the imposing and expensive pageantry that attended its various manifestations. It now seems to us, however, that the time is ripe for a really serious appraisement of the so-called aeroplane and for a withdrawal by the government from all further participation in its financial and scientific calamities."

So it went from coast to coast. In the shadow of Langley's public failure, the Wrights' private success stood as nothing. Readers wouldn't have believed it, didn't even want to hear of it—or so newspaper editors seemed to believe.

Most accounts say that Harry Moore sent queries to twenty-one newspapers to try to interest them in the *Virginian-Pilot* story. He found only five takers.

The reaction in the Wrights' hometown was particularly frustrating. Rather than giving the story a banner headline and front-page treatment, the *Dayton Daily News* placed it in the section reserved for local news and headlined it "Dayton Boys Emulate Great Santos-Dumont."

Lorin Wright had even worse luck peddling the story in person. The response the local Associated Press representative gave him is legendary: "Fifty-seven seconds, hey? If it had been fifty-seven minutes then it might have been a news item."

An abbreviated version of the *Virginian-Pilot* account bearing an Associated Press credit finally began appearing in isolated papers in North Carolina and elsewhere around the time the Wrights packed up camp and headed home just before Christmas. The coverage was still sparse.

David Lilienthal, chairman of the Atomic Energy Commission in the late 1940s, liked to tell the story of how one of the Wright family approached a local paper with the earth-shattering news that two local residents had accomplished the world's first heavier-than-air flights. "Popular local bicycle merchants home for holidays," an item in the personals column read the next day. Lilienthal's tale was fiction, but it illustrates the level of mistrust the public felt on the subject of flight in December 1903.

There was one well-qualified gentleman who was chafing to spread the news. "I am deeply grateful to you for your telegram of this date advising me of the first successful flights of your brothers. It fills me with pleasure," Octave Chanute wired Katharine Wright in Dayton on December 17. "I am sorely tempted to make the achievement public, but will defer doing so in order that they may be the first to announce their success."

"Immensely pleased at your success," he telegraphed the brothers in Kitty Hawk the next day. "When ready to make it public please advise me."

"Pleased at your success. When ready to make public please advise me," he wired Wilbur the following day.

Given Chanute's connections in high places, perhaps Wilbur and Orville should have allowed him the role he desired. The Wrights were quickly finding that their simple story was either being ignored, misunderstood, or misrepresented.

In a way, it was a fitting primer for their return to the Outer Banks in 1908.

To date, their great invention had not changed the world in the slightest.

Four and a Half Years

The success of December 1903 led the Wrights to a change in attitude. Back home, they took stock of the progress they'd made and the problems yet to be solved. Wilbur was now thirty-six and well aware of the physical demands of building and flying airplanes. He was concerned with reaching the goal of practical flight while he was still vigorous. Slow progress had doomed others before him to failure.

The Wrights decided to devote themselves full-time to flight, making little further pretense of supporting themselves through their bicycle business. That being the case, they would also expect some financial gain from their work. Flying was no longer to be a sportsmen's vacation, but a business proposition.

The first step was consolidating their operation close to home. After scouting the open areas around Dayton, they decided on a hundred-acre cow pasture eight miles east of town, a place familiar to Orville and others of his generation from school field trips. Called Huffman Prairie, it belonged to Torrence Huffman, a Dayton banker. Though not a believer in flight, Huffman allowed the Wrights free use of his land, the only stipulation being that they chase his cows to safety before they try to take to the air.

By April 1904, the brothers had cut down the tall grass, built a hangar much like their second Outer Banks structure, and begun assembling a new airplane, Charlie Taylor already having made considerable progress on an improved engine.

Flying so close to home, the Wrights could now run a year-round operation. They would also be spared the expense of camping on the Outer Banks, as well as the aggravation of having inadequate repair facilities on hand when something broke. They could depend

The scene at Huffman Prairie
LIBRARY OF CONGRESS

on having decent meals. Additionally, if their invention was ever to find a market, they needed to make it work outside the special conditions present on the Outer Banks.

But quitting North Carolina had a downside, too. There were significant differences in geography and climate between the prairie and the Outer Banks.

Wilbur once described their new site as looking like "a prairie dog town," pocked with small, grassy hummocks, a surface less forgiving than the Outer Banks sand. When their airplane crashed, it tended to suffer greater damage.

And the indifferent winds of western Ohio made it tougher to get off the ground. Having used a 60-foot starting track on the Outer Banks, the Wrights first tried a 100-foot track at Huffman Prairie, eventually extending it all the way to 240 feet. They often found that by the time they completed the painstaking process of laying track, the wind had changed direction or died altogether.

Lastly, there was some advantage to experimenting at sea level during dry, cold conditions, as on the day of the famous flights. The difference in elevation between Huffman Prairie and Kill Devil Hills is only 815 feet. However, Wright biographer Harry Combs took the trouble to calculate the difference in density altitude between the sites on two separate days—December 17, 1903, and May 23, 1904—taking humidity and air temperature into consideration. He found that on the latter date, with warm temperatures and high humidity, it was as if the Wrights were trying to take off from an altitude 4,700 feet higher than on December 17, 1903. Though the dates in question are not entirely representative of conditions at the two sites, the point is well taken: the air at Huffman Prairie was simply less buoyant than that at Kill Devil Hills.

Problems were quickly evident. On May 23, the first day the Wrights tried their new machine, it failed to lift at all, simply running off the end of the track and into the grass. Three days later, Bishop Milton Wright came to the pasture, his first chance to see his sons fly. "Went at 9:00 [on] car to Huffman's farm," he noted soberly in his diary. "At 2:00 Orville flew about 25 ft. I came home on 3:30 car."

The frustrations continued beyond the end of July, with most flights only in the two-hundred-foot range. This was also the most dangerous work the Wrights had ever done. For example, in eight days of trials in early August, they broke their "tail stick," "disarranged" their tail wires, "injured" a runner, broke their rudder, broke a propeller, and broke their elevator. Many such mishaps brought bumps and bruises to the pilot.

The Wrights blamed their craft's lack of lift on a shallower wing camber than they'd used in 1903. They blamed its fragility on the substitution of pine spars for spruce.

Mid-August brought a definite improvement, with four flights over 1,250 feet, exceeding their best effort at Kill Devil Hills. In fact, their main limitation soon came to be the length of the pasture.

The revelation came on September 7, when the Wrights began using a simple catapult launch system. They built a twenty-foot derrick and placed it behind the craft, at the rear end of the starting rail. In preparing to launch, they would raise nearly a ton of weight to the top of the tower. A rope led down to the base of the derrick, out to the far end of the track, and then back to the front of the craft. When the weight dropped, the airplane, engine running wide open, as always, was accelerated quickly and reliably to flight speed using only a sixty-foot rail.

Just thirteen days after they began using the catapult, Orville made the first circular flight in history, covering a little over four thousand feet in a little over a minute and a half. Though the 1904 craft was unstable, and though the Wrights found the mechanics of turning difficult to master, they made a couple of flights exceeding five minutes and encompassing several circuits of the pasture by the time they suspended operations in early December.

They didn't get back into the air until late June 1905, using a new airframe but the same motor as the 1904 machine.

Their 1905 craft is widely regarded as the world's first practical airplane, though Orville would hardly have believed it on July 14, when he suffered the brothers' worst crash to date, losing control of the elevator and diving into the prairie at thirty miles an hour. It was the modifications to the elevator after this crash—it was enlarged and moved farther in front of the wings—that finally made for a stable craft and allowed the rapid progress that followed.

During one trial in late September, the craft stayed up for over eighteen minutes. On October 3, that record was broken with a twenty-six-minute flight. The following day saw a flight exceeding thirty-three minutes. The Wrights were now actually running their gas tank dry. Lying prone for such spans of time was growing uncomfortable. Though it must have been a temptation to point the craft upward, gain some altitude, and venture out over the countryside, the brothers were always careful to remain low and to stay within the confines of the pasture.

Their best flight came on October 5, when Wilbur made thirty circuits, staying up more than thirty-nine minutes and covering a little over twenty-four miles, at an average speed of about thirty-seven miles per hour. John Daniels, Johnny Moore, and the other Outer Banks witnesses probably wouldn't have believed it.

Nearly as amazing as these breakthrough flights is the scant attention they received.

The Wrights' flying field outside Dayton was alternately known as Simms Station, in reference to the trolley stop adjacent to the prairie. Though the field was located in a rural area, the trolley line running past it served two small towns to the east and hundreds of passengers daily. Since the Wrights were more concerned with catching a breeze than scheduling their flights between trolley runs, it would seem they couldn't escape notice now.

In a departure from the way they usually conducted business, they wrote the Dayton and Cincinnati newspapers to invite reporters—but no photographers—to their first trials in 1904. About forty spectators were on hand to witness the failed flight of May 23, with a few still present to see the twenty-five-foot hop three days later.

It has been suggested that these were deliberate failures staged for the press. If newsmen were on hand to witness a humbling attempt at flight, the argument goes, then they wouldn't get excited about reports of activity at Huffman Prairie over the coming months, and the brothers would be left in peace. But though the Wrights had their faults, disingenuousness is rarely taken to be one of them. Most likely, the failed public flights of May 1904 just represent miscalculation or overconfidence on their part.

Whatever the reason, the Wrights found themselves more alone than they could have hoped. A couple of farmhouses looked onto the prairie, and trolley patrons and other local people knew of their activities, but the media remained unaware or indifferent. It is one of the strange facts of the Wright brothers' story that the first eyewitness accounts of their flights were written by Amos Root, the publisher of a beekeeping journal called *Gleanings in Bee Culture*. Having heard rumors of the brothers, Root traveled by car from Medina, Ohio, and was rewarded on September 20, 1904, by seeing history's first circular flight. Through the following year, he was the only man to regularly cover the Wrights, using their flights as a kind of moral tale to inspire his readers to better beekeeping.

Finally, after the great flights in the fall of 1905, the brothers' activities began to attract interest, though even then press coverage was mostly confined to Dayton and Cincinnati.

Meanwhile, the Wrights were busy on other fronts.

In early 1904, they renewed their effort—begun between the 1902 and 1903 seasons—to secure a patent for their invention, this time hiring a patent attorney to prepare their application. That October, they made their first try at selling an airplane, to a representative of the British government. Their sales efforts continued between the 1904 and 1905 seasons.

With the great flights of 1905, the Wrights proved they could launch their airplane, ascend and descend, turn, fly long distances, and land, all reliably and under control. Having mastered the basics, they believed they could build airplanes to buyers' specifications— airplanes that would fly farther, faster, and higher than anything they had constructed to date.

The brothers now had more to lose than they had to gain by further flying. Without patent protection, the spread of accurate information about their airplane could only hurt them. Until they sold their invention and reaped their reward, they would retire from flying.

That retirement lasted longer and was filled with more frustration than they anticipated.

The Wrights are often said to have been marginal or even poor businessmen. In fairness, it should be noted that they undertook to introduce a radically new technology to the entire world, a task few small-time entrepreneurs would be equipped to handle. To their credit, they consistently resisted financial assistance and offers of partnership, always maintaining full control over their invention. They didn't become fabulously wealthy off airplanes, but they made about as much money as they cared to. They were scrupulously honest, and they remained dignified ambassadors of flight throughout their lives.

That said, they did have shortcomings as businessmen. According to their critics, their excessive secretiveness so delayed their sales negotiations that they lost their technological advantage and let their competition catch up with them. The greatest aeronautical engineers the world had ever seen, they ultimately spent more time in courtrooms defending old designs than in the workshop pioneering new ones. They were essentially past their heyday by the end of 1909. Their main American rival, Glenn Curtiss, a more astute businessman, remained at the forefront of the industry much longer than did the Wrights.

Their business failings first came to light after 1905.

Octave Chanute still hadn't seen the Wrights fly, but he was well aware of their progress, and he believed it was time for them to flaunt their invention before the world. He encouraged them to announce a public flight or to compete for flight prizes being offered in St. Louis and France. Failing that, he encouraged them to reveal photographs of their machine in the air, which likely would have been revelation enough to bring the governments of the world to their doorstep. At the very least, they might release eyewitness statements from some of the people who had seen them fly at Huffman Prairie.

The Wrights were reluctant to consider any of those options.

From late 1905 through the end of 1907, they worked full-time trying to sell airplanes to the United States, Great Britain, France, Germany, and Russia, usually to the respective governments but occasionally to private syndicates, usually through their own efforts but sometimes with the help of agents. They hosted potential customers in Dayton and traveled to New York, Washington, and assorted sites in Europe.

They made it a condition of negotiations that they would reveal no particulars of their invention or stage any demonstrations until they had a contract. They wouldn't show drawings of their airplane, and they certainly wouldn't show the craft itself, even to representatives who had sailed across the ocean to meet them. Honorable men not given to making exaggerated claims, they expected to be taken at their word. And in fact, to a man, those officials who met face to face with the Wrights came away believing they could do what they said they could do.

From the brothers' perspective, there was little risk on the buyers' part, as no money was to be paid until they proved their airplane could perform according to the terms specified in the contract.

From the buyers' perspective, they were being asked to stake their careers on the claims of two self-taught men from Dayton, Ohio. Embarrassment had always been the reward for those who believed in flight. The Wrights may have convinced the representatives they met face to face, but those officials were front men for networks of decision makers, not free agents. In the wake of Samuel Langley's failure, it was unreasonable to expect that Washington might contract for an airplane sight unseen. And though foreign governments did not have a Samuel Langley in their closet, a considerable risk still attended the official who signed his name to a contract.

The Wrights felt at liberty to dictate the terms of sale because they believed they had the field to themselves. "We are convinced that no one will be able to develop a practical flyer within five years," Wilbur wrote Octave Chanute on October 10, 1906.

He drove home the point a few sentences later: "It is many times five years."

Actually, it was thirteen days from the time of that writing. While the machine in question was by no means a "practical flyer," it covered a distance somewhere between 150 and 200 feet on October 23, then flew 726 feet on November 12. That was legitimate heavier-than-air flight even by Wilbur Wright's standards.

It was Alberto Santos-Dumont who made the breakthrough, piloting a craft called the *14-bis*. In airworthiness, Santos-Dumont's machine was a major step backward from even the Wrights' early gliders. He operated it standing upright in a wicker basket, like something out of *Ben Hur*. Already famous as a balloonist, Santos-Dumont reasserted his claim as the world's foremost aeronaut with the longer of his two powered flights in France.

Though Octave Chanute was not involved with Santos-Dumont's effort, he helped bring about the success of it and other projects. Since 1902, experimenters in France—the world's hotbed of aeronautics—had been building gliders patterned after those of the Wrights. Chanute published articles in Europe detailing the brothers' success, including photographs he had taken of their 1902 glider and partial drawings of their craft. French aeronauts took those bits and pieces as their starting point. The Wrights grew more famous abroad through the old news delivered by Chanute than they were in their own hometown through their exploits at Huffman Prairie.

Other experimenters in France were close behind Santos-Dumont. On November 5, 1907, Léon Delagrange made a flight covering over 1,600 feet.

More significant than the efforts of Santos-Dumont and Delagrange was that of Henri Farman. In mid-October 1907, Farman flew over 900 feet, then improved that mark to 2,350 feet before the end of the month. At a field outside Paris on November 18, he fell just short of flying a complete circle, covering over 4,900 feet in the process—nearly a mile. Among the spectators in the crowd that day was Orville Wright, in France trying to tie up business with the government. He was not among those who mobbed Farman after his triumph.

Criticism of the Wright brothers flowed naturally from these events. Asked how their accomplishments compared with the reported flights of the Wrights, the aeronauts in France, reluctant to share their glory with men who had never flown publicly, generally asserted that the brothers were fakes.

For their part, the Wrights considered the French efforts primitive and remained confident that their rivals were several years removed from the standard they had set. Nonetheless, their reputation took a beating.

Finally, two days before Christmas 1907, the United States government, after consultation with the Wrights, put out a public bid for a heavier-than-air flying machine. The brothers were ready with a proposal before the end of January 1908.

And in late March, an agent working for the Wrights closed a deal with a private French syndicate.

The performance standards set forth in both contracts far exceeded any flying the Wrights had ever done. But they were well prepared, with five new airplanes in various stages of construction.

After their two-and-a-half-year layoff, some flying practice was in order before the official trials in the Washington area and France. Experiencing the full force of public pressure for the first time, the Wrights found that privacy concerns again outweighed convenience. Seven and a half years earlier, they had turned to the Outer Banks mostly for the wind and sand. No longer needing those commodities, they would now return strictly for the isolation.

The world was closing in. A major push for powered flight was under way in western New York, led by the talented Glenn Curtiss. By the time the Wrights were finished with the Outer Banks in 1908, at least four other Americans had flown.

The Fourth Estate

Having staked out a position in the vanguard of aeronautical reporting with its story of the powered flights of December 1903, the *Norfolk Virginian-Pilot* ran the following item on its front page on May 2, 1908. Headlined "WRIGHT BROTHERS SAIL OVER LAND AND SEA WITH AEROPLANE," it was accompanied by a couple of photographs of the brothers' gliders in flight.

> With their machine under perfect control, John and Wilbur Wright, of Ohio, has [sic] mastered the air, and yesterday morning down at Nags Head, N.C., not only sailed their airship over the land, but ventured ten miles out on the ocean, and steering

their aerial navigator back to terra firma as easily as a harbor captain steers the ordinary little tugboat.

The Wright brothers have been at Nags Head for the past ten days, daily experimenting with their airship, or aeroplane. Newspapers up North have been waiting almost with breathless anxiety for some tidings of the results of their experiments, but up to last night not a word had gone out from the camp of the experimenters, which is as closely guarded as the cell of a condemned murderer. . . .

The two brothers yesterday not only sailed their ship overland, but steered her out to sea. From the shore the life-savers at Nags Head watched the peculiar shaped thing sail away in the distance until it resembled only a black speck on the horizon, like some bird that inhabits the seashore in search of food for itself and young.

Fearing something might befall the two men who defied the wind and angry waters below them, the brave men who guard the coast prepared to launch their life boats and pull in the direction of the thing in the air, ready to save its two passengers should they be thrown into the sea. Hardly had they got in readiness for the trip, when the little black speck, magnified through the glass of the captain of the life-saving station, was seen to turn and make for the shore.

Coming like a bird and as straight as an arrow, the thing gradually took on size, until it resumed its natural proportions and sailed peacefully back to the place from which it had started.

Unlike the 1903 account, which at least had a basis in fact, no one ever came forward to claim credit for this story. On the date in question, the Wrights were ground-bound in a rebuilt hangar at Kill Devil Hills, the pieces of their airplane spread around them. The wings were assembled and the engine—less the radiator—mounted, but work on the elevator and the tail assembly was only partially completed. They were still a week from flying. Wilbur had been on the North Carolina coast a little over three weeks, and "John," his younger brother, barely a week.

The Wrights would also have been surprised to learn that they made a visit to the Outer Banks in 1904 or 1905—at least according to ninety-year-old Charlie Rose in a *Raleigh News and Observer* article in 1983. The eleven- or twelve-year-old Rose and his two cousins were mending fishing nets on Core Banks, near the southern end of the Outer Banks, when an airplane came roaring over their heads and landed on the flats nearby. The pilot was Wilbur Wright, who generously offered to take the boys for rides, making them the first North Carolinians to fly and giving them a spectacular view of the Cape Lookout Lighthouse in the process.

Assuming it started at Kill Devil Hills, such a fantasy flight would have been remarkable not only for its distance—roughly 110 miles, most of it probably over the vast Pamlico Sound—but also because Wilbur must have found a way to transport a complete set of starting rails with him, else he never would have gotten back off the Core Banks sand.

Actually, many people suppose that the Wright brothers' association with the Outer Banks ended in 1903. Their return trip in 1908 was in some regards their most interesting visit, featuring the first two-person flights in history and a new cast of secondary characters. It also stands as their only visit entirely devoted to powered flight.

Their French contract demanded that they "make two flights, each of 50 kilometers within an hour," according to Wilbur. Their American contract required that their airplane fly 125 miles at an average speed of 40 miles per hour and be able to carry two men. The craft also had to be constructed in such a manner that it could be transported on a standard army wagon, which meant that its wings had to be easily removable. At that time, the primary military use of airplanes was understood to be in scouting enemy positions.

The Wrights had no intention of meeting these strict requirements during their Outer Banks trip. In fact, they were bringing what amounted to a secondary airplane: their 1905 craft, fitted with a larger motor and equipped for upright seating and a passenger. Practice time was their primary goal. They also needed to familiarize themselves with the new controls demanded by the upright seating. The levers were now to the right of the pilot, and the passenger's position to the right of that.

With his name known—if not universally respected—around much of his own country and in Europe, Wilbur found himself in the same kind of predicament he had experienced seven and a half years earlier. Shipping men and supplies to the Outer Banks and setting up camp there were attended by all the usual frustrations, along with a few new ones.

Wilbur left Dayton alone on Monday, April 6, and arrived in Elizabeth City the following evening. A couple of minor disasters were close on his heels: his trunk was lost in transit, and he was informed at the depot that the camp buildings at Kill Devil Hills were in ruins. There were even three fires in Elizabeth City that night, though none affected Wilbur directly. That was the good news.

After buying lumber and gasoline, Wilbur shipped across the sound aboard the *B. M. Van Dusen*, arriving in Kitty Hawk on April 9. When he reached camp the following day, he found the 1903 hangar laid practically flat, the 1901 building without a roof and with only three walls standing, the water pump gone—appropriated by the Kill Devil Hills lifesavers—and the camp's contents, including

The camp in 1908. The 1903 building (rear) had been completely repaired by the time this photograph was taken. In better days, the Wrights' kitchen and dining space were located in the back portion of the 1901 building, on the far left here.

the various gliders in storage, either damaged by weather or picked over by local residents.

The lumber to repair one of the camp buildings was sent from Elizabeth City aboard the *Lou Willis* on April 10, but owing to conditions in the sound, it couldn't be brought to a point on shore opposite the camp, and it proved to be only a partial shipment at that. Some of the remainder of the wood, Wilbur learned, was still aboard one of the boats plying the sound, and the rest was back in Elizabeth City. Further delays were caused by a storm that blew the sails off the *Lou Willis*, another blow that left it aground, and a headache suffered by a member of the Midgett family, who left work the day he was expected to deliver the missing lumber. It took ten days to get the goods from Elizabeth City to Kill Devil Hills.

Meanwhile, the barrel of gasoline Wilbur had purchased was now less than half a barrel, owing to a leak caused by rough handling. Without shelter of his own, he stayed at the Kill Devil Hills Lifesaving Station, where the food gave him diarrhea.

Whether referring to his besieged intestines or the general state of affairs, Wilbur pronounced conditions "almost intolerable." Set to take the international stage later that year with the engineering miracle of the new century, he was finding himself thoroughly beaten by mundane matters.

The only bright spot was the arrival of Charlie Furnas, a Dayton mechanic and friend of the Wrights.

Wilbur was at the Kill Devil Hills Lifesaving Station on April 15 when someone spotted a man milling around the camp a mile away. Expecting it to be one of the local men he'd hired to do carpentry work, Wilbur trekked across the sand and was completely surprised to discover Furnas.

It is unclear whether Furnas made the trip out of curiosity or whether Orville had dispatched him to help his brother. Regardless, Charlie Furnas stayed for the duration. He proved his usefulness almost immediately by making the long walk to Kitty Hawk to try to expedite the shipping of the lumber, as Wilbur was too ill to do so himself. He also helped hammer together some of the furnishings once the camp building was completed.

For his efforts, Furnas was rewarded more handsomely than he could have imagined. The Wrights' American contract demanded that their airplane carry two men, but their father had made them promise that they would not fly together. They needed to test two-man flight before their official trials, and Wilbur now found the answer right in front of him.

On the other hand, Furnas may have unwittingly deprived some local resident—perhaps one of the Wrights' friends among the life-savers—of the honor of being the world's first airplane passenger.

Things began looking up around April 25. That was the date the building was complete enough for Wilbur and Furnas to bring their belongings over from the lifesaving station and set up housekeeping, and also the day Orville arrived with the airplane parts.

Wilbur was anxious to get into the air by then. For two and a half weeks, while his nearest flying machine was being packed into crates in Ohio, he had faithfully begun his daily diary entries by recording the wind speed and direction, a fruitless exercise. Now, at last, he had an outlet for his energy.

April 26 was a Sunday. Work on the airplane began immediately after that.

The Wrights may have received a visit from Bill Tate and his family around this time. In interviews with *Outer Banks Magazine* in 1984 and the National Park Service in 1990, Pauline Tate Woodard, one of Bill's daughters, recalled that it was in 1908 that her father loaded the children aboard the *Dixie*—a powerful boat belonging to the owners of the Martins Point property where the Tates were living—and took them down the sounds to Kill Devil Hills to meet the Wright brothers.

"I remember that Sunday well," Elijah Tate said in the 1984 interview in *Outer Banks Magazine*.

> It was a fine autumn afternoon and Father took all four of us children: Irene, eleven, Pauline, ten, myself, six and the youngest, my brother Lewis, then four. . . . Well, the brothers had a kind of experimental surface, a fabric and wood panel about six feet wide with a hand hold on each end. They used it to test the angle of incidence, the inclination with the horizon, to see how much lift they could get at various strengths of wind. The brothers

set the wing section on edge and said to me, "Lije, take hold of it," but just as I was about to reach up to the top edge they said, "Here, let Lewis do it; he's lighter." So Lewis held on to the leading edge and lay on the wing and they ran with it against the wind, one on each side.

The Wrights kept running until the wing rose to arm's length above their heads.

At least one source places this visit in 1911, not 1908, which fits with Elijah Tate's memory of an autumn afternoon; the 1908 trip was in the springtime. Then again, the "Wright brothers" in question in 1911 would have been Lorin and Orville, not Wilbur and Orville, and all the Tate children would have been three years older than Elijah remembered.

Whichever the case, Lewis Tate still set the mark as the youngest member of the clan to fly, surpassing ten-year-old cousin Tom Tate and his glides of 1900.

False as it was, the account of the Wrights' daring ocean flight that ran in the *Norfolk Virginian-Pilot* on May 2 awakened attention in high places. That same day, the *New York Herald* telegraphed the Weather Bureau operator in Manteo—presumably Alf Drinkwater, who now held that position—asking for news of the brothers' activities.

The *Herald* also ran a muted version of the *Virginian-Pilot* story. The editors there supposedly disbelieved the tale, but living as they did in mortal fear of James Gordon Bennett—the *Herald's* famous owner, also an aeronautical enthusiast—they didn't dare let the matter pass without sending a reporter. Rather than dispatching a regular staffer, they compromised, engaging the services of D. Bruce Salley, a reporter for the *Norfolk Landmark* who had previously worked as a stringer for the *Herald*.

The thirty-five-year-old Salley, described as "long" and "loose-jointed" by one of the reporters who soon joined him to cover the Wrights, was a good man for the job. A lifelong resident of Tidewater, Virginia, and a veteran of at least three Norfolk newspapers, he already had contacts on the Outer Banks.

He promptly shipped to Manteo and checked into the Tranquil House. On May 5, he began a routine that grew all too familiar over the next week and a half, rising early, taking a skiff across Roanoke Sound, and then tramping overland toward the Wrights' camp.

That first time, unlike the days that followed, he entered camp directly, escorted by one of the Midgett family, his captain on the trip across the sound. Salley introduced himself and stated his purpose. What passed between the Wrights and Salley was not recorded by either party, but Salley came away with the impression that re-

The modified 1905 machine on the Outer Banks in 1908

porters were unwelcome around camp. He resolved to take a more secretive approach from that point onward—though he violated his cardinal rule just three days later.

The Wrights were not quite ready for flying the Tuesday that Salley visited, but they were the following day, Wilbur making a flight of a little over 1,000 feet in twenty-two seconds—their first effort since 1905. Thanks to a more powerful motor and the strong winds of Kill Devil Hills, they didn't require the catapult they'd used at Huffman Prairie, employing instead a 120-foot rail.

Bruce Salley, sent to the Outer Banks for one specific purpose, was resting on his laurels in Manteo at the time. Luckily for him, he received a telephone call—most likely from one of the Kill Devil Hills lifesavers—informing him of the flight. He then wrote his copy and delivered it to Alf Drinkwater at his home, which doubled as the Manteo telegraph office. Salley's description of the Wrights' machine was reasonably accurate, as were the details of the flight he'd received over the phone, but the embellishments he added were conjecture.

"Wright brothers, the aeronauts, now at Kill Devil Hill, near here, made their first flight in their new aeroplane this afternoon," his account began. "Although but a test flight it was successful in every respect, the machine under the perfect control of its two makers traveling a distance of 1000 feet. Apparently it could have flown a thousand times as far as easily as not. . . . After several preliminary tests made during the next two or three days a durance [sic] test of the machine will be made, and on this test an effort will probably be made to fly the machine to cape Henry, a distance of about seventy five miles and return."

A flight to Cape Henry, Virginia, was out of the question. Salley further claimed that the craft bore both Wilbur and Orville that day, which was also mistaken.

The Wrights were back at it on Friday, May 8, making nine short flights that morning, assisted by lifesavers Willie Dough, Uncle Benny O'Neal, and Avery Tillett. Wilbur reported trouble getting used to the new "cockpit" controls.

Bruce Salley nearly managed to miss his assignment again, arriving around noon, after the first nine flights. This time, acting on the assumption that the Wrights wouldn't fly if they knew he was present, he staked out a position in the brush some distance from camp. That afternoon, he secretly watched as Orville made a flight of 945 feet in thirty-one seconds. Actually, he didn't manage to keep his secret for long. Finding the spectacle of flight even more marvelous than he had imagined it in his dispatch two days earlier, he burst from cover and hustled into camp, where he "interrupted experiments," as Wilbur put it.

During his visit, Salley apparently asked for and received specific information about the craft, as his second telegraph from Manteo corrected a few errors he'd made in the first. For example, he stated that the motor produced thirty horsepower, rather than the twenty previously reported, a fact only the Wrights could have provided him. In his enthusiasm, he also inquired about the prospect of a transatlantic hop, a flight roughly twenty thousand times the length of the one he'd just witnessed. "Wilbur Wright gave it as his opinion today that a machine could not be made to fly across the ocean until something better than a gasoline engine has been found to drive it," he noted in his dispatch.

Salley's opinion that the Wrights wouldn't fly if they knew a reporter was anywhere in the vicinity was quickly proven wrong, as Wilbur made the last and longest flight of the day—covering a little less than half a mile in about a minute—after their visitor departed camp.

In his dispatch that day, Salley also told of seeing a herd of cattle scared into Roanoke Sound by the noise from the Wrights' motor. He further reported that they were planning a flight fifteen miles south to Oregon Inlet and back, a tidbit nearly as fantastic as the proposed jaunt to Cape Henry.

Another mixture of fact and fiction, Salley's telegram of May 8 stands as the first eyewitness account of the Wrights by a representative of a major news source.

The story was suddenly judged too hot for Bruce Salley. His first account—the absentee story of May 6—appeared on the front page of the *New York Herald* and was also picked up by the *New York Times*. His account of May 8 was telegraphed to the *Herald* and then distributed nationally by that paper, picking up embellishments along the way according to the whims of the editors whose desks it crossed.

A handful of major publications thought enough of the events at Kill Devil Hills to send staffers. Byron Newton of the *Herald* and Bill Hoster of the *New York American* were the first to arrive, checking into the Tranquil House on May 10. Newton and Hoster were on hand to accompany Bruce Salley the next time the Wrights took to the air, Monday, May 11. How Salley—in Manteo at the behest of the *Herald*—felt about being one-upped by star reporter Byron Newton is a matter for speculation.

The forty-six-year-old Newton was a native of Allegany County, New York, and had attended Oberlin College in Ohio, which was also Katharine Wright's school. He was well traveled as a journalist, having begun his career in Buffalo in 1887 and served as an Associated Press correspondent covering the Spanish-American War in 1898. He had been at the *Herald* since 1902. As for his opinion of the Wright brothers, he was skeptical that they had ever achieved sustained flight.

Perhaps feeling the effects of his difficult trip from Elizabeth City to Manteo, Newton initially looked upon coastal North Carolina with big-city disdain. In an article most definitely not intended for local consumption, he pronounced the citizens of Roanoke Island "well nigh as ignorant of the modern world as if they lived in the depths of Africa. The sound of a steam locomotive is as unknown to them as the music of Mars. The automobile is as much a myth to them as Noah's Ark and the flying machine across the sound they regarded as a sea serpent yarn invented by Yankee reporters, the first strangers since the Civil War to invade their island domain."

Newton, Salley, and Hoster rose at four in the morning on May 11 for the boat ride to the Outer Banks. Perhaps enlarging on his African theme, Newton described the walk to the observation point near the Wrights' camp as a perilous safari through "noisome swamps and jungle" and among "thousands of moccasins, rattlers and blacksnakes, the blinding swarms of mosquitoes, the myriads of ground ticks and chiggers, the flocks of wild turkey and other fowl, the herds of wild hogs and cattle and the gleaming white sand mountains." Indeed, according to Newton, "two of the men narrowly escaped the poisonous fangs of moccasins." Once in hiding, they lay "devoured by mosquitoes and ticks, startled occasionally by the beady eyes of a snake." The local folk would have been amused.

And that was before the real action began. "As we crept into our hiding place we could see the doors of the aerodrome were open and the machine standing on its monorail track outside," Newton wrote.

> Three men were working about it and making frequent hurried trips to the aerodrome. Presently a man climbed into the seat while others continued to tinker about the mechanism. Then we saw the two propellers begin to revolve. . . .

For some minutes the propeller blades continued to flash in the sun, and then the machine rose obliquely into the air. At first it came directly toward us, so that we could not tell how fast it was going except that it appeared to increase rapidly in size as it approached. In the excitement of this first flight men trained to observe details under all sorts of distractions, forgot their cameras, forgot their watches, forgot everything but this aerial monster chattering over our heads. As it neared us we could plainly see the operator in his seat working at the upright levers close by his side. When it was almost squarely over us there was a movement of the forward and rear guiding planes, a slight curving of the larger planes at one end and the machine wheeled about at an angle every bit as gracefully as an eagle flying close to the ground could have done. . . .

After the first turn it drove straight toward one of the sand hills as if it were the intention of the operator to land there, but instead of coming down there was another slight movement of the planes and the machine soared upward, skimmed over the crest of the mountain, 250 feet high, and disappeared on the opposite side. For perhaps ten seconds we heard distinctly the clatter of the propellers, when the machine flashed into view again, sailed along over the surf, made another easy turn and dropped into the sand about one hundred yards from the point of departure.

Summarizing the experience, Newton gave the opinion that "thinking men and women of our generation have in store a great treat when they shall have the good fortune first to witness this marvel of man's creation. . . . It brings a special exhilaration. It is different from the contemplation of any other marvel human eyes may behold in a life time."

What Newton, Salley, and Hoster had seen was a flight by Orville

Byron Newton

*The Outer Banks press corps hiding
in the woods . . .*

*. . . and seeking relief from
aching feet and bug bites*

covering a little more than half a mile. An hour later, around nine
o'clock, they saw Wilbur make a flight of nearly two miles, lasting
two and a half minutes. At eleven, they saw Orville make a flight a
quarter-mile short of that.

They also saw the first recorded instance of taxiing in history.
Newton described how, at the end of each flight, "two wide tired
trucks . . . were placed under the machine, the motor started and
the aeroplane at once became a wind-wagon rolling itself back to
the starting track with the power of its own propellers." Bruce Salley
confirmed this in his dispatch that evening.

As for the newsmen's secret hiding place, Wilbur Wright noted in
his diary that same day, "It is said that Salley, the newspaperman,
spent the day in the woods over by Ha[y]man's old place."

With a few days' hard experience, Bruce Salley was for the moment perhaps the most seasoned newspaper reporter in the world
on the subject of aeronautics. His May 11 telegram to the *Herald*
showed it. While Byron Newton was forgetting his watch in the
excitement of witnessing flight, Salley was putting his own to good
use in measuring the time the Wrights were in the air. He also estimated distance by means of the telegraph poles spaced along the
sand, thus providing an independent record of the length of the
flights that day. He even calculated the airplane's average speed, and
to three decimal places at that—on Wilbur's flight, the longest of the
three, he made the speed to be 46.774 miles per hour.

But it seems that the more professional Salley became, the less his
stories were believed.

Understanding the controversial nature of his material, he attached
a postscript to his May 11 dispatch: "Editor *Herald*: Stories you are
getting from Manteo are accurate. Should you wish to substantiate
correctness of my information wire Mr. Drinkwater, officer in charge

Weather Bureau service here, or Captain Jesse Ward keeper of Kill Devil Hill Life Saving station. Big fakes have been concocted in Norfolk. If you want to know anything about me personally write S. S. Nottingham editor *Norfolk Landmark*."

The reference to the "big fakes . . . concocted in Norfolk" presumably means the *Virginian-Pilot*, where the staff was busy finagling more stories on the Wrights. It is interesting to note how that paper, having run the fantasy flying story that resulted in Bruce Salley's being sent to the Outer Banks on behalf of the *New York Herald*, did not dispatch a reporter to cover a major event in its home territory. Editor Keville Glennan later claimed he proposed going himself or having someone else sent, but was told it wasn't worth the expense.

Making the best of their situation, Glennan and a *Virginian-Pilot* reporter named Benjamin Myers, who knew Morse code, supposedly made nightly visits to the Weather Bureau office in Norfolk. According to Glennan, it so happened that the men's room was close enough to the telegraph machine for someone to spy on the incoming transmissions. Glennan and Myers would repair to the bathroom, leave the door ajar, and make a transcription.

Back at the *Virginian-Pilot*, Glennan would "rewrite Salley's stuff, enlarging and embellishing," as he put it. It was a matter of pride to Glennan that his paper "got better stories than the *New York Herald* because I could fill in with more background than the *New York Herald*'s rewrite staff."

Meanwhile, Bruce Salley's reputation was suffering. His May 11 dispatch, sent to the *Herald* and then offered nationally, received a strong negative response from the *Cleveland Leader*, which refused to pay the telegraph toll on the story, amounting to a third of a cent per word at night rates. The *Leader* apparently bypassed the *Herald* and wired Salley directly in Manteo, admonishing him to "cut out the wild cat stuff." Salley promptly fired back, "Where did you get idea I have been filing you wild cat stuff. Am not in habit of filing such matter."

Even Byron Newton was having difficulty with editors. In addition to his reporting for the *Herald*, he tried to sell longer versions of the story to some of the leading magazines of the day. One of the rejection letters he later received went as follows:"While your manuscript has been read with much interest, it does not seem to qualify either as fact or fiction and we are therefore returning it with thanks for your consideration of us." Newton grew so frustrated that he put the story in a trunk and made no further effort to sell it for twenty-four years.

As for his status at the *Herald*, some accounts have it that on his return to New York, Newton was briefly suspended from the staff for his exaggerated reporting.

When Newton, Salley, and Hoster arrived back at the Tranquil House after the flights of May 11, they found that three more colleagues had arrived during the day: writer Arthur Ruhl and photographer Jimmy Hare, both representing *Collier's* weekly magazine, and P. H. McGowan of the *London Daily Mail*. Arthur Ruhl was already known and liked by the Wrights, having made their acquaintance in New York in the fall of 1907.

The newsmen's predicament was growing more curious all the while. Arthur Ruhl described the routine beginning with the daily boat trip from Manteo:

> At five the next morning you catch the launch that chug-chugs out to Nag's Head and Kitty Hawk with the mail. . . . Out of the chug-chug half a mile from shore and into a skiff, across the gunwales of which, as it is poled miraculously shoreward with one oar, the rollers sleepily climb and deposit themselves in your lap. If you stand, the skiff will sink, and to sit

requires fortitude and repose of manner almost superhuman. At the precise moment of swamping, the boat conveniently touches bottom and you wade ashore.

Then comes the tramp through the woods to the Kill Devil sand-hills. Geographically, this may be only four or five miles, but measured by the sand into which your shoes sink and which sinks into your shoes, the pine-needles you slip back on, the heat, and the "ticks" and "chiggers" that swarm up out of the earth and burrow into every part of you, it seems about thirty-five.

Ruhl also told how the newsmen wrestled dead limbs through the forest to try to bridge a boggy area, and how they hotfooted it across sparsely vegetated sections to keep the Wrights from seeing them.

All this to set up a spy post about a mile from the brothers' camp, to suffer insects, heat, and humidity, and to face rainstorms unprotected, with no guarantee that the Wrights would even take a notion to fly that day. Jimmy Hare's memorable photographs show the reporters tramping across the sand in various stages of undress, struggling up a dune, camping in the woods, and, pant legs rolled, applying medication to their badly bitten legs.

Of course, these hardships were endured in the belief that the Wrights would do no flying if they knew reporters were nearby. Yet Bruce Salley had already been to camp twice, and the brothers had received at least one report of his hiding in the woods. In case there was any doubt, Arthur Ruhl left cover and walked into camp after witnessing his first couple of flights.

It was a painful charade for the men of the press. The Wrights were in a position where they had to get in flying practice no matter who was watching.

It might be supposed that sharing such an experience would have
led the newsmen to mutual understanding and a common sense
of purpose—a kind of brotherhood of misery—but that was not
entirely the case. They were covering a big story in a competitive market.

In later years, Alf Drinkwater was fond of telling of hot tempers
in his telegraph office. According to Drinkwater, P. H. McGowan
managed to scratch out his story in pencil on the boat ride back to
Manteo one day and was therefore the first to deliver his completed
copy to the telegraph office. Drinkwater dutifully transmitted
McGowan's eighteen-hundred-word story while the other newsmen
were arriving with their copy.

McGowan had only recently arrived in the United States after
serving as a correspondent in Japan and Russia, where it was the
custom that the first man in line could occupy the transmitter as
long as he cared, effectively blocking his competitors from getting
their stories on the wire. While his copy was flashing northward,
McGowan picked up a magazine, marked off a couple of pages for
Drinkwater to send, and informed the other newsmen that his story
was to be an "exclusive" that day.

Bill Hoster grabbed a chair and threatened to break it over
McGowan's head.

Drinkwater threatened to make Hoster pay for the chair if he did.

Byron Newton and Bruce Salley intervened to separate McGowan
and Hoster.

Agitated, Drinkwater informed the newsmen that he was operating a government office that was only required to remain open until
four o'clock, and that he was continuing to transmit well after that
only as a courtesy to them. From that point onward, he told them,
stories would be limited to five hundred words.

Alf Drinkwater was very much at the center of things in 1908. He later claimed to have transmitted forty-two thousand words related to aeronautics that May. It was not an easy job. Once all six newsmen were on the scene, Drinkwater was sometimes occupied until two in the morning, relieved occasionally at the telegraph key by his wife or Bruce Salley. When the wire to Norfolk got damp at night, he found it almost impossible to transmit.

As usual, Drinkwater's slant on the events is not without controversy. The claim that Byron Newton was suspended from the *Herald* for his reporting of the Wrights' activities may have originated with the Manteo telegrapher. The more popular view is that it was Newton who severed the tie, over the *Herald's* sensationalized coverage of the brothers. Drinkwater further claimed to have sent an affidavit to the paper testifying to the Wrights' long flights, which got Newton his job back. And in one interview, he even stated that, due to illness, Newton was confined to the Tranquil House during his entire visit and never made it to Kill Devil Hills at all; Drinkwater claimed he went in Newton's place.

In fact, Alf Drinkwater did make a visit to the Wrights' camp that month. After the morning flights of May 11, he showed up with a Mr. Grant, whom he introduced as an attaché of the Weather Bureau office in Norfolk—most likely the Charles C. Grant who was on the receiving end of the famous telegram in 1903, and who was now being spied on from the men's room by Keville Glennan and Benjamin Myers of the *Virginian-Pilot*. Drinkwater and Grant told the Wrights they were in the area to make repairs on the telegraph line, but when they learned the brothers would be doing no flying that afternoon, they departed quickly. Wilbur found the visit suspicious.

Tuesday, May 12, was the first day the full complement of reporters made the early-morning trip from Manteo to Kill Devil Hills. It wasn't worth the effort. As Wilbur put it in his diary, "The wind was high all day, and as we were very sore after the long hauls of yesterday we did not get the machine out."

The following day proved more fruitful, though exceedingly long. The Wrights made the first of their four flights early in the morning and the last, owing to wind conditions, at nearly seven o'clock at night. The longest was a flight by Orville of nearly two and a half miles. This was the day Arthur Ruhl left cover and walked to camp after his first experience of flight.

That night in his dispatch, in a dark bit of foresight the inventors themselves hadn't even considered, Bruce Salley postulated that an airplane might "soar over any given point, such as a man of war, upon which it may drop a destroying explosive."

Though he noted that "at no time today did the machine ascend to a greater elevation than twenty feet above the ground," Salley speculated that it could fly "at least 1000 miles" and that it could soar "five miles above ground."

May 14 was the Wrights' best day on the Outer Banks in 1908. Just before eight o'clock that morning, Wilbur took Charlie Furnas up for the world's first two-man flight, covering a little less than half a mile in a little less than half a minute. Furnas then accompanied Orville on a circular flight covering over two and a half miles and lasting more than four minutes.

Of course, the historic event of a two-man flight was already old news, Bruce Salley having erroneously announced it in his absentee story of May 6, and the *Virginian-Pilot* having proclaimed it four days before that. Now, witnessing the event with his own eyes, Salley still didn't get it quite right, remarking on "the presence of both the Wrights in the machine. They were unmistakably seen in it as the machine soared by a group of responsible observers and they were seen to step from the machine when it lit."

It was Bill Hoster who correctly identified "Furness [*sic*], their mechanic" as the passenger.

After dinner, Wilbur made a solo flight that stands as the Wrights' longest in North Carolina, covering a little over five miles in about seven and a half minutes. Describing the craft on that flight, Bill Hoster wrote of how "her motions were like clock work, and she sailed along serenely under the bright blue skies like a thing endowed with life. Behind her floated a flock of gulls and crows that seemed at once amazed and jealous of this new thing of the air."

The flight came to an end when Wilbur, still learning the new control levers, pulled the elevator handle the wrong way and dove when he meant to climb, plowing into the sand at between forty and fifty miles per hour.

The crash occurred out of sight of the newsmen. Learning of it later through the lifesavers, Bruce Salley took it lightly: "Wilbur Wright . . . escaped without a scratch, and he has passed safely through other accidents. If a life is ever charmed, his must be."

Wilbur himself was less sanguine: "I was thrown violently forward and landed against the top surface. . . . I received a slight cut across the bridge of my nose, several bruises on my left hand, right forearm, and both shoulders. The next day I felt a little stiff all over."

Their upper wing ruined, the Wrights' season on the Outer Banks was at a close. The career of their 1905 craft—the world's first practical airplane—was also ended.

Most of the newsmen checked out of the Tranquil House and headed home. An exception was P. H. McGowan, whom the Wrights discovered in camp on May 15 seeking to photograph the remains of the 1902 glider. With McGowan was a reporter who identified himself as Gilson Gardiner of Washington. The newsmen tried to photograph the Wrights, Orville wearing what he called his "Merry Widow" bonnet and Wilbur hitched in a "dog harness" and pulling a cart bearing the wreck of the 1905 machine. Not dressed to their usual standards, the Wrights declined.

Also visiting camp that year was J. C. Burkhart of Ithaca, New York, who came "disguised as a native," in Wilbur's words. Wilbur took him to be a newsman, though he was apparently affiliated with Cornell University. And Fred Essary, a colleague of Bruce Salley's at the *Norfolk Landmark*, is sometimes listed among the Outer Banks press corps of 1908, but his exact role is unclear.

By now, the Wrights were about as interested in the newsmen as the newsmen were in them. On their way through Manteo on May 17 after breaking camp, they stopped at the Tranquil House and checked the guest register to determine exactly who had been watching them from the woods.

Traveling from Manteo to Elizabeth City, the Wrights enjoyed their first trip aboard the *Hattie Creef*, an institution on that part of the North Carolina coast for nearly eighty years. Designed for sail, later fitted with an engine, later sunk in the Pasquotank River and resurrected, the *Hattie Creef* saw service as an oyster boat, a passenger, mail, and freight vessel, a tugboat, a pleasure cruiser, and a small museum honoring the Wrights, operated by Elijah Tate, Bill's older son. It lived out its days as part of a restaurant in Avon, on the Outer Banks near Cape Hatteras.

Unaware of all this pending history, Wilbur Wright misidentified it in his diary as the *Hattie Cruf*.

With two sets of government trials facing them, the Wrights decided they had no choice but to work separately. Wilbur would head for France. Orville would return to Dayton, crate up one of the new machines for shipment to his brother, and head to Virginia with a second machine for the American trials.

The Wrights' strange relationship with the men of the press on the Outer Banks that year seems to have been mutually agreeable.

Upon arriving in Norfolk on his way to New York and France, Wilbur took dinner with Bruce Salley at the Monticello Hotel.

When Arthur Ruhl's account of the Outer Banks flights appeared in *Collier's* later that month, the brothers pronounced it the best thing yet written on them.

Upon reaching home, Byron Newton wrote the Wrights a personal letter expressing his admiration.

Orville's reply to Newton crystallized the entire affair: "We were aware of the presence of newspaper men in the woods at Kill Devil Hills, at least we had often been told that they were there. Their presence, however, did not bother us in the least, and I am only sorry that you did not come over to see us at our camp. The display of a white flag would have disposed of the rifles and shot guns with which the machine is reported to have been guarded!"

CHAPTER 6

1 9 1 1 _____

Mr. Lorin Wright, of Dayton, Ohio, one of the Wright brothers, famed for aerial navigation and flying machines, spent Wednesday here the guest of the Southern hotel, and has gone to Kitty Hawk on a little outing. He will be joined there by his brother Orville Wright, who is now returning from Europe accompanied by one of his aviators. Kitty Hawk is the scene of the first successful flight of the Wright brothers. Here they spent a few years ago much time perfecting their invention.

The words Kitty Hawk and flying machines are very closely associated; and, when the people of this section hear that any of the Wrights are heading for Kitty Hawk, they expect some wonderful developments in flying machines.

Elizabeth City Weekly Advance,
September 22, 1911

Fame

Seeing an aircraft in flight was once a wonderful, frightening thing. There's a good story from 1783, the first great year of ballooning in France. That August, Jacques Alexandre Cesar Charles constructed an unmanned hydrogen balloon and announced plans to launch it from Paris. Not knowing where the craft would be taken by the wind, and understanding that rural folk would be mystified upon seeing it, the French government issued a proclamation to be delivered to outlying areas: "Anyone who should see in the sky a globe, resembling the moon in an eclipse, should be aware that far from being an alarming phenomenon, it is only a machine, made of taffeta, or light canvas covered with paper, that cannot possibly cause any harm, and will some day prove serviceable to the wants of society."

Soon after launching, the balloon rose to an estimated height of three thousand feet and disappeared into the clouds. Forty-five minutes later, it descended in a place called Gonoesse, a farm village that the proclamation had somehow missed. Seeing the craft coming to earth, the local citizens took it to be a monster bird or flying dragon. Coming out of their fields, they surrounded it with scythes and pitchforks, being sure to keep a safe distance. Finally, one man retrieved his trusty fowling piece, crept within range, and fired. The craft writhed about the ground and gave off a foul odor in its death struggle, which further convinced the villagers of its evil nature. They advanced on the balloon and cut it to ribbons with their field tools, then tied the remains to the tail of a horse and sent the animal running across the fields, until the balloon was good and dead.

Among the scientists of the day, it was believed that ascending in a balloon would result in fainting, hemorrhages, and heart failure. The first "manned" ascents were made by animals, and the historical distinction of being the first human to fly was originally going to be awarded to a condemned criminal.

Much of that innocence was still intact during the Wright brothers' day.

After leaving the Outer Banks in 1908, Wilbur traveled through New York and arrived in Paris near the end of May. The news was all bad at first. The French firm hired to assemble the motor shipped over by Orville had damaged it. The airframe was in even worse condition; French customs officials had gone through the Wrights' crates, then repacked them so poorly that the wing fabric was torn in various places and just about every other part—from ribs to radiator to seats—was battered in some way. Unable to explain assembly procedures to the French mechanics assisting him, Wilbur had to do most of the work himself. On the Fourth of July, he was badly burned on the arm and side by boiling water sprayed from a radiator hose. It took nearly ten weeks from the time of his arrival to get his airplane in order.

Wilbur finally flew on Saturday, August 8, at Les Hunaudières, an automobile race course near Le Mans, making two circuits of the field in about two minutes—the Wrights' first public flight ever. He continued testing the new craft through the following Thursday, achieving a best flight of over eight minutes, then moved his operation to a better facility at Camp d'Auvours, an artillery testing ground, also near Le Mans. Enthusiastic crowds cheered him at both sites.

Meanwhile, Orville prepared for the American trials at Fort Myer, Virginia, near Washington. Charlie Taylor and Charlie Furnas were on hand to help. Orville first flew on Thursday, September 3, making a circuit of the field in a little over a minute. He progressed rapidly from there, making solo flights of fifty-seven, sixty-two, sixty-five, and seventy minutes and flights with a passenger exceeding six, then nine minutes by September 12. Reaction was initially more subdued in the United States than in Europe, but Orville, too, was drawing large crowds by the time of his long flights.

In fact, enthusiasm grew to such a level that it didn't dampen even when tragedy struck. Orville was flying with Lieutenant Thomas Selfridge of the United States Army on September 17 when he heard tapping sounds coming from the rear of the airplane. Unknown to Orville, his right propeller had developed a crack, which flattened the blade slightly and created unequal thrust between the left and right blades. Sensing something was wrong, he began making preparations to land. Next, the right propeller brace deformed, throwing the blade out of its proper rotation; it cut through a wire bracing the rudder at the rear of the craft, causing the rudder to twist and sending the craft into the ground at a speed approaching fifty miles an hour.

As fate would have it, the crash occurred along the border of Arlington Cemetery, where Thomas Selfridge was buried a few days later. Selfridge, the victim of severe head injuries, was the first fatality in a powered, heavier-than-air machine. Orville, knocked unconscious, counted a broken leg, broken ribs, a cut head, and a hurt back among his injuries. His leg and back troubles stayed with him the rest of his life.

Having seen a Wright airplane fly, and understanding that the crash was more the result of misfortune than unreliability on the part of the inventors, the American government didn't hesitate in granting the brothers until the following summer to fulfill their contract.

Still in France, Wilbur was in a position where he had to fly absolutely safely, yet spectacularly enough to overshadow Orville's crash. Performing under considerable pressure, he did the best flying of his career. Just four days after the tragedy, he set world records for distance flown and time aloft. On December 31, he made a flight lasting two hours and eighteen minutes.

In early 1909, he relocated his operation and made numerous flights at Pau, a resort in the south of France, where he was joined by the recuperating Orville and their sister, Katharine.

Orville was back in the air in late June 1909 for the rescheduled American trials at Fort Myer. On July 12, he stayed aloft with a passenger for an hour and twelve minutes. On July 30, he fulfilled the last requirement of the Wrights' contract by covering a ten-mile course at an average speed in excess of forty miles per hour.

The upshot of all these public flights was a level of fame beyond anything the Wrights had ever imagined.

Among the first crowds at Les Hunaudières were some of the most sophisticated flight observers in the world, men who understood Wilbur's tight figure-eights and steeply banked turns to be qualitatively different from anything they'd ever witnessed. Upon seeing Wilbur in the air, many of the French aeronauts who had previously denounced the Wrights as fakes issued apologies in the newspapers, declaring the brothers to have brought the aeroplane and the art of flying to perfection.

Hard-bitten newsmen in the crowds found tears streaming down their cheeks. Other spectators fell to their knees and prayed.

The citizens of the world had been given a great gift.

That was only the beginning. Wilbur Wright dominated the news in France. The kings and millionaires of Europe came calling. Never having claimed expertise in anything but aeronautics, he suddenly found his opinions sought on art, literature, medicine, and world affairs.

Songs, poems, and plays were written about the Wright brothers.

Women sent descriptions of themselves and proposals of marriage.

A frying pan in which Wilbur did some of his cooking in France was supposedly displayed in the Louvre.

His manner of dress spawned a line of commercial clothing.

When Wilbur, Orville, and Katharine returned to the United States in early 1909, a flotilla awaited them in New York Harbor. A major civic celebration was scheduled in Dayton.

Upon the brothers' arrival in the Washington area for Orville's second attempt at fulfilling their American contract, one of their first stops was the White House, where President William Howard Taft spoke in their honor. One day, the entire United States Senate adjourned and made the trip across the Potomac in hopes of seeing Orville fly. President Taft came another day. When Orville crashed into a bush during one trial, the crowd rushed forward to strip its branches for mementos.

Many experts consider the Wright brothers the first great international

celebrities of the twentieth century. Biographer Harry Combs is of
the opinion that their first public flights had a greater effect on human consciousness than Neil Armstrong's walk on the moon.

But the Wrights quickly lost their edge.

One of the principal reasons was their involvement in lawsuits.
The Wrights' patent was unusually broadly drawn. Rather than pat-
enting a particular system for presenting an airplane's wings at different angles to the wind, they had effectively been allowed to patent
the general principle behind such systems. But it wasn't long after
the Wrights started flying publicly that aviators like Glenn Curtiss
began expanding on their wing-warping system with ailerons—
moveable surfaces usually placed at the trailing edges of the wings,
designed to control the craft in the roll axis.

In the Wrights' view, mastery of the roll axis was absolutely vital
to controlling an airplane, and as they were solely responsible for
solving the problem, they deserved compensation for any system
growing out of their work. But as their competitors saw it, ailerons
were qualitatively different from the Wrights' wing-warping system,
and the brothers were merely seeking financial gain from the ideas
of others, as well as impeding the progress of aviation. There was no
doubt that ailerons were an advancement. The Wrights' system was
well suited for slow speeds, but the brothers could not build wings
that were both flexible enough to permit warping and strong enough
to endure the stress of great speeds. Ailerons allowed the use of
more rigid wings.

Public opinion generally favored the Wrights. The courts invariably did. The primacy of the brothers' control system was upheld
both in the United States—most notably in a suit against the Herring-Curtiss Company, a principal figure of which was 1902 Outer
Banks camper Augustus Herring—and in Europe. The Wrights' op-

ponents generally managed to circumvent injunctions and continue
flying while their suits were pending, but all the same, the Wrights
were publicly vindicated. They were ultimately compensated for the
use of their patents through fees and royalties.

Having instigated numerous patent suits, the Wrights found them
to be an extraordinary drain on their time. While other men were
busy advancing the science of aviation, they found themselves preparing legal actions.

The formation of companies to produce Wright airplanes placed
additional demands on their time. The Wright Company, organized
in 1909 and backed by such powerful men as Cornelius Vanderbilt
and August Belmont, was easily the best of the lot, producing new
designs and quality-built planes at a plant in Dayton. But the various
Wright companies in Europe were a constant source of concern.
Workmanship was sometimes shoddy. Unauthorized modifications
were made to the Wrights' designs. And business practices were even
worse. It was an important point for the Wrights that their participation in the companies allow them ample time for pursuing new
design ideas, but as matters developed, overseeing business operations became a full-time source of worry.

After introducing a major new industry to the world, the Wrights
found they exercised little control over its direction. There was as
yet no practical use for airplanes, which severely limited sales of the
craft manufactured in their plants. The short-term market lay in exhibition flying, a pastime the Wrights had always scorned. Keenly
aware of the prize money Glenn Curtiss and other aviators were
earning at staged events, the Wrights organized an exhibition team,
Orville assuming the responsibility of training new pilots.

Their worst fears proved true. Seeing an airplane perform low-
altitude laps of a field was enough of a spectacle for people witnessing

flight for the first time, but crowds soon began to develop a thirst for steep dives and the pursuit of speed and altitude records. The Wrights had always emphasized safety in their own flying, and Orville tried to impress the same attitude on the members of their exhibition team. Instead, the Wright pilots, in direct competition with Glenn Curtiss's men, grew into daredevils of the highest order. Many paid with their lives. Five of the nine original members of the Wright team perished in crashes in the first two years of exhibition flying. Wright airplanes began to get a poor reputation for safety, though that was mainly a problem with craft of European manufacture and those that had been modified.

Despite these setbacks, the Wright brothers enjoyed their share of triumphs after their French and American contract trials of 1908 and 1909. Orville flew for crowds of nearly a quarter of a million people in Germany in September 1909. That same month, on September 29, Wilbur took off from Governors Island and buzzed the Statue of Liberty. The word of his takeoff was sent by wireless to many of the ships crowding New York Harbor by Guglielmo Marconi. On October 4, Wilbur flew ten miles up the Hudson River to Grant's Tomb and back, a flight witnessed by a crowd estimated at a million people.

The members of the Wright exhibition team had their successes, too. In June 1910, for example, Walter Brookins established a world altitude record of over six thousand feet. Four months later, Ralph Johnstone climbed to over nine thousand feet.

Records were broken and rebroken quickly in those days. Aviation technology advanced with amazing speed in the years after the Wrights' first public flights. Yet the Wrights were becoming spectators. With Wilbur doing most of their legal maneuvering and Orville training pilots, their engineering days were largely past. Whether, under different circumstances, they would have made further significant contributions to flight will never be known. But it is a fact that the next important advances—ailerons, of course, but also enclosed fuselages, monoplane design, and tractor propellers—were all pioneered by other men.

The Wright brothers were receding toward the middle of the pack. By the fall of 1911, when Orville returned to the Outer Banks, he was again flying gliders. Wilbur, who was busy pursuing a couple of lawsuits, and who was all but finished with flying anyway, did not accompany him.

Soaring

Though Orville Wright was one of the most famous men in the world when he came to Kill Devil Hills in 1911, his arrival was still secondary news on the local level.

In August or early September, J. D. Hathaway of Elizabeth City, a physician and amateur archaeologist, was walking the beach a couple of miles north of Nags Head when he stumbled upon the remains of an ancient Indian village apparently destroyed by fire. It is not unusual for the Outer Banks winds to shift the sand from atop shipwrecks and other relics buried for many years, then to cover them again beyond discovery just as quickly.

Dr. Hathaway and other investigators initially found Indian pottery, arrowheads, a tomahawk, a pipestem, and what they tentatively identified as petrified sweet potatoes. As the story developed through September and October, however, a piece of flowered earthenware of English design was also discovered, along with what appeared to be an English dagger of the period of Edward IV. This anlace, or dagger, was partly consumed by rust, and a portion of its edge was broken away. According to the *Elizabeth City Weekly Advance* of September 29, it was "a very unwieldy instrument—but a very effective one, if it ever landed on the cranium of an enemy." Their memory jogged, other local residents recalled finding old brass buttons in the vicinity in years past.

It was only a small leap from the discovery of English artifacts to the claim that Nags Head was the ultimate destination of the Lost Colony of 1587. If so, Dr. Hathaway's archaeological find was highly significant. According to his theory, Virginia Dare and her elders had traveled across the sound from Roanoke Island to live among

Orville and his 1911 guests, invited and otherwise. Seated are Buster Wright, Orville, and Alec Ogilvie. Lorin Wright is at left in back. The others are the newsmen who came to the Outer Banks that fall. The reporter standing next to Lorin is Van Ness Harwood.

LIBRARY OF CONGRESS

friendly Indians while awaiting relief ships from Great Britain. The Lost Colonists and their Indian friends later perished in a fire set by a rival tribe.

While the discovery at Nags Head was interesting, it ultimately didn't lay to rest North America's oldest mystery. After leading the local news in late summer and early fall, it took its spot among the numerous theories that place the Lost Colonists at points north, south, east, and west of Fort Raleigh and Roanoke Island—wherever blue-eyed Indians, unexplained accents, and cryptic words carved into trees have dared rear their heads.

Orville left Dayton for North Carolina on Saturday, October 7. Accompanying him this year were his older brother Lorin, on his second trip to the Outer Banks; Horace "Buster" Wright, Lorin's ten-year-old son; and Englishman Alec Ogilvie, invited to make the trip as Wilbur's replacement. They reached Kill Devil Hills on October 10, Orville's glider parts arriving three days after that.

Travel to the Outer Banks was improving by this late date, the Eastern Carolina Transportation Company providing year-round, daily boat service between Elizabeth City and Manteo, with a stop in Nags Head both ways.

Organizing camp also proved easier than in years past. The buildings were a shambles, as always, but matters were apparently set straight within a few days, and the glider was fully assembled and ready to fly three days after its arrival.

The most interesting addition to camp in 1911 was Alec Ogilvie. If a brief biographical account in the July 1910 issue of *The Motor*, a British journal, is to be believed, Ogilvie began flying not long after the Wrights, gliding from the hills of Sussex, a county in southeastern England. In the winter of 1901, he supposedly moved his operation to a spot near the ruins of Camber Castle, a fortress in

Sussex on the Strait of Dover, built by Henry VIII around 1514. There, Ogilvie constructed a large shed, apparently with a view to setting up camp and doing some gliding over the square mile of beach available at low water.

He met Wilbur Wright in France in 1908. The following year, the Wrights contracted with British balloon manufacturers Oswald and Eustace Short to build a total of six Wright airplanes for British customers. One of the purchasers was Charles Rolls, of Rolls-Royce fame. Another may well have been Alec Ogilvie, as the account in *The Motor* has him flying a British-built Wright plane on the beach and out over the water near Camber Castle in the summer of 1910.

Ogilvie's career is more certain after that. In September 1910, he traveled to Dayton, where he took flying lessons from Orville and arranged to purchase a Wright Roadster, a one-seater version of their standard airplane. The following month, he traveled with Orville and Katharine Wright to Belmont Park on Long Island, New York, to participate in the International Aviation Tournament, the first international flying competition to be held in America. The major award at stake was the Gordon Bennett Trophy, a speed prize awarded by James Gordon Bennett, the publisher of the *New York Herald*. The Wrights were intent on winning the trophy, building a special racer called the *Baby Grand*, which had a scant 140 square feet of wing area but a motor delivering between fifty and sixty horsepower. In testing, Orville flew it at seventy miles per hour. Unfortunately, the *Baby Grand* crashed in practice with ace pilot Walter Brookins aboard. In its absence, Alec Ogilvie, though not a member of the Wright exhibition team, carried the torch for the brothers, finishing third in the trophy race. This was a respectable achievement given that his new Roadster's engine had barely a third the horsepower of the winning French plane.

In June 1911, Wilbur stayed with Ogilvie during a trip to England. Ogilvie was preparing for a flying meet to be held in Eastchurch. Wilbur's main purpose was an inspection of the Wrights' British operation.

With regard to his trip to the Outer Banks, Alec Ogilvie was simply someone Orville trusted enough—even in the highly competitive atmosphere of aeronautics in 1911—to help test a development he hoped would put the Wrights back in the industry lead.

In their early experiments, the brothers had avoided systems that promoted automatic stability, feeling it was paramount to establish three-dimensional control over an airplane. But once they perfected three-dimensional control, they began to see an advantage in relinquishing some of the moment-by-moment operations of an airplane, freeing the pilot from making manual adjustments for every gust of wind.

They began tinkering with an automatic-stability system about 1906 and applied for a patent in 1908. Their system had two components: a pendulum that sensed changes in the roll and yaw axes and a vane that sensed changes in pitch. When the airplane veered from straight and level, the pendulum and vane activated the wing-warping and elevator systems by means of compressed-air cylinders, which restored the craft on course.

The purpose of Orville's 1911 trip was to test this system. Returning to the Outer Banks and using a glider, rather than a powered craft, would allow him to experiment over a forgiving surface and at slow speeds.

These plans quickly came to nothing. When Orville went to Kitty Hawk to pick up his glider parts on October 13, sailing up the sound from Kill Devil Hills in a rented motorboat, he found four newsmen waiting at the dock: John Mitchell of the Associated Press;

Van Ness Harwood and another reporter named Mitchell, both representing New York papers; and Bruce Salley, on his second trip covering the Wrights. Seeing such a crowd gathered in his honor, Orville apparently decided on the spot that there would be no testing of the automatic-stability system.

Unlike the 1908 trip, Orville was not faced with deadlines that compelled him to proceed with testing regardless of whether reporters were present. Revealing the secrets of his new system without patent protection in place would have jeopardized years of work.

On the other hand, after his 1908 experience with reporters on the Outer Banks, and after apparently having sent his brother Lorin on an advance trip to North Carolina in September 1911, it is a mystery why Orville did not expect to be bothered by newsmen.

Their primary plans canceled, Orville and Alec Ogilvie resolved to have some fun and go gliding. The 1911 craft, once it was modified with parts cannibalized from the ruined machines lying around camp, had a different configuration from other Wright gliders. For the first time, the elevator was at the rear of the craft, with the tail having both horizontal and vertical surfaces. This gave the machine a more modern look than their old gliders. A vertical stabilizer replaced the elevator at the front of the craft.

The first day of trials was Monday, October 16, when Orville made three glides. He immediately noticed that the tail surfaces were too small. He made modifications between the first and second and second and third flights, adding the vertical vane in front and then replacing the original elevator with a larger surface in back. The reward was a third glide lasting twenty-three seconds and covering over twelve hundred feet.

Alec Ogilvie got his turn the following day, making three glides to Orville's two.

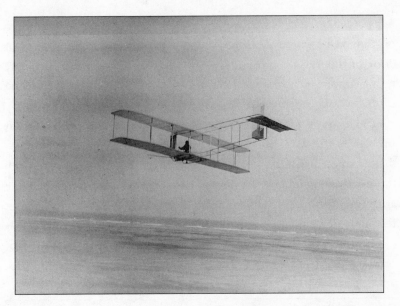

This view shows the 1911 craft's new tail assembly
LIBRARY OF CONGRESS

Orville was aboard on October 18 when the craft flipped over in midair and careened straight into a dune, breaking the elevator and both of the left-hand wings. Repairs and modifications—the tail frame was lengthened and both tail surfaces were further altered—consumed the next three days. Two more newsmen arrived during this period: Arnold Kruckman and a man named Berges, both representing the *New York American*.

If Lewis Tate's flying adventure took place in 1911, rather than 1908, then Sunday, October 22, was the magic day, Orville noting simply in his diary, "Tate & family called in morn." Ten-year-old Buster Wright would have been a year older than Elijah Tate, Lewis's brother. Whether Buster was ever given a chance at mounting a wing was not recorded. However, his stay in camp was memorialized on film, as he posed wearing a floppy hat and standing in the open door of the 1903 camp building, looking very much like Tom Tate in his famous picture from 1900, in which he was captured showing off his whopper fish.

Orville was back in the air on October 23. There was a further mishap on the second flight that day, as the craft flipped over immediately upon being let go by Lorin Wright and Alec Ogilvie. Both the horizontal and vertical portions of the tail were broken. Orville attributed the crash to different wind velocities at the surface and six feet above ground.

The following day saw the best gliding ever done by a Wright brothers craft, and some feats not surpassed for ten years. The suc-

Buster Wright

LIBRARY OF CONGRESS

cess emphasized just how far the technology had come since 1900.

Orville took a variety of anemometer readings that Tuesday, find-ing the wind to range from twenty-five miles per hour at ground level, to forty miles per hour six feet above the top of the dune, to fifty miles per hour six feet above that. While hardly suitable for man or beast, those conditions were ideal for soaring craft. The briefest glide that day lasted a minute. One flight lasted five and a half minutes, the craft rising fifty feet above the top of the dune. Two others lasted seven and a half minutes. And topping all of these was a glide by Orville that lasted a full nine minutes and forty-five seconds, the craft remaining virtually stationary relative to the ground.

When the flight was over, it was determined that the glider had traveled forward only 120 feet. That was exactly the same distance as the first powered flight of December 17, 1903, but of a duration almost fifty times greater. It was the Wrights' longest-standing record, not broken until 1921 in Germany.

Aside from the greatest of these glides, which is universally cred-ited to Orville, it is not entirely clear who made each of the approximately twenty flights that day. Some accounts suggest that all of them were Orville's, while others split them indiscriminately be-tween Orville and Alec Ogilvie.

The good times continued with fifty-five glides over the follow-ing two days, though lower winds did not permit the kind of feats performed October 24. Nine of the flights on October 26 lasted over a minute.

One of the strangest visits during all the Wrights' experiments on the Outer Banks occurred around this time, as reported by Orville in a letter on November 18. The interloper this time was Victor Lougheed, the older half-brother of Malcolm and Allan Lougheed, who later founded what eventually became the Lockheed Corporation—a

The 1911 glider at work

worldwide leader in aviation and aerospace technology. Victor Lougheed was a minor force in aeronautics himself, having published two books on the subject in 1909 and 1910.

He was, however, an ardent supporter of California aeronaut John Montgomery and just as strong a detractor of the Wright brothers. Thanks to a brief glide way back in 1885, Montgomery held the distinction of having made the first heavier-than-air flight of any kind in the United States. In the fall of 1911, while Orville was setting up operations at Kill Devil Hills, Montgomery was undertaking some glider experiments on the West Coast.

When Victor Lougheed learned that Orville Wright had made a glide of nearly ten minutes, he announced his opinion that the reports coming out of Kill Devil Hills were false and promptly headed to the Outer Banks to prove them so. The exact date when he reached North Carolina was not recorded, but since he could not have read of Orville's great flight until October 25 at the earliest, he certainly did not arrive before testing wrapped up on October 26.

Upon making his way to camp, Lougheed "learned at first-hand from a half dozen different persons who had been eyewitnesses of the flights that the reports were really true," according to Orville. Lougheed immediately turned around and headed back home without even bothering to have a look at the record-setting craft—and presumably without congratulating Orville.

Had records been kept for the shortest stay at the Wrights' camp, Victor Lougheed would have easily set the standard. He must also go down as their most frustrated visitor.

Orville and his more agreeable guests broke camp sometime around the end of the month.

John Montgomery, the man championed by Victor Lougheed, died in a glider crash in California on October 31.

Orville eventually did put his automatic stabilizer to a public test, after his patent came through in the fall of 1913. The device worked just as advertised. On the last day of the year, before a crowd at Huffman Prairie, he made numerous laps of the field with his hands held high, completely off the controls.

However, he was upstaged six months later by a twenty-one-year-old: Lawrence "Gyro" Sperry.

Lawrence Sperry's family was living in Cleveland, Ohio, in December 1903 when the *Cleveland Press* was one of the few papers to carry the news of a couple of bicycle mechanics and their flights in a powered airplane. Ten-year-old Lawrence, the story goes, was so moved that he gave up his newspaper route and began making plans to open a bicycle repair shop in the family basement.

Aside from his early interest in aeronautics, Sperry could hardly have been more different from Orville Wright. He was the son of famous inventor Elmer Sperry, a pioneer in electric automobiles, streetcars, mining machines, and railroad equipment, and most notably in gyroscopic navigation systems for ships. A daredevil and innovator from a young age, Lawrence Sperry was recruited by Glenn Curtiss to develop a gyroscopic stabilizer in 1912. He came up with a brilliant system of two gyroscopes, one sensing movement from side to side and operating the rudder, the other sensing movement in the roll and pitch axes and operating the ailerons and elevator.

Like Orville Wright, Sperry publicly demonstrated his stabilizing system with his hands off the controls, but he went Orville one better by standing in the cockpit and having an assistant crawl several feet out onto one wing. It was Sperry's system that became the basis for subsequent developments in the field.

His star was still rising in America and Europe through the early 1920s, with his marriage to a well-known actress, his landings and takeoffs in streets and public parks, and his advances in seat-pack parachutes, detachable landing gear, and aerial torpedoes.

Sperry was crossing the Strait of Dover in December 1923 when his engine failed. He washed up dead on the Sussex shore not far from where Alec Ogilvie learned to fly in the shadow of a ruined castle.

Orville Wright's automatic-stability system was his last big idea for advancing the technology.

CHAPTER 7

1932

Reports reach this newspaper that some vandal called a souvenir hunter has already chipped a piece of granite from the base of the beautiful Wright Memorial on Kill Devil Hill.

. . . Every one connected with this undertaking has taken something akin to a religious pride in making this monument one of the outstanding things in America. Every piece of the beautiful Mt. Airy granite used in the construction was especially selected and especially quarried.

And now, unless carefully guarded it is to be ruthlessly despoiled by these loathsome creatures who must have a souvenir to tote around with them as evidence that they have visited the very birthplace of aviation. Their word for it would not suffice; people of such low mentality are such infernal liars that no one would believe them.

Elizabeth City Independent,
August 19, 1932

Wilbur Wright, 1867–1912

Contrary to warnings like that in the *Elizabeth City Independent*—or perhaps in part because of them—Wright Brothers National Memorial has weathered the attention of millions of visitors in fine shape for more than six decades.

Only one of the men it was built to honor lived to see its dedication. In August and September 1896, Wilbur Wright watched his brother Orville nearly die from typhoid. Orville's fever reached 105 degrees and then held for an extended period at 103. He was delirious for about a month. The infection was ascribed to bad well water at the family home in Dayton.

After that experience, Wilbur took great care about what he ate and drank while traveling. In 1900, during his first trip to the Outer Banks, he wouldn't eat food prepared in Israel Perry's galley, and he

Wilbur Wright

NATIONAL AIR AND SPACE MUSEUM

wouldn't drink the water at Bill Tate's home without having it boiled. Beginning in 1907, when he made his first visit to Europe, he was equally meticulous about his diet abroad.

In April 1912, Wilbur became ill while on a trip to Boston, perhaps the result of eating contaminated shellfish.

His father, Milton Wright, documented the uneven course of the illness in his diary beginning on May 2: "Wilbur began to have typhoid fever."

Six days later, he noted, "Wilbur is some better. . . . There seems to be a sort of typhoidal fever prevailing. It usually lasts about a week."

Two days after that, Wilbur dictated his will.

On May 18, the news was grim: "Wilbur is no better. He has an attack mentally, for the worse. It was a bad spell.

"He is put under opiates. He is unconscious mostly."

On May 24: "Wilbur seems, in nearly every respect, better."

On May 27: "His fever was higher and he has difficulty with the bladder, and his digestion is inadequate. . . . We thought him near death. He lived through till morning."

On May 28: "Wilbur is sinking. The doctors have no hope of his recovery."

On May 29: "Wilbur seemed no worse, though he had a chill. The fever was down, but rose high. He remained the same till 3:15 in the morning [on Thursday, May 30], when, eating his allowance 15 minutes before his death, he expired, without a struggle.

"His life was one of toil.

"His brain ceased not its activity till two weeks of his last sickness had expired. Then it ceased."

Orville was there, as was the rest of the family.

Condolences came from the president of the United States and the kings of Europe. Wilbur was eulogized on front pages around the world. But for succinctness and eloquence, no one summed up the life of the real visionary behind the airplane better than did Milton Wright in his diary on the day of his son's death: "This morning at 3:15, Wilbur passed away, aged 45 years, 1 month and 14 days. A short life, full of consequences. An unfailing intellect, imperturbable temper, great self-reliance and as great modesty, seeing the right clearly, pursuing it steadily, he lived and died."

Ceremony

After Wilbur's death, Orville took over the presidency of the Wright Company. He was so reluctant a businessman that he maintained an office above the old bicycle shop, rather than in the company headquarters. It was during his tenure that the long-running patent suit against Glenn Curtiss was finally adjudicated in the Wright Company's favor. There was a brief opportunity when some experts believe Orville might have established an industry-wide monopoly and charted the course of aeronautics for many years to come, but he instead opted for the short term, collecting a royalty from all competitors who wanted to continue in the airplane business.

The Wright Company began a downward spiral characterized by a loyalty to old designs that had fallen behind the leaders in the industry. Orville finally borrowed a large sum of money to purchase a controlling interest, then turned around and sold the company. In the rapidly growing aviation industry, all this transpired rather quickly. Orville was essentially out of the company by October 1915.

The following year, the Wright Company merged with the Glenn L. Martin Company to become the Wright-Martin Company. In 1917, the company headquarters was moved from Dayton to New Jersey.

Ultimately, in the late 1920s, the company started by the Wright brothers merged with that of their longtime rival, Glenn Curtiss, to become the Curtiss-Wright Company, a major force in aeronautics for years. But Wilbur was dead and Orville was out of the picture by then.

Meanwhile, Orville spent the World War I years helping organize the Dayton-Wright Company. As it developed, this company's main purpose was not pioneering new technology but manufacturing craft of foreign design for the war effort. It had limited success even at that, the number and quality of its airplanes coming into question. Orville remained a peripheral figure in the company into the early 1920s.

During World War I, he worked toward developing an unmanned, self-propelled bomb, an effort that was discontinued when the war ended. His most successful invention after Wilbur's death was the split flap, designed to slow the speed of an airplane during a steep dive. The device was widely and successfully used on dive bombers during World War II.

Orville spent most of his later years at Hawthorn Hill, a large home in a Dayton suburb, begun around the time of Wilbur's illness. An engineering genius when it came to airplanes, Orville was in matters of home improvement the kind of tinkerer the Wrights' detractors had always accused them of being. The heating, plumbing, and electrical systems he designed for the estate were the picture of complexity. Upon his death, most of his work was replaced by more sensible substitutes.

As his days of active experimentation wound down, Orville served on a variety of aeronautical boards, his travels taking him frequently to Washington. But it is rather difficult to track his visits back to the Outer Banks. He made at least three trips after his glider experiments in 1911, and perhaps more.

In his 1990 interview with the National Park Service, Elmer Woodard, Jr.—grandson of Bill Tate—recalled that Orville made four or five trips to Kill Devil Hills in connection with the national memorial honoring the Wright brothers, as well as one trip strictly for nostalgia. Those are more than are usually reckoned.

According to Woodard, at least a couple of visits were intended mostly as a private matter between Orville and Bill Tate, who worked from 1915 onward as keeper of the Long Point Lighthouse at Coinjock, North Carolina, located on the mainland in Currituck County. Orville would supposedly telephone Tate at the lighthouse to arrange a meeting time, always referring to himself cryptically as "the main party" or some other such name, so his identity would not be picked up by people listening in on the party line. At the appointed hour, Orville would whisk Tate off toward Kill Devil Hills in his custom automobile. The exact nature and dates of any such private visits will probably never be known.

On the other hand, Orville's visit in December 1928 for the celebration of the twenty-fifth anniversary of powered flight is fully documented. The occasion was the laying of the cornerstone of the national memorial at Kill Devil Hills and the unveiling of the granite boulder marking the 1903 takeoff point.

The national memorial is without a doubt the best-known tribute to the Wrights. Conceived in 1926 by Congressman Lindsay Warren of North Carolina, the project was intended to serve the dual purpose of honoring the Wrights and opening the Outer Banks to development. In 1927, a bill sponsored by Warren and Senator Hiram Bingham of Connecticut, the president of the National Aeronautic Association, received an initial appropriation of fifty thousand dollars toward the establishment of a national memorial.

On the home front, Elizabeth City newsman W. O. Saunders and a group of local citizens formed the Kill Devil Hills Memorial Association and set about raising funds for what eventually became the Wright Memorial Bridge, which stretches three miles across Currituck Sound from Point Harbor to the Outer Banks north of Kitty Hawk. The bridge was conceived mainly to provide access to the site of the first powered flights. Artist Frank Stick of Dare County, the Carolina Development Company, and a pair of New Jersey sportsmen—Charles M. Baker and Allen R. Heuth—donated the land for the national memorial at Kill Devil Hills.

The trip for the laying of the cornerstone was as fraught with complications as any Wilbur and Orville had ever taken. It showed just how little the Outer Banks had changed in a quarter-century.

Orville left Dayton by train in mid-December 1928 to attend the International Civil Aeronautics Conference in Washington. At the conclusion of the conference, he and two hundred of the delegates, representing forty nations, set out for the North Carolina coast. It was a carefully orchestrated affair. Just after midnight on Sunday, December 16, the party departed the nation's capital aboard the steamship *District of Columbia*. Assistant Secretary of Commerce William P. MacCracken, Jr., led church services on board the ship that morning, Senator Hiram Bingham banging out hymns on the piano.

Early that afternoon, they disembarked at Old Point Comfort, Virginia, and traveled by car to Langley Field, where they were given a tour of the world's foremost wind-tunnel facility. They then returned to the *District of Columbia* and steamed the rest of the way to Norfolk, where they spent the night.

The following morning, they continued south, apparently by bus. At the border, they were met by Governor Angus McLean of North Carolina and escorted to the village of Currituck, where they transferred to sixty-five private automobiles for the rough drive to Point Harbor on Currituck Sound.

The boat trip to the Outer Banks was as difficult as always. At one point, Woody Hockaday of Wichita, Kansas, fell overboard and was dragged under the frigid water by his heavy coat, only to be saved by a quick-thinking sailor wielding a boat hook. The ferry also grounded in the shallow sound. It was during this grounding that Governor McLean and Congressman Warren supposedly conceived the idea of establishing America's first national seashore park, a dream later realized in Cape Hatteras National Seashore.

Finally landing on the Outer Banks, the members of the party made their sixth transfer since leaving Washington, boarding a hundred cars donated for the occasion by local citizens. They then proceeded through woods and swamps and down the sand to Kill Devil Hills. En route, they were joined in their pilgrimage by a crowd estimated by the *New York Times* at three to four thousand people, traveling mostly on foot. It was a spectacle unlike any ever seen in the area. As the *Times* put it, "There were hundreds of boys and girls who some day will learn to fly, mothers trudging through the blowing, stinging sand with babies in their arms, and old men who have never yet seen an airplane fly."

Amelia Earhart was at the ceremony. So was faithful friend Bill Tate. So were first-flight witnesses John Daniels, Adam Etheridge, and Willie Dough. Johnny Moore was supposedly on the premises but "got away before he could be introduced," according to the *Times*. As for the ceremony itself, neither Orville Wright nor anyone else present had much of an idea what they were laying the cornerstone to, as the design of the national memorial had not been decided upon yet.

Across the ocean, the Paris chapter of the United States National Aeronautic Association gathered to observe a moment of silence and drink a toast to the Wrights.

In England, where the 1903 Flyer was being stored in exile, a hundred prominent men of aviation gathered at tables set up under the wings of the old airplane to eat a celebratory dinner.

Orville was unmoved by such a show of devotion. As was always his custom at official functions, he gave no speech or public thanks, his only surviving comment caught in a private conversation: "I wonder if this whole thing isn't a mistake. Fifty years from now might be soon enough to determine if this memorial should be built. To do it now seems like an imposition on the taxpayers."

Matters took a somber turn on the ferry ride back across Currituck Sound after the celebration. Allen R. Heuth, one of the donors of the land for the national memorial, dropped dead on the deck while talking with Secretary of War Dwight F. Davis.

As for the proposed monument, the most perplexing problem centered around what to do with Kill Devil Hills—or, more precisely, Kill Devil Hill. Of the four dunes present at the turn of the century, only the largest remained, and it had migrated an estimated four hundred to six hundred feet southwest since 1903. Left to its own devices, the hill could be expected to walk away from the site of the famous flights and eventually go swimming in Roanoke Sound, burying the new cornerstone lying atop it somewhere along the way.

Assigned the task of halting a ninety-foot-tall, twenty-six-acre pile of sand, the United States Army Quartermaster Corps dispatched Captain John A. Gilman, whose previous credits included the Tomb of the Unknown Soldier at Arlington National Cemetery, and Captain William H. Kindervater, his assistant, to Kill Devil Hills. They began work in early 1929. Kindervater moved his family to Kitty Hawk during the project.

Their first move involved building a fence around the base of the dune to keep feral cattle, horses, and hogs from wandering in and eating the vegetation they proposed to plant. Next, they laid a two-inch-deep, 250-foot-wide strip of pine straw, rotted leaves, and rotted wood around the base. They sowed it with rye and tough imported grasses from Puerto Rico and Australia, gradually working the vegetation up the northeastern slope, then around the entire dune.

Anchoring the hill cost $27,500, or nearly thirty times what the Wrights had spent on all their aeronautical experiments up to and including the 1903 Flyer. And that didn't begin to include the cost of the monument itself.

Meanwhile, a jury provided by the American Institute of Architects selected the design of New York architects Robert P. Rogers and Alfred E. Poor from the thirty-five entries submitted to Quartermaster General Frank B. Cheatham. Rogers and Poor's design was said by the jury to be "not only the most original and impressive as seen from land, but would also be extremely effective as seen from the air." Indeed, it was no mean feat to conceive a five-thousand-ton monument suggestive of lightness and flight.

The construction contract went to the firm of Willis, Taylor, and Mafera of New York. Beginning in February 1931, workers sunk a concrete foundation thirty-five feet into the top of the dune, then laid a star-shaped base that extends twelve feet into the sand. The base is similar to the one supporting the Statue of Liberty.

The curving slope of the monument's walls and the wings carved in bas-relief on two sides presented special problems for the stone cutters in Mount Airy, North Carolina, where the great granite blocks were quarried. To guarantee a proper fit, technicians had to make individual drawings of each block in the monument, then make zinc patterns for four or five faces of nearly every block—the two ends, the top and bottom, and the outer face, if it contained a portion of the bas-relief—before the stone was ever lifted out of the mountain and moved by aerial cable and railroad car to the cutting sheds. The

*Two views of the monument
at Kill Devil Hills*

OUTER BANKS HISTORY CENTER

finished blocks were then crated, shipped by rail to Norfolk, and loaded on barges for delivery near the monument site. Then came the difficult task of transporting the blocks—the greatest of which weighed ten tons—up a steep, soft pile of sand for assembly.

The inscription on the monument's exterior reads, "In commemoration of the conquest of the air by the brothers Wilbur and Orville Wright, conceived by genius, achieved by dauntless resolution and unconquerable faith." Life-size bronze busts of the Wrights rest on pedestals outside the monument. The original busts, installed in 1960, were damaged by vandals in 1985 and stolen three years later. The First Flight Society, a commemorative organization based in Kitty Hawk, subsequently raised twenty-five thousand dollars for four new busts, two of which are kept under lock inside the monument.

Aerial view of the monument

The interior saw such heavy use during the days when it served as the park's visitor center that it had to be closed permanently to the public. The bronze doors leading inside feature eight engravings, among them a depiction of Icarus falling from the sky and one of the French locksmith and fledgling aeronaut Besnier paddling his way through the air.

The chief attraction in the interior was the second-floor map room, reached by a pair of curving stairways. There, a stainless-steel map designed by Rand and McNally showed the location and path of the world's historic flights between 1903 and 1928, beginning with the Wrights and including such figures as Louis Blériot, the first man to fly across the English Channel; Glenn Curtiss; Calbraith Perry Rodgers, the first man to fly across the United States; French aviator Roland Garros; and Charles Lindbergh.

From the map room, an iron stairway leads to another landing, from which a spiral lighthouse stairway extends to the top. The small platform outside once allowed visitors a spectacular view of the area.

One of the most noteworthy features of the monument's design was the thousand-watt beacon that shone from the roof, visible for up to thirty miles. However, once put into use, the light only served to confuse boat captains sailing the shipping lanes, who were accustomed to a dark coast between the Currituck Beach Lighthouse to the north and the Bodie Island Lighthouse to the south. The beacon at Kill Devil Hills was soon shut down for good.

The sixty-foot monument carried a final price tag of $225,000, the cost of the entire park coming in at $285,000.

Orville Wright returned to North Carolina to listen to more speechifying in November 1932, when the national memorial was dedicated. The last leg of the trip was easier this time, thanks to the Wright Memorial Bridge. Opened in 1930, the bridge was initially a toll span. There was also a new asphalt road running from Kitty Hawk to Kill Devil Hills.

The heavy rains that fell that November 19 did not cast the new memorial in its best light. At one point, the wind tore the covering off the platform where the ceremony was being held, much of the crowd getting soaked as a result.

Again, Orville had little to say, other than a simple "Thank you" upon being handed a letter from President Herbert Hoover.

Over the years, a 431-acre park has grown around the monument and the First Flight Area, with its five boulders marking the takeoff point and the four landing points of the flights of December 17, 1903.

Before 1953, the park was known as Kill Devil Hills Monument National Memorial. That year, the name was changed to Wright Brothers National Memorial. The two replica camp buildings, lying between the current visitor center and the First Flight Area, also date from the fiftieth anniversary. Their authenticity—down to the bunks in the rafters and the canned goods on the shelves—can be vouched for by anyone who has ever seen photographs of the Wrights' 1903 camp.

Ground was broken for the current visitor center in 1957.

The year 1963 saw the opening of a three-thousand-foot airstrip running parallel to the path of the 1903 flights. Among the noteworthy events at the anniversary celebration that December were a visit from John Glenn and the installation of a replica of the Flyer in the visitor center. It is noteworthy that, while the original Flyer was built by two self-taught brothers and a hired mechanic prone to foul language, some thirty manufacturers were enlisted to help in constructing the replica. It and a replica of the 1902 glider are the feature attractions in the visitor center today.

According to National Park Service figures, approximately half a million people visit the park annually, with double that number anticipated at the approach of the centennial anniversary of the first powered flights.

The Competition

The countless tributes to the Wrights notwithstanding, their claim of being first in flight is not universally accepted.

In his native Brazil, Alberto Santos-Dumont is still held to be the father of flight. A museum there is dedicated to him, and a city is named in his honor. In putting forth Santos-Dumont as the true pioneer of heavier-than-air flight, Brazil is effectively denying that the Wright brothers ever left the ground before 1908, either at Kill Devil Hills or Huffman Prairie.

At the height of Santos-Dumont's popularity in Europe, his influence was such that his drooping-brimmed hats and high double collars were widely imitated by fashionable men, who also took to parting their hair in the middle like the famous aeronaut. A monument erected at the Bagatelle field in France where he flew in November 1906 bears an inscription that translates, "Here, the first Aviation world records were established under control of the Aero Club of France by Santos-Dumont."

Around the time of Wilbur Wright's inaugural public flights, some of the more patriotic members of the French aeronautical establishment also put forward countryman Clément Ader as the first to fly. Ader's claim of having flown approximately a thousand feet back in 1897 was laid to rest by 1912.

The Russians were not to be left out either. In 1953, at the approach of the golden anniversary of the first powered flights, the following statement was issued by *Red Star*, the newspaper of the Soviet army: "Careful study of our archive documents show that more than 20 years before the Wrights the Russian inventor A. F. Mozhaisky built an airplane in Russia." The upcoming ceremonies, at Kill Devil Hills and elsewhere were thus no more than "American propaganda to prove the priority of the Wright brothers."

On July 20, 1882, at an army field near St. Petersburg, a craft designed by Alexander Mozhaisky, a captain in the Russian Imperial Navy, supposedly made a powered flight of indeterminate length. Though Mozhaisky's airplane apparently took off down an inclined ramp, the Russians considered the trial of sufficient length to qualify as sustained flight.

Of course, the Cold War was just heating up when Mozhaisky's story came to light around 1950. The Soviets were also claiming the first balloon, the first dirigible, the first parachute, the first aviation magazine, the first automatic pilot, the first helicopter, the first seaplane, and the first jet.

Ominously for Mozhaisky's case, his craft had checked in at over two thousand pounds—nearly three times the weight of the 1903 Flyer and Samuel Langley's Great Aerodrome—and was driven by only thirty horsepower, split between a twenty-horse motor for a large tractor propeller and a ten-horse motor for two smaller pusher propellers.

In the mid-1950s, Soviet investigators conducted interviews at the site of Mozhaisky's flight and discovered, to their embarrassment, that some of the people listed as eyewitnesses had not even been born in 1882. The oldest among them was only three at the time of the flight.

Whatever Alexander Mozhaisky accomplished in 1882, it would very likely not meet any reasonable definition of powered, sustained heavier-than-air flight.

Even New Zealand has a claimant. Richard Pearse was a farm boy who was obsessed with flight from the time of his youth. He had no formal training, his only link to the larger world being *Scientific American* magazine, which he read while plowing behind his family's horses. In the early years of the century, Pearse is said to have made a powered flight estimated at anywhere from 100 to 440 yards. On another occasion, he supposedly took off from a 50-foot bank and flew half a mile on a gradually descending course before landing in a dry riverbed. Most notably, witnesses also said he made two and a half circuits of a field sometime in 1903, a feat that would rank him among the engineering geniuses of all time.

Parts of two of Pearse's airplanes were displayed in the Museum of Transport and Technology in Auckland, New Zealand.

The claims made for Pearse are impossible to verify. No camera ever photographed him in the air. A reclusive man, he kept no diary or logbook and wrote few letters. Though the date most often put forward for his first flight is March 31, 1903, witnesses' recollections made it anywhere from 1902 to 1904. In letters to two newspapers, Pearse himself recalled it was 1904.

There is no proof he ever flew at all.

At the approach of the centennial anniversary of the first powered flights, the most strident counterclaims are sure to be heard from the supporters of Gustave Whitehead, a German-American most closely associated with the town of Bridgeport, Connecticut.

Around 1895, having claimed he made some glider flights during his days as a seaman in Brazil, Whitehead was hired as a mechanic by the Boston Aeronautical Society, an organization that stood near the forefront of the field. His chief project there was an 1897 bamboo glider that apparently had either flapping wings or paddles designed to beat the air.

The most persistent claims for Whitehead date from 1901 and 1902, when he was living in Connecticut. His 1901 machine had two motors, one to supply power to its four wheels on the ground and the other to drive its twin propellers. Sometime before mid-June 1901, he supposedly made a flight of half a mile. Shortly after midnight on August 14 of that year, at a site near Fairfield, Connecticut, he is said to have made another flight of half a mile—later amended to a mile and a half. Then, on January 17, 1902, with a new machine featuring a forty-horsepower motor, he supposedly made separate flights of two and seven miles over Long Island Sound, the longer flight following a circular course and reaching an altitude of two hundred feet.

The Wright brothers knew of Gustave Whitehead at least as early as July 1901, when Octave Chanute mentioned one of Whitehead's engine-building projects in a letter to Wilbur. However, the alleged flights of 1901 and 1902 received little play. Whitehead was an obscure figure at the time of his death in 1927, and his legacy troubled Orville Wright not in the slightest.

Until 1935, that is. That was the year a story on Whitehead was published in *Popular Aviation* magazine. In 1937 came a book-length treatment, *The Lost Flights of Gustave Whitehead*, which received attention in such newspapers as the *Washington Herald* and the *Los Angeles Times*. If Whitehead wasn't national news by then, he certainly was in 1945, when he was the subject of a *Reader's Digest* story and when his son was interviewed on network radio about his father's work.

Meanwhile, the Whitehead story began to irritate Orville. In 1937, he criticized Stella Randolph, the author of the initial article and book on Whitehead, partly on the grounds that she "work[ed] in a doctor's office in Washington" and "ha[d] no particular interest in aviation." These were strange objections from a former bicycle mechanic who had no particular reason to be interested in aviation himself.

The strongest evidence in favor of Whitehead's claim is a fuzzy photograph purportedly showing one of his craft in flight.

The debit side of the ledger is much more heavily weighted. The affidavits Stella Randolph collected for her book were easily picked apart. One "eyewitness" denied he had ever seen Whitehead fly and explained that the stories of the August 17, 1901, flight merely reflected what Whitehead said he *planned* to do, not what he had actually accomplished. When members of Whitehead's family were later interviewed, none of them could recall his mentioning any powered flights at the time they were said to have taken place. But the most damning evidence against his claim is that, having supposedly built a craft that flew seven miles in a circular course, he then abandoned his airplane design for lesser ones pioneered by other men.

In recent years, a segment aired and later repeated on the television program *60 Minutes* has made Whitehead's case and kept him in the public eye.

Even in the unlikely event that Richard Pearse, Alexander Mozhaisky, or Gustave Whitehead—or all three of them, or any of the many other claimants—flew before the Wright brothers, it probably wouldn't matter. Such men, talented as they may have been, entered and departed the scene without leaving a ripple. Had all of them succeeded as claimed and the Wright brothers failed, the dream of powered flight would have been just as distant from the people of their time as if they had never existed.

Frivolous challenges were one thing, but what happened at America's national museum was more serious, and more personal.

The most painful blow struck against the Wrights started as part of a patent suit and later assumed a momentum of its own. To invalidate the brothers' patent, it was necessary that their opponents prove that other aeronauts had either flown or designed wing-warping-type systems before the Wrights. By the time the suit against Glenn Curtiss was in full swing, all the reasonable candidates for such an honor had been rejected in various courts of law.

With that avenue exhausted, Curtiss hit upon the idea of proving that, while Samuel Langley's Great Aerodrome had not actually *achieved* sustained flight, it had been *capable* of sustained flight. If the craft *might* have flown under favorable circumstances, then the Wrights' claim of primacy in aeronautical design might be given a narrow interpretation, opening the field for men like Curtiss.

Samuel Langley had his supporters and the Wrights their detractors among the staff at the Smithsonian. They granted Curtiss the opportunity to take the professor's old machine and try to make it fly.

The plan was to restore the Great Aerodrome to its original condition, but Curtiss soon began nibbling around the edges of that distinction. Ultimately, he rebuilt the wings with a different camber, retrussed and rewired them, installed a new system of cockpit controls, changed the tail, and rebuilt the engine with upgraded parts. Additionally, the Great Aerodrome, launched from a catapult atop a houseboat in 1903, was now a seaplane. Curtiss made these modifications in early 1914 at his facilities in Hammondsport, New York.

On May 28, 1914, with a crowd of reporters and photographers present, Glenn Curtiss and the Great Aerodrome lifted off nearby Keuka Lake for a flight of about 150 feet. On June 2 came two more flights, probably covering a shorter distance than the first trial. Next, the craft was fitted with a state-of-the-art, eighty-horsepower Curtiss motor. That fall, Curtiss pilot Elwood Doherty made several flights in the thousands of feet.

Early the following spring, the craft was fitted with runners to

Glenn Curtiss flying the Great Aerodrome

NATIONAL AIR AND SPACE MUSEUM

take off from the ice covering Keuka Lake. Lorin Wright, registered under a fake name in a local hotel, was present at those trials on behalf of Orville. When he attempted to take photographs of the craft, he was confronted by Curtiss's men and his film confiscated.

Three years later, in 1918, the Great Aerodrome was returned to its 1903 condition and put on display in the Smithsonian. The written material accompanying it boasted, "The first man-carrying aeroplane in the history of the world capable of sustained free flight. Invented, built, and tested over the Potomac River by Samuel Pierpont Langley in 1903. Successfully flown at Hammondsport, N.Y., June 2, 1914."

This state of affairs grated on Orville for years. Finally, in 1925, understanding that the Smithsonian was not going to budge from its position, he took the radical step of sending the Flyer to the Science Museum of London, making it clear that the plane would not be returned to America until the controversy over the Langley craft was ended.

An estimated fifteen million people saw the Flyer during its stay in Great Britain.

A man not usually given much credit for his public-relations sense, Orville created an avalanche of sentiment in his favor. The Flyer had been largely ignored in the United States for years, but once it was sent abroad, it became a national treasure of the first magnitude, and its loss was felt deeply. Considerable pressure was brought to bear on Smithsonian officials to clarify the nature of the 1914 trials of the Langley craft. During the 1930s, the museum issued a couple of resolutions that went halfway toward a public recantation, but Orville held out for full disclosure of the specifications of the 1903 Langley machine and the 1914 version, to be published side by side so people could judge the modifications for themselves.

The matter was not resolved until after Orville's final visit to the Outer Banks. The Flyer remained on foreign soil until after his death.

CHAPTER 8

BEYOND

Let us hope that the advent of a successful flying machine, now only dimly foreseen and nevertheless thought to be possible, will bring nothing but good into the world; that it shall abridge distance, make all parts of the globe accessible, bring men into closer relation with each other, advance civilization, and hasten the promised era in which there shall be nothing but peace and good-will among men.

Octave Chanute in
Progress in Flying Machines,
1894

Myth: Flight is one of the most beneficial technological advances made by man.

Baloney. The airplane is and has always been primarily a military weapon, capable of horrendous destruction. The atom bomb project would never have been started if there were no airplanes to deliver them; the British and Americans in one day and night in 1945 killed 135,000 civilians in Dresden solely by use of airplanes. . . .

Illustrious men in high offices will gather Sunday at Kitty Hawk to praise Wilbur and Orville Wright and the airplane. Those who listen might well wonder why they talk so proudly.

New Bern (N.C.) *Sun Journal*,
December 16, 1978

The Professionals and Their Fate

The course of the Wrights' relationship with Octave Chanute was a sore spot to all concerned.

Having devoted twenty full years to the flight problem, and fifteen years of part-time study before that, Chanute lived to see airplanes flying long distances, carrying passengers, and performing acrobatics. Better yet, the problem had been solved by two close friends. From the days when they first established contact with what passed for an aeronautical establishment, the Wrights had considered Chanute their primary resource. Chanute came to camp for parts of three seasons on the Outer Banks. He also visited Dayton. Wilbur stayed at Chanute's home on Dearborn Street in Chicago when he spoke before the Western Society of Engineers in 1901.

Octave Chanute
NATIONAL AIR AND SPACE MUSEUM

But pressure had been building for some time. The Wrights had long been bothered by Chanute's willingness to publicize their design ideas and his reluctance to correct the impression that they were his pupils. Chanute thought the Wrights should more freely share their advances for the good of the science; he also felt the brothers publicly undervalued his contribution to their efforts. Still, these grievances did little to harm a relationship that had prospered through hundreds of letters.

However, questioning the originality of the Wrights' ideas was another matter altogether. At issue was a French patent issued to Louis-Pierre Mouillard in 1896. The Wrights' rivals claimed that Mouillard's patent covered a control system that presented an airplane's wings at different angles to the wind, and so invalidated the brothers' claim of having been the first to develop the concept. But the Wrights had pointed out many times—and been upheld in court—

that Mouillard's system allowed only flat turns and had not taken the roll axis into account at all.

Wilbur dropped a bombshell in a letter to Chanute dated January 20, 1910:

> The *New York World* has published several articles in the past few months in which you are represented as saying that our claim to have been the first to maintain lateral balance by adjusting the wing tips to different angles of incidence cannot be maintained, as this idea was well known in the art when we began our experiments. As this opinion is quite different from that which you expressed in 1901 when you became acquainted with our methods, I do not know whether it is mere newspaper talk or whether it really represents your present views. So far as we are aware the originality of this system of control with us was universally conceded when our machine was first made known, and the questioning of it is a matter of recent growth springing from a desire to escape the legal consequences of awarding it to us.

Chanute fired back three days later: "I did tell you in 1901 that the mechanism by which your surfaces were warped was original with yourselves. This I adhere to, but it does not follow that it covers the general principle of warping or twisting wings, the proposals for doing this being ancient."

He then opened some additional wounds, new and old. As for the Wrights' practice of bringing suit against aeronauts using aileron-type control systems, his opinion was succinct: "I am afraid, my friend, that your usually sound judgment has been warped by the desire for great wealth." As for his own role in the Wrights' success, Chanute had a complaint, too:

> In your speech at the Boston dinner, January 12th, you began by saying that I "turned up" at your shop in Dayton in 1901

and that you invited me to your camp. This conveyed the impression that I thrust myself upon you at that time and it omitted to state that you were the first to write to me, in 1900, asking for information which was gladly furnished, that many letters passed between us, and that both in 1900 and 1901 you had written me to invite me to visit you, before I "turned up" in 1901. . . . I hope, that, in future, you will not give out the impression that I was the first to seek your acquaintance, or pay me left-handed compliments, such as saying that "sometimes an experienced person's advice was of great value to younger men."

Chanute having broadened the field of argument, Wilbur responded on January 29 with a letter as hard-edged as any he ever wrote. He first restated the brothers' position on the Mouillard patent, then moved quickly to other incendiary topics. "As to inordinate desire for wealth," he wrote, "you are the only person acquainted with us who has ever made such an accusation. We believed that the physical and financial risks which we took, and the value of the service to the world, justified sufficient compensation to enable us to live modestly with enough surplus income to permit the devotion of our future time to scientific experimenting instead of business."

As for Chanute's place in the Wrights' scheme of things, Wilbur wrote this:

I several times said privately that we had taken up the study of aeronautics long before we had any acquaintance with you; that our ideas of control were radically different from yours both before and throughout our acquaintance; that the systems of control which we carried to success were absolutely our own, and had been embodied in a machine and tested before you knew anything about them and before our first meeting with you; . . . that you built several machines embodying your ideas in 1901 and 1902 which were tested at our camp by Mr. Herring, but that we had never made a flight on any of your machines, nor your men on any of ours, and that in the sense in which the expression was used in France we had never been pupils of yours.

Wilbur tried closing on a hopeful note—"If anything can be done to straighten matters out to the satisfaction of both you and us, we are not only willing, but anxious to do our part"—but he had probably lost his audience long before then.

Three months passed, and Chanute did not respond.

Finally, on April 28, Wilbur sent a conciliatory note: "My brother and I do not form many intimate friendships, and do not lightly give them up. . . . We prize too highly the friendship which meant so much to us in the years of our early struggles to willingly see it worn away by uncorrected misunderstandings." He proposed a joint public statement by the brothers and Chanute precisely detailing Chanute's involvement in their work.

Responding two weeks later, Chanute vowed that, upon returning from an upcoming trip to Europe, he would do his part to try to resume the friendship.

It never happened. Traveling in France with his three daughters, Chanute fell ill and consulted a Paris physician. Told that his heart was failing and that he should sharply curtail his activities, he disregarded the advice and soon found himself in the hospital, where it was discovered he had double pneumonia. His convalescence at the American Hospital in Paris took two months. Back home in Chicago, after showing such signs of improvement that his nurse was dismissed, he died on Thanksgiving Day 1910, at age seventy-eight.

The tribute Wilbur wrote for *Aeronautics* magazine better reflected his true feelings than his last letters to Chanute:

> If [Chanute] had not lived, the entire history of progress in
> flying would have been other than it has been. . . . His writings

were so lucid as to provide an intelligent understanding of the nature of the problems of flight to a vast number of persons who would probably never have given the matter study otherwise, and not only by published articles, but by personal correspondence and visitation, he inspired and encouraged to the limits of his ability all who were devoted to the work. His private correspondence with experimenters in all parts of the world was of great volume. No one was too humble to receive a share of his time. In patience and goodness of heart he has rarely been surpassed. Few men were more universally respected and loved.

Today, a town in Kansas, a memorial in Gary, Indiana, and an air-force base at Rantoul, Illinois, bear Chanute's name. The Wright brothers might never have gotten off the ground without his steady encouragement.

Like Chanute a three-time Outer Banks camper, George Spratt was the Wrights' best friend among the outsiders who came to North Carolina to experiment with them.

They remained in contact after Spratt's last Outer Banks visit in 1903, the Wrights spending a weekend at his home in Coatesville, Pennsylvania, in 1906 during a sojourn from their first effort at selling an airplane.

Unfortunately, the friendship followed the same course as the brothers' relationship with Chanute.

The point of contention with Spratt was a measuring apparatus the Wrights used in the wind tunnel they built after the 1901 season. Where other experimenters had designed separate tests to determine the lift and drag of wing sections, Spratt told the Wrights of a way to measure the ratio of lift to drag in a single test. The Wrights' wind-tunnel tests constituted some of the most important work they ever did, and Spratt's tip was vital to unlocking the secrets of wing design.

Spratt was repaid, appropriately enough, with the complete data tables from the brothers' wind-tunnel experiments, which were far more accurate than anything the Pennsylvanian had arrived at himself. But once the Wrights achieved world fame, that somehow wasn't enough. Spratt wrote them in 1909 complaining that he had never been given proper credit for his contribution. Aside from Spratt's participation in some of the Wrights' legal proceedings, the relationship was effectively ended.

In 1922, when Orville was thinking of authoring a personal account of the development of the airplane, he reestablished contact, writing Spratt to ask him for copies of letters the Wrights had sent him in the early days. Spratt declined, and went on to lay into Orville for what he considered the Wrights' secretiveness and their general obstruction of the progress of aviation.

"Not wishing to add to the sorrow of an already unhappy life," Orville wrote to a friend after receiving Spratt's letter, "I have refrained from making any reply."

"He doesn't want those letters just to make photostats," Spratt told a reporter for the *Coatesville Record*, his hometown paper. "What he wants is to get his hands on those letters, and if I send them to him I'll never get them back."

Meanwhile, Spratt was busy developing his own design ideas, his work proceeding at the kind of pace that had doomed many experimenters to failure before the Wright brothers came on the scene.

An advocate of parabolically curved wings early in his career, Spratt later switched camps and began touting wings with a circular curve, which he now believed would lend greater stability in the air. Having spent his early days in aeronautical study removing the tail feathers from live birds and seeing how they flew without them, Spratt had another pet notion: a tailless airplane. He envisioned what he called a "controllable wing" craft. It would have no ailerons or wing-warping system and either a small, fixed tail or no tail at all; its wings—featuring a circular curve and mounted on a universal joint, so they could tilt forward, backward, and from side to side— would assume all conventional aileron and tail functions.

The goal, as it developed over the years, was an inexpensive craft that would be stable at low speeds. Since it was to be operated by a single control, roughly analogous to the steering wheel of a car, flying it would require virtually no training.

In those days, with the future course of aeronautics a matter for speculation, some observers believed that every American home would eventually have an airplane in the garage, right beside the automobile. George Spratt was one of the men who hoped to open aviation to the masses.

His first step was a "controllable wing" biplane glider, built in 1908. Spratt flew the craft himself, towed into the air alternately by an automobile and a horse.

The next step, though exceedingly slow in coming, brought Spratt the greatest attention he ever received. In 1934, he introduced a powered "controllable wing" biplane. The craft flew under its own power to much local fanfare in early October, the inventor's son, George G. Spratt, at the controls. It was a selling point that the younger Spratt, entirely untrained to fly conventional airplanes, could pilot his father's craft with minimal practice.

Newsreel photographers came to Pennsylvania in 1934 and 1935 to record the tests; a reporter for the *New York Times* came, too. The 1935 newsreel photographer captured the airplane taking off and flying. He also recorded it in its "roadable" mode, driving happily down a conventional roadway powered by its propeller, its wings rotated to run along the length of its body from front to back, rather than from side to side in flying position.

In mid-November, it was demonstrated that the airplane could fly

George Spratt's "roadable" biplane of 1934

NATIONAL AIR AND SPACE MUSEUM

backward as well as forward. "The only changes that were made in the structure of the ship to make it fly backwards were to turn the seat around so that the pilot could see where he was going, to replace the tractor propeller with a pusher type and to put the tail on the front end," the *Coatesville Record* reported.

George Spratt lived just long enough to see his airplane in newsreels at a local theater. His health was always poor. He endured numerous hospital stays over the years, and he supposedly witnessed one of the first trials of 1934 from a stretcher. Never having made a dime off his forty years in aeronautics, he lived his last years in a small room at the Coatesville YMCA. He died of heart failure at his son's home in late November 1934, at age sixty-five.

George G. Spratt continued his father's work. In 1945, he

developed a "controllable wing" airplane for the Consolidated Vultee Aircraft Corporation. Nicknamed the *Doodle-Bug*, it looked more than a little like a Volkswagen Beetle with a wing on top. Strangely enough, the craft was built and tested in and around Elizabeth City, North Carolina, just up Albemarle Sound from where Spratt's father had camped with the Wright brothers.

Of course, those were the days when the Nazi war machine, heading toward its last days, was making revolutionary breakthroughs with jet aircraft. A new era of aviation was set to begin. The future did not rest upon craft designed for slow speeds and pilots with minimal training, but upon high-performance planes flown by specialists. The Spratt airplanes were interesting, but they didn't make a major contribution to the progress of the science.

When the 1903 Wright Flyer was brought to the Smithsonian from England after World War II, George G. Spratt was one of the guests at the ceremony.

Spratt, age ninety, was still making occasional news as of January 1995, when *Air and Space Smithsonian* carried an article on his and other designers' efforts at popularizing "controllable wing" airplanes. At that time, he was a living testament to the ease of operating such craft, having logged hundreds of hours without ever acquiring a pilot's license or even taking a single flying lesson.

As for Edward Huffaker, George Spratt's fellow camper in 1901, he dropped out of aeronautics for a decade and a half upon returning home from the Outer Banks. With his wife dead and two children to raise, he took up his old career as a surveyor for a means of support. He also served for a time as postmaster of Chuckey City, Tennessee.

His interest in flight was rekindled upon being called to testify in behalf of Glenn Curtiss in the Wright brothers' patent suit against Curtiss. Back home in Tennessee, Huffaker started building and testing

model airplanes as in the old days, his goal being to design an inherently stable craft. These efforts culminated in 1920, when he was
issued a patent for a new stabilizing device. However, he never managed to interest manufacturers in his invention.

In 1930, Huffaker moved to Oxford, Mississippi, to be with his
daughter, Mary Ada, wife of the chancellor of the University of
Mississippi. A teacher like her late mother, Mary Ada supposedly
gave music lessons to William Faulkner's children in their home.

When he wasn't taking long walks around campus, Edward
Huffaker was a familiar figure at the university library, where he is
said to have read the entire collection of books in Greek and Latin.
He also continued his interest in airplane design, contacting his
former employer, the Smithsonian, about the possibility of securing
grant money to develop a "flying wing."

Edward Huffaker died in 1937, at age eighty-one.

To all appearances, Augustus Herring, a camper on the Outer Banks
in 1902, was a talented man who ran out of ideas early, then tried
to hang onto his position in the aeronautical establishment by any
means he could, to the point of becoming a general nuisance.

When Herring left the Wrights' camp, he headed to Washington
with a view to exchanging information on the brothers' work for a
job at the Smithsonian.

The following year, he moved from St. Joseph, Michigan, to
Freeport, Long Island, his wife's home territory, where he lived the
rest of his life.

The 1902 season on the Outer Banks didn't end the Wrights'
dealings with Herring. In late December 1903, about a week after
arriving home following their historic flights, they received a letter
from Herring proposing they form a three-way business partnership. According to Herring, he had already received feelers about
selling his rights in future patent suits against the brothers. Bringing

Herring on board might thus serve as a hedge against litigation. The Wrights didn't bite.

Then, after the United States government issued a bid for a powered, heavier-than-air flying machine in December 1907—a bid tailored to the Wrights but open to all comers—Herring stepped forward with a proposal. Most observers doubted he even had an airplane, much less one that could fulfill the government's strict requirements. Herring's supporters claim he did in fact have a craft in

Augustus Herring
NATIONAL AIR AND SPACE MUSEUM

the works—a light biplane with twin five-cylinder engines—and that he later tested it at a field near his home, at which time it crashed and was destroyed.

In early 1909, Herring approached Glenn Curtiss with the same kind of partnership offer he had tendered the Wrights. Claiming he had patents that predated and invalidated the Wrights', he assured Curtiss that a jointly held company could not be successfully sued for infringement. The Herring-Curtiss Company soon became a major force in the aeronautical industry. However, with Glenn Curtiss the principal designer, Herring still found himself in the background.

When the Wright brothers brought suit against the Herring-Curtiss Company, Curtiss quickly learned that his partner had no patents at all. He dissolved the partnership to free himself from Herring, upon which Herring turned around and sued Curtiss for illegally kicking him out of the company. This monumentally long suit lasted until 1932, after both men were dead. Curtiss's widow ultimately agreed to pay a settlement of half a million dollars. After legal and administrative fees were siphoned off, thirty thousand dollars filtered down to Herring's heirs.

In February 1910, when the Herring-Curtiss partnership was about to reach the boiling point, Herring did achieve one last, if minor, aeronautical triumph. Backed by W. Starling Burgess, a yacht designer, he built and flew a biplane off Chebacco Lake in Essex, Massachusetts. His supporters claim it was the first powered flight in New England, though it lasted only five seconds and covered just forty yards—little better than what he had accomplished on the shore of Lake Michigan nearly twelve years earlier.

Soon afterwards, Herring suffered the first in a series of paralytic strokes. Despite his health problems, he was able to do a little engineering consulting and to continue participation in his lawsuits. He died in 1926.

His son, Bill, was a major-league pitcher for the New York Giants.

Augustus Herring never conceded the Wright brothers the high ground, summing up his opinion on the birth of flight in one memorably pithy comment during court testimony: "The airplane had a good many daddies."

The fortunes of radio experimenter Reginald Fessenden continued their rise and fall.

Unlike the Wright brothers, who became famous almost instantly upon going public with their invention, Fessenden reaped little reward when he made the first two-way Morse transmission across the Atlantic, when he became the first to send voice across the ocean, and when he made the world's first radio broadcast. In fact, his new employer, the National Electric Signaling Company, required that he sign over all the patents he developed during his tenure, so he didn't even have the rights to some of his greatest radio inventions. After much in-fighting, he was squeezed entirely out of the company shortly after Christmas 1910. As during his tenure with the Weather Bureau, his employment came to an ugly end, an officer of the court serving him legal notice forbidding him to have further dealings with the company.

A couple of lean years followed. Without steady employment, Fessenden took to gimmickry, inventing things like aluminum bags to hold tea and violins with built-in amplifiers. He and his family lived in cheap rooming houses and gradually sold off their possessions to pay for food, rent, and legal fees for Fessenden's never-ending patent suits. It was during this hard-luck period that Fessenden approached Orville Wright about the prospect of building an airplane motor.

Things picked up in the middle of 1912, in the wake of the greatest tragedy of the time: the sinking of the *Titanic*. Fessenden was standing in a train station in Boston when he bumped into an old friend who worked for the Submarine Signal Company. The friend inquired as to whether radio waves might be used for communication between submarines, and whether they might have some use for locating icebergs and dangerous rocks. A new door open to him, Fessenden went back to serious work, eventually producing a pair of noteworthy breakthroughs: the sonic depth-finder, or fathometer, and elementary sonar.

The outbreak of World War I led him to one of his most productive periods. One of his first war proposals had to do with airplanes. At a time when factories were building only a few dozen planes a month, he came forward with plans for a Canadian plant that would

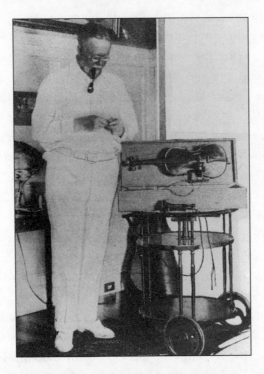

Reginald Fessenden and one of his lesser inventions,
the electric-assisted "radio talking violin"

produce them like Henry Ford produced automobiles—two hundred a day, for the purpose of dropping bombs on the enemy. Of course, training pilots to keep up with such a pace was another matter entirely, and the plant never came to pass.

Other ideas were better. Back in 1908, Fessenden had invented the turbo-electric drive, which was later used to power battleships and other vessels. Now, he put his radio waves to use in designing wireless communication systems between artillery batteries and in devising a means to locate enemy zeppelins in the air. He also invented the tracer bullet. When poison gas was used on Canadian forces, it was Fessenden who came up with the idea of igniting petroleum in front of the trenches, which caused the gas to rise out of harm's way on the heated air.

In the years after the war, he saw the first financial ease of his life. His fathometer brought him a good income. And in 1928, he finally won a major suit against violators of some of his old radio patents, which netted him a sum reported at anywhere from several hundred thousand dollars to two and a half million. While the award left him comfortable, it barely tapped the value of his many inventions over the course of his lifetime.

In his later years, with his heart failing, he moved to Bermuda, his wife's home. For a time, he tried self-treating his heart with electrical stimulation, but his principal interests were experimenting in agriculture and theorizing about ancient civilizations. His principal anthropological writing was a tome called *The Deluged Civilization of the Caucasus Isthmus*. He died July 22, 1932.

Today, outside of a couple of state historical markers—one on Roanoke Island and the other near Cape Hatteras—Reginald Fessenden is little remembered around North Carolina. In 1964, the Coastal Carolina Emergency Network issued its first Fessenden Memorial Public Service Award, presented at a performance of the famous *Lost Colony* outdoor drama in Manteo. In the 1980s, a coastal group tried to generate interest in developing a Fessenden memorial on Hatteras Island, but the effort has yet to bear fruit. Some say the base of the old boiler at his Roanoke Island facility is still visible in Croatan Sound at low tide, but if so, it is difficult to find.

The Word Men

The news coverage of the flights of December 17, 1903, remained a source of controversy around Norfolk at least as late as 1928. That December, the *Virginian-Pilot* ran a series of articles in celebration of the twenty-fifth anniversary of the birth of flight. Included in the series were a couple of pieces by Harry Moore, who told how he had scooped the world with his coverage of the event.

That brought a response from Keville Glennan, the *Virginian-Pilot's* city editor back in 1903 and a part-owner of the paper in 1928. He stated his position in a letter to the editor: "For the purpose of keeping the record straight, I would like to inform you that the credit for the magnificent 'beat' which the *Virginian-Pilot* scored on that occasion does not belong to any individual man—no one person 'scooped the world'."

Having said that, Glennan hastened to cast his vote for Edward Dean, the man who had received the news of the flights from the local Weather Bureau office. Dean, Glennan pointed out, was the first to report the story to the city desk. "And that's the finish line in news races," he wrote.

The following day, the paper started backpedaling, running a statement from the publisher apologizing for "any erroneous impression" the anniversary series might have created and stating that "Mr. Glennan's description of the event is entirely correct."

This did not please Harry Moore, who felt his contribution to the historic scoop was being slighted. A sharp exchange of letters in the *Virginian-Pilot* followed. Moore went so far as to collect statements from staffers who had been at the paper back in 1903, whose main contribution was to air old grievances against Glennan. "Don't let anything Glennan has to say worry you in the least," one former colleague wrote Moore. "I know him of old. He waits 25 years to claim credit for himself and Dean for the hard and excellent work you did on the Wright flight story." Another former co-worker claimed Glennan had thrown the first-flight story in the wastebasket and had to be persuaded to retrieve it.

For his part, Edward Dean was the voice of reason, assigning credit as it was most likely due: in three equal parts. Dean claimed that he had been first to report the event, that Moore had supplied the essential details, and that Glennan had written the story.

Of course, the prize was hardly worth the fight. Harry Moore once met Orville Wright and asked him what he thought of the first-flight story in the *Virginian-Pilot*. "It was an amazing piece of work," Orville said. "Though 99 per cent wrong, it did contain one fact that was correct. There had been a flight."

The three newsmen went on to varied lives.

Though Keville Glennan never got closer to an early Wright brothers flight than spying on the telegraph reports of their 1908 Outer Banks season from the men's room at the Weather Bureau office in Norfolk, he did manage to be present at one of aviation's great events. On November 14, 1910, Eugene Ely, one of Glenn Curtiss's pilots, came to Hampton Roads, Virginia, to attempt the first takeoff from the deck of a ship. Glennan was there to cover and snap a photograph of Ely as he left the deck of the USS *Birmingham*, dipped so low that the plane's wheels got wet, and then gained altitude and made it to dry land.

Harry Moore, only nineteen or twenty years old in 1903, was

offered a five-year contract by the *Norfolk Dispatch* when his role in
the first-flight story came to light. However, he elected to stay at
the *Virginian-Pilot*. In fact, he stayed so long that he eventually became the paper's oldest reporter, covering a number of important
maritime stories over the course of his career. He attended the
celebration of the twenty-fifth anniversary of flight at Kill Devil
Hills in 1928, then didn't attend again until the forty-ninth anniversary in 1952.

Edward Dean was the most quietly ambitious of the men involved
with the first-flight story. He soon moved to a position with the
New York Times. Reaching age forty-five and feeling he had yet to
accomplish anything of significance, he wrote a pair of books for
Harper and Brothers in a two-year span. Still, he considered his
career a failure. He wrote Keville Glennan in 1927 saying how he
hoped to leave the workaday world and find time to write a great
novel. That never came to pass. Crossing a street one night on his
way home from work, at about age fifty, he was hit by a truck
and killed.

Byron Newton was the brightest star among the reporters covering the Wrights in the early days.

Having grown up learning how to plow with oxen in rural New
York State, Newton had apparently distanced himself from his roots
by the time he arrived on Roanoke Island in 1908 and pronounced
the local people "well nigh as ignorant of the modern world as if
they lived in the depths of Africa."

No one who knew Byron Newton ever doubted he was going
places. He was locally famous from the time he began publishing
poetry in his teenage years. A skeptic of the Wrights before he saw
them fly on the Outer Banks, he was soon a faithful supporter, even
becoming, in the view of some, the first newspaper specialist
in aviation.

If Newton's success wasn't surprising, his ultimate direction was: big-time politics. In 1912, he served as the director of publicity for Woodrow Wilson's successful presidential campaign. The following year, he became assistant secretary of the treasury. Beginning in 1917, he served as collector of the port of New York, a demanding job during the World War I years.

Through all this, Newton never lost his artistic urge, continuing to publish poetry and play the violin.

He and Alf Drinkwater grew into longtime friends, Newton supposedly visiting the old telegrapher in Manteo for a week every year.

Another of Drinkwater's friends was Van Ness Harwood, who came to the Outer Banks to cover Orville Wright's glider trials in 1911. Harwood eventually moved to Manteo with his wife.

It is unfortunate that Bruce Salley, the first professional newsman to cover a Wright brothers flight in person, saw the most untimely end of all the journalists who came to the Outer Banks. Salley parlayed his flight stories of 1908 and 1911 into a job with the *New York Herald*. His promising career was cut short in 1917, when he died of a massive heart attack at age forty-four.

The Local Folk

First-flight witnesses Willie Dough, Adam Etheridge, and John Daniels might have been amused to learn of their posthumous reunion in 1974. The occasion was the release of a model kit depicting the historic events of December 17, 1903, manufactured by the Tonka Corporation and distributed through a Smithsonian mail-order catalog. Orville and the Flyer were the feature performers, of course, but the three Kill Devil Hills lifesavers were of a stature equal to Wilbur's—they were all two-inch-tall figurines. Daniels, who snapped the famous first-flight picture, was to be posed behind a toy camera and its tiny tripod. The color key indicated that he was to be painted wearing a dark gray hat, a white shirt, a gray jacket, a dark green sweater, dark gray pants, and black shoes. The kit sold for about seventeen dollars.

John Daniels retired from the Coast Guard in 1918 due to disability. After that, he captained several vessels plying North Carolina's inland waterways, including the ferry running between Beaufort and Morehead City.

Often praised for his landmark photograph, Daniels seemed equally proud of his status as the world's first airplane casualty, having been trapped in the wind-driven Flyer as it cartwheeled across the sand after the fourth powered flight.

Elizabeth City newspaper editor W. O. Saunders rode Daniels's ferry in 1927 and opened a conversation with the former lifesaver by saying, "I rather expected to find you piloting an aircraft by this time."

"Who, me?" Daniels asked. "No, sir, the only way they'll ever get me in one of them airplanes again will be to put me in irons and strap me in. I reckon I'm the proudest man in the world to-day because I was the first man ever wrecked in an airplane, but I've had all the thrill I ever want in an airplane; I wouldn't take a million now for that first thrill, but you couldn't give me a million to risk another."

Daniels changed his mind about flying in 1937, when he and Adam Etheridge were invited to attend an air race in Cleveland, Ohio. Though first inclined to make the trip by bus or train, they finally decided to fly, an experience Daniels described as "the most pleasant ride we ever had. Why, when we got about to Pittsburgh, I went sound asleep."

Daniels and Etheridge were back on tour in April 1938. Henry

Former surfmen Adam Etheridge and John Daniels at Greenfield Village in 1938

WRIGHT STATE UNIVERSITY

Ford had purchased the Wright brothers' home and bicycle shop and moved them from Dayton to Dearborn, Michigan, where they were to become part of Greenfield Village, Ford's collection of historic structures associated with noteworthy Americans. The two former lifesavers were guests at the dedication.

According to a 1970 article in the *Eden* (N.C.) *News*, it was on this trip that Daniels was inducted into the Early Birds, an association of old-time aviators. In a departure from his customary silence at public gatherings, Orville Wright supposedly introduced Daniels at the Early Birds banquet by making use of his friend's favorite subject: "The man is present tonight who rode further in the plane than either of the inventors."

As a distant cousin of Josephus Daniels, a longtime Raleigh newspaper publisher and secretary of the United States Navy under

Woodrow Wilson, John Daniels could boast another connection with aeronautical history. In 1913, the year he was appointed to his high post, Josephus Daniels became the first cabinet-level official to fly in an airplane. "Daniels, did you want to get yourself killed?" President Wilson supposedly asked him upon learning of his flight. It was also during Josephus Daniels's tenure, in 1919, that a United States Navy plane made the first flight from America to Europe, starting on Long Island and ending in Plymouth, England, with stops in Nova Scotia, the Azores, and Portugal. This preceded Charles Lindbergh's solo, nonstop flight by eight years.

Orville Wright, John Daniels, and Josephus Daniels all died in January 1948, Orville and John Daniels within twenty-four hours of each other.

Adam Etheridge, John Daniels's good friend, died in 1940, as did first-flight witness and Manteo resident W. C. Brinkley, a lumber broker in 1903 and a dairy farmer in later years.

Johnny Moore was the junior member of the first-flight witnesses. He was also the least prepared for the attention that came his way in

later years. Though he lived on Colington Island less than a mile from the national memorial honoring the Wright brothers, he often declined invitations to participate in commemorative ceremonies held there, ceremonies well attended by his fellow witnesses.

That changed in 1948. Orville Wright and John Daniels were

Johnny Moore

OUTER BANKS HISTORY CENTER

dead, leaving Johnny Moore the only man alive who had seen the famous flights. And it just so happened that 1948 was also the year that the Flyer was to be brought back to the United States and installed at the Smithsonian. A witness to the events of December 17, 1903, was desired at the ceremony in Washington, and pressure mounted on Moore to make the trip.

He finally agreed, bringing his wife, Chloe, with him. And after that, he attended the anniversary ceremonies at the memorial in Kill Devil Hills in 1950 and 1951.

This brief fame was a mixed blessing to Moore. An unpolished man at events where sophistication was called for, he was as much a curiosity as a figure of respect. He signed autographs, met important people, and received royal treatment in his official capacity, but he also took a few knocks. His offhand comment upon seeing the rebuilt Flyer—widely reported as either "I seen it before," "I seen it once," or "I seen it onct"—was taken as a sign of either boredom or backwardness. His reply when asked whether it was true that he really had fourteen children—"Sounds right to me, but I ain't counted lately"—also received play. A piece in the *Washington Evening Star* covering the 1951 ceremonies at Kill Devil Hills cruelly introduced him as "rheumy-eyed John Moore" and said he was "undoubtedly the least eloquent of all the speakers who looked back upon the 48th anniversary of the airplane."

In an event entirely unconnected to these public doings, Johnny Moore, in ill health, took his own life by shooting himself in the head with a shotgun in February 1952.

The *Raleigh News and Observer* eulogized him in a manner befitting a private man who found attention thrust upon him, calling him "the dean of freshwater fishing guides" and noting how "he often told visitors he would charge them nothing if they didn't catch the legal limit of fish."

Alf Drinkwater continued to lead one of the most interesting lives of the North Carolina people associated with the Wright brothers. Forced to retire from his position as a Coast Guard communications official around 1946 because of his age, Drinkwater quickly found other pursuits. He became involved with the Civil Air Patrol, eventually assuming the mantle as that organization's oldest warrant officer in the entire United States. He worked as a stringer for the Associated Press through the age of eighty-six, undoubtedly becoming one of the senior writers in the business. He also sold real estate and insurance from an office in Manteo, his window displaying the slogan "See Me Before You Buy or Burn."

Throughout his life, Drinkwater continued to tell how he had sent the telegraph announcing the first powered flights, a story generally more doubted than believed. But no matter. No one ever questioned his role in transmitting the news of the Wrights' 1908

Alf Drinkwater with some of his admirers, cadets of the Civil Air Patrol

NATIONAL AIR AND SPACE MUSEUM

Outer Banks season, and that brought him plenty of attention in itself.

According to accounts in the *Greensboro Daily News* and the *Raleigh News and Observer* in the 1940s, future president Herbert Hoover once came to Drinkwater's home to examine the transcripts prepared by the newsmen who covered the Wrights in 1908. This visit supposedly took place in the early 1920s. In 1945, during a Manteo dinner held in Drinkwater's honor, some of those transcripts were displayed in glass-topped cases borrowed from Fort Raleigh.

He also received invitations to attend dedication ceremonies at airports in Charlotte and elsewhere. At the opening of a new Eastern Air Lines passenger terminal at New York International Airport in 1959, he tapped out the official message kicking off the celebration on his old Morse key. When someone asked his opinion of the Big Apple, Drinkwater conceded that it was "mighty big," but was sure to mention how "you folks . . . never saw an airplane until 1909."

Drinkwater was a noted party host on Roanoke Island. Over the years, he accumulated a number of monikers, among them "the Old Salt of Dare," "Cap'n Alf," "Drink of Dare," and "the Fig Wizard of Roanoke Island."

He took great pride in his leisure-time hobby—the cultivation of figs. Shortly after World War II, the British ambassador supposedly visited Drinkwater's home and liked his fig preserves so well that he took some home to the queen, who wrote the old telegrapher a complimentary letter.

Drinkwater was a newsman to the end. According to an account in the *Raleigh News and Observer*, he was sick with cancer when he awakened at two-thirty one morning in September 1962. Sensing his approaching death, he called his daughter, Dorothy, to his side and asked her to contact well-known Outer Banks publicist Aycock Brown, who was in turn to notify the Associated Press of Drinkwater's impending event.

He died three hours later, at age eighty-seven.

Though their correspondence lagged at times, Orville Wright and Bill Tate seemed to grow closer as the years passed. In one of his final letters, addressed to Tate, Orville expressed his desire to pay one more visit to his oldest North Carolina friend.

Bill Tate was not quite done nurturing flying men when he joined the United States Bureau of Lighthouses and moved to Coinjock to tend the Long Point Lighthouse in 1915.

Bill Tate with Elijah Baum, who worked as a carpenter and contractor in later years

His grandson, Elmer Woodard, Jr., later told an old family story, passed down through the years, about a chance meeting on Currituck Sound. A young man of eighteen or nineteen was bailing his boat on the sound one day in 1917 when he heard a voice calling, "Hello, there!" across the water. He was more than a little surprised to see two men a few hundred yards away rowing a seaplane toward him. It seems the men had been flying through the area that day when they began having trouble with their propeller. They were now looking for a place to go ashore and get repairs.

They must have been pleased to find an easy solution to their problem in such a remote place. The young boatman turned and pointed toward the Long Point Lighthouse two miles away, telling them they could find a man there who had quite an interest in aviation, someone who had a lot to do with it in the early days.

True to form, Bill Tate took the men ashore, told them where they could get the parts they needed, and put them on a train.

One of the aviators soon returned to the lighthouse and his seaplane but showed an inclination to linger at the Tates' longer than was necessary to make repairs. During his two-week stay, he appar-

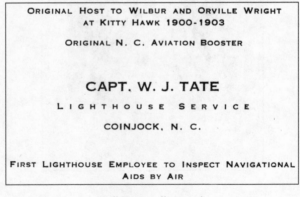

ORIGINAL HOST TO WILBUR AND ORVILLE WRIGHT
AT KITTY HAWK 1900-1903

ORIGINAL N. C. AVIATION BOOSTER

CAPT. W. J. TATE

LIGHTHOUSE SERVICE

COINJOCK, N. C.

FIRST LIGHTHOUSE EMPLOYEE TO INSPECT NAVIGATIONAL
AIDS BY AIR

Bill Tate's calling card

NATIONAL AIR AND SPACE MUSEUM

ently took Bill up for a flight to inspect the local aids to navigation, sparing him a four- or five-hour job by boat.

As it turns out, this aviator, Bennett Severn of New Jersey, was after more than Bill Tate's friendship. He returned the following spring to marry Bill's elder daughter, Irene. Bennett Severn eventually gave up barnstorming in the interest of safety, but before he did, Irene grew into as avid an enthusiast as her husband, flying some ten thousand miles with him and becoming the first woman to fly round-trip between New York and Miami.

The teenager in the boat who directed Bennett Severn to the lighthouse was supposedly Elmer Woodard, Sr., who married Bill's younger daughter, Pauline. It was a fortuitous meeting of the future sons-in-law of Bill Tate.

Bill was a tireless supporter of the Wrights and the cause of aviation throughout his life, eventually heading the Kill Devil Hills Memorial Association and the North Carolina branch of the National Aeronautic Association and becoming a member of the North Carolina Aviation Committee. His last wish was that he be present at Kill Devil Hills for the fiftieth anniversary of the birth of flight on December 17, 1953, but he died about six months short of that date, at age eighty-four.

Bill's son Elijah, the boy who was judged too heavy to ride a wing during the family trip to Kill Devil Hills that took place in either 1908 or 1911, eventually became a mechanic for Glenn Curtiss's company, and a pilot as well.

Orville Wright, 1871–1948

Orville Wright returned to the Outer Banks in April 1939. As covered in *U.S. Air Services* magazine, this little-known trip was exactly the kind of private, nostalgic visit described separately by Elmer Woodard, Jr.

Orville left Dayton in his eight-cylinder Hudson on Friday, April 14, to attend the Gridiron Dinner in Washington, where he sat at Table A, just to the right of President Franklin Roosevelt's table. On Sunday, he boarded a steamer for Old Point Comfort, Virginia, where he visited Langley Field.

Tuesday morning, he drove south from Norfolk, picking up Bill Tate at the Long Point Lighthouse in Coinjock before heading to the Outer Banks and Kill Devil Hills.

There was no separate visitor center at the national memorial in those days, the big monument on top of the dune serving that function. Arvin O. Basnight, the uniformed National Park Service guide on duty that day, was more than a little surprised to recognize Orville Wright trudging unannounced up the dune. It is unclear whether Orville saw the interior of the monument during the dedication ceremony in 1932, but Basnight was under the impression he was giving the great man his first tour that Tuesday in 1939.

After their visit, Orville and Bill Tate continued south. At Nags Head, they turned west onto the bridge across Roanoke Sound—the first on the Outer Banks, constructed in 1927—and drove to Roanoke Island, where they visited historic Fort Raleigh and Manteo. Orville then returned Tate to his home and made a solo visit to Elizabeth City—which he hadn't seen since the 1911 glider trip—before heading back to Norfolk for the night.

This was very likely Orville's last visit to the Outer Banks.

In 1942, one of his fondest wishes was granted when the Smithsonian finally came clean about the flight trials of the rebuilt Langley craft, effectively admitting that the Wrights were the first to fly and clearing the way for the installation of the 1903 Flyer in our national museum.

Of course, wartime Great Britain was in peril just then, and there was concern over whether the Science Museum of London and the Wrights' aged craft would survive German bombing. Still, it was decided that it was safer to keep the Flyer where it was than to try to ship it home during the war.

Orville didn't live to see the day in 1948 when the Flyer was crated up and put aboard the *Mauretania* for the voyage back across the Atlantic. In Halifax, Nova Scotia, it was transferred to the carrier *Palau* for the trip to Bayonne, New Jersey. From there, a military honor guard and a motorcycle escort led the Flyer on an overland trip to Washington, where it was finally welcomed at the Smithsonian on December 17, 1948, the forty-fifth anniversary of the famous flights.

One of the stipulations under which it was given to the museum was that, should the Smithsonian ever recognize another airplane as capable of sustained flight before the Flyer, Orville's estate could reclaim possession of the craft.

Orville Wright lived to see nonstop transatlantic flights, reliable commercial air service, early jet propulsion, and rocketry. He also saw the air attack on Pearl Harbor, the heavy World War II bombing of much of Europe, and the leveling of Hiroshima and Nagasaki.

He was asked during World War II whether he ever regretted his invention. His reply was a classic: "I feel about the airplane much as I do in regard to fire. That is, I regret all the terrible damage caused by fire. But I think it is good for the human race that someone discovered how to start fires, and that it is possible to put fire to thousands of important uses."

A practical joker around his family, Orville was extremely humble in his public doings. Once asked to list what he considered the ten most important inventions from the past hundred years, he named things like the linotype machine, radio, the air brake, the telephone, and the telegraph. Conspicuously absent was the airplane.

He suffered a heart attack in Dayton on October 10, 1947, while

Orville Wright and Charles Lindbergh
NATIONAL AIR AND SPACE MUSEUM

running up some stairs to keep an appointment. He was hospitalized for four days. On January 27, 1948, he had another heart attack. He died in the hospital on January 30, at age seventy-seven.

The airplane would have come about without the Wright brothers, of course.

Their success with gliders was in no way a product of the period in which they lived. The materials they used had been available for centuries. But for lack of insight, someone might have designed efficient wings and a three-dimensional control system long before they did.

But powered, sustained flight was impossible before their time. Lightweight engines were just reaching a state of refinement around the turn of the century. In fact, engines soon grew so efficient that, within certain bounds, they could overcome inferior design in other

Orville with his Saint Bernard, Scipio

areas. Some of the Wrights' competitors flew remarkably well with second-rate propellers and wings.

Author Harry Combs estimates that without the Wright brothers, the airplane would not have been developed for ten to twenty more years, with important—if unknowable—consequences for both world wars. Some experts have questioned whether the Nazis could have been stopped with air power in a more primitive state than it was in the early 1940s.

There is also room for debate about how the Wrights are to be credited for the development of qualitatively different forms of flight. Most authorities would say that airplanes and rockets are no more similar than the principles of lift and thrust. But in carrying a piece of wing fabric from the Flyer with him during his historic walk on the moon, Neil Armstrong demonstrated the view that the Wrights are at least the spiritual fathers of more advanced forms of travel.

Gifts among Friends

The Wright brothers' work has been commemorated in more ways—large and small, public and private—than can be recounted.

Among the major literary figures who have written about the Wrights are John Dos Passos and Ogden Nash. One of the best-known tributes is Robert Frost's poem "Kitty Hawk"—the central poem in his final book, *In the Clearing.* A depressed, lovelorn Frost wandered his way through the Great Dismal Swamp to Elizabeth City and ultimately to Nags Head as a nineteen-year-old in 1894. Later a supporter of the Wrights, he met Orville in the 1930s. He wrote the poem after a return visit to the Outer Banks in 1953.

If you prefer screen adaptations, you can take your pick between Michael Moriarty and David Huffman or Stacy and James Keach as the brothers from Dayton in a couple of the film treatments of their story. The *Washington Post* described Stacy Keach's cigar-chomping Wilbur Wright as "bullying, petulant and repressed" in the 1971 production *Orville and Wilbur*. And petulant Wilbur was, admonishing his younger brother, "Orville, if I told you a thousand times, I cannot stand lumps in my gravy!" A few concessions to modernity were made in the show's flight sequences. For safety's sake, the Flyer replica, made of metal, was tethered to a Jeep and powered by a 750cc Honda engine. The younger crowd would likely prefer the animated television program in which the Wrights had the honor of meeting Charlie Brown and the "Peanuts" gang.

For a roving advertisement of the Wrights' accomplishments, it would be hard to top the six million "First in Flight" license plates currently worn by North Carolina vehicles. Though the "First in Flight" campaign may come across as a bit of regional bravado, it started as an act of self-protection. North Carolina license plates put in circulation in the mid-1970s bore the slogan "First in Freedom," which drew a storm of legal challenges and sent officials scrambling for a motto to replace it. "The matter of Kitty Hawk and First in Flight is a historical fact, a fact that we can prove," said Henson Barnes, the floor manager for the bill in the state senate that brought the new plate into being in the early 1980s.

The Wrights' influence on the Outer Banks runs deep. The fine beaches of Dare County would surely have seen development if Wilbur and Orville had never paid them a visit, but it is equally certain that the Wrights influenced the course of that development.

Kill Devil Hills, with no permanent population whatsoever when the Wrights first saw it, is now the largest community in the county, approximately 4,200 people living within its corporate limits. Dare County, with the major resort area stretching from Kitty Hawk to Kill Devil Hills to Nags Head as its principal draw, is host to between 100,000 and 140,000 visitors on any given day during peak season. A good many area businesses use the region's connection to the Wright brothers in their advertising and even in their names.

The local development that would likely have been of greatest interest to the Wrights is the hang-gliding industry centered around Jockey's Ridge, just south of Kill Devil Hills. With a height varying from 110 to 140 feet, the big dune at Jockey's Ridge is the tallest in the eastern United States. Though the dune and its smaller sisters do not offer the advanced challenges of mountain hang gliding, their forgiving landing surface and the strong winds in the area—qualities the Wrights recognized long ago—have made them one of the premier training grounds in the world. An estimated hundred thousand pilots have tried hang gliding at Jockey's Ridge. Some of the major figures in the sport are regular visitors.

The state of North Carolina established Jockey's Ridge State Park in 1975, after a grass-roots effort led by Carolista Fletcher Baum—the granddaughter of novelist Inglis Fletcher—saved the dunes from being bulldozed for development. Today, there is lingering concern over whether the big dune—unanchored, unlike the dune supporting the monument to the Wright brothers at Kill Devil Hills—will migrate beyond the boundaries of the park. Or it may dwindle to nothing, having no source of new sand to replenish what blows away.

Francis Rogallo, a former NASA engineer, is the man considered the father of modern hang gliding. In the 1960s, during his effort to design a parachute system for the recovery of rockets, he developed what is called the "Rogallo wing" or the "flex wing." His wing design was tested with hang gliders primarily in California.

After his retirement, Rogallo moved to Southern Shores, just north of Kitty Hawk. He witnessed and learned of some amazing flying at Jockey's Ridge. In the early 1980s, Jim Johns of Marina, California, took off from Jockey's Ridge, circled to heights of a thousand feet on rising air currents, and landed four miles away—at the foot of the monument to the Wright brothers. In altitude and distance, this flight exceeded any gliding the Wrights had ever done by about a factor of twenty-five.

Francis Rogallo, still busy designing kites and testing them at Jockey's Ridge during his later years, subsequently offered a cash prize for the first pilot to fly round-trip between the state park and Wright Brothers National Memorial. Not yet claimed, that prize is still on deposit in a bank.

Mementos of the Wrights are scattered up and down the Outer Banks.

Fate has been kind to the two lifesaving stations they frequented.

The former Kitty Hawk station, located at Milepost 4 on N.C. 12 in Kitty Hawk, now houses a well-known restaurant, the Black Pelican Seafood Company. Though the building has been added to and is not as easily recognizable as the second-generation stations that followed four years later, the Wrights would still be able to identify the main dining room as the place where they were welcomed by their first friends among the North Carolina lifesavers.

It was to the Weather Bureau office housed at this station that Wilbur Wright addressed his initial inquiry about Kitty Hawk. And three and a half years later, it was from this place that Joe Dosher, the recipient of that inquiry, telegraphed the news of the flights.

Its neighbor, the Kill Devil Hills station, fell into disrepair after it was replaced by a newer structure in the 1930s. In fact, it was in such bad shape when local realtor Doug Twiddy expressed interest in buying it in the mid-1980s that he was advised not to waste his time. Furthermore, he was informed that it wasn't the original station at all, but rather a boathouse. That opinion was quickly disproved, as Twiddy removed the Coast Guard sign gracing the building and discovered the old U.S. Lifesaving Service sign underneath.

Restoring the structure was more difficult. First came a change of scenery. Twiddy wanted to use the station as a realty office in Corolla, located thirty miles north at the end of the Outer Banks road, so he arranged to have it moved by flatbed truck in three separate pieces: a wing, the top floor, and the bottom floor. That accomplished, a preservation architect set about returning the building to as near its original state as was possible.

Today, the old station—still a working building—is immediately familiar to anyone who has ever seen photographs of the classic lifesaving stations of the late 1870s.

Less permanent reminders of the Wright brothers have had varied fates. Some exist only in memory.

Its usefulness past, the 1900 glider provided material for Bill Tate's daughters' dresses—complete with French knots around the collar and bows tied at the back. When worn out, the dresses were casually discarded.

Wood from the 1900 glider supposedly came into the possession of John Daniels. According to his son, Archie, the family carved it into toothpicks and splinters and gave them out as souvenirs.

In 1975, ninety-eight-year-old Lillie Swindell of Manteo, formerly of Kitty Hawk, made headlines around North Carolina with the claim that her family had been the final recipient of the world-famous 1903 craft. However, with the Flyer having been held by the Smithsonian for more than a quarter-century, and by a major British museum for many years before that, her story was obviously mistaken. But on closer examination, her basic memory of the events—that the Wrights had given a flying machine to her former husband, first-flight witness Adam Etheridge—rang true. As best as could be determined, it was the 1902 glider she once possessed.

Mrs. Swindell told how she had given the wing cloth to neighbors for use in making children's clothes. Some of the wood was used to make quilting frames, and the rest was sent to the attic. Later, she asked Adam Etheridge to move it. When he was slow in doing so, she burned it herself.

Sometime between the Wrights' 1908 Outer Banks season and 1912, Margaret Hollowell of Elizabeth City was summering at her family's cottage in Nags Head when she learned that other vacationers were bringing souvenirs from a deserted camp up the beach. She and a small group of girlfriends took a pony and cart and went to have a look. At the camp, they saw where local residents had stripped away boards from the buildings for use at their own homes. Pieces of flying machines and miscellaneous papers were scattered around the ground.

Hollowell took a few samples of wood and a stack of papers away with her that day. Back in Elizabeth City, she stored them in her attic, where mice got into the papers over the years.

It was 1927 before she resolved to do something with them. By that time, about the only papers she could identify were shooting targets initialed "O. W.," "W. W.," and "Chas."—the latter for 1908 camper Charlie Furnas. She boxed up everything she had and mailed it to Orville Wright in Dayton, asking him to keep what he wanted and to send the rest back, identifying whatever he could.

A notoriously slow correspondent, Orville was ten years in replying. Two of the pieces of wood were rudder struts from the 1905 powered machine, flown on the Outer Banks in 1908. They would prove useful in a planned reconstruction of that craft, the world's first practical airplane. The miscellaneous bits Orville sent back became part of the collection at an Elizabeth City museum.

Over the years, Margaret Hollowell was not the only person to retrieve some priceless artifact from the sand and ship it back to its famous owner. Orville was pleased to receive the packages that came his way, but he made no serious effort to clean out the camp and retrieve what was his. The Wrights attached little sentimental value to their craft, the 1903 Flyer excepted. Each was a means to an end, becoming dispensable as soon as they learned what they could from it.

Frugal men in small matters, the Wright brothers were generous, even careless, with their possessions of greatest worth. Their camp buildings and the objects within them were left to rot or to be stripped of anything of value.

In the years since Orville's last camp in 1911, those haphazard gifts to their Outer Banks friends have been stored in attics, hung on walls, donated to museums, and incorporated into buildings—carved, trampled, resewn, tinkered with, burned, washed away by storms, dispersed by the wind. Mostly, they are part of the sand supporting the great monument to the Wrights.

Perhaps the best gift the brothers received in return came courtesy of Bill Tate.

In 1912, he wrote the custodian of the Hall of History in Raleigh,

> I want to put myself on record by saying that we North Carolinians are lacking in civic pride. . . . If Virginia Dare had been born in Massachusetts instead of North Carolina, a shaft piercing the sky would mark the spot instead of the simple monument that now exists. If Wilbur Wright had begun the assembly of that first 1900 experimental glider which led to man's conquest of the air on the front yard of some citizen in California, as

he began it in my front yard here in North Carolina, tons of printers ink would have been spread over the event, a monument would have marked the spot, and tourists would have come from thousands of miles, just to see and stand on the spot. Verily, we Tar Heels are very much lacking along the lines of the preservation of our epoch-making events of history.

When the plans for a national memorial at Kill Devil Hills were announced, Tate was spurred to action. He favored a monument sponsored by the people who had actually known and hosted the Wrights. The federal government had a head start on him, but this was to be a simpler project.

With the help of Elijah Baum—the first local citizen to welcome Wilbur Wright ashore after his ride with Israel Perry back in 1900—Tate set about raising funds. Contributors had to be Kitty Hawk residents. A good many of them were schoolchildren.

The result was a five-foot marble obelisk purchased from a monument dealer in Elizabeth City. Placed in the front yard of Bill Tate's old home, the monument featured an engraving of a Wright glider above an inscription reading, "On this spot on Sept. 17, 1900, Wilbur Wright began assembly of the Wright Brothers first experimental glider which led to man's conquest of the air. Erected by citizens of Kitty Hawk, N.C. 1928."

It was the first monument to the Wrights on American soil and the second in the world, following one erected in France. It cost all of $210. The monument was unveiled by Elmer Woodard, Jr.

Of course, the Tates were no longer living in the home, having sold it to the local Methodist church for use as a parsonage when they moved to Martins Point in the early years of the century.

Sometime between the erection of the monument and 1930, the resident preacher spent an idle day cleaning up the yard, piling trash

The locally sponsored monument to the Wright brothers
in the yard of the Tates' former home.
The house burned not long after this photograph was taken.

OUTER BANKS HISTORY CENTER

on the north side of the house, and setting fire to it. When the
fickle Kitty Hawk wind changed direction, sparks blew under the
home. The resulting blaze not only destroyed the house but cracked
the monument as well.

Over the years, water repeatedly leaked into the crack and froze
during winter. In the 1980s, local officials resolved to replace the
deteriorating monument.

The original is now housed inside Kitty Hawk's town hall. The
replica can still be seen in the yard of a home on Moore Shore
Drive, fifty or seventy-five feet from its original site. Few visitors to
the area know it exists.

Orville Wright was still alive when the monument was created, though he did not attend its simple dedication.

His elder brother, too, would have appreciated the gift's humbleness, the good taste it represents, and the sacrifice, the frugality, and the deep feelings that brought it into being.

Contrary to the long tradition of the Outer Banks as a place of refuge from calamity at sea, the Wright brothers were among the first persons of note to wash up from the west. Like new arrivals before them, they ate poorly, did without comforts, and endured wicked storms with little protection—and cherished their isolation and reveled in their self-sufficiency.

Elijah Baum showing off the Kitty Hawk monument in later years

OUTER BANKS HISTORY CENTER

Unlike the local people, who enjoyed the bounty of the sea but endured the poverty of the land, the Wrights had a need of the barren dunes and the sandy open spaces. The course of their experiments was sometimes as uneven as the local wind, but they found Bill Tate's promise of "a hospitable people" to be thoroughly dependable. In fact, their success owed a great deal to the kindness of new friends.

Through much of the century, there has been a controversy of sorts over whether Dayton or Kitty Hawk has a greater claim to the Wright brothers. Had the Wrights themselves ever been asked, it seems certain they would never have let another place supplant their Ohio home. But with less success than they found on the Outer Banks, there's a fair chance they would have eventually returned to their lives as local small businessmen, and such questions never would have been posed.

In that light, a little regional competition looks good.

Bibliography

The North Carolina Collection at UNC-Chapel Hill has excellent clipping files on the Wright brothers and many of the local people involved with them during their time on the Outer Banks. Unpublished letters between Orville Wright and Reginald Fessenden are held in the North Carolina State Archives and the Library of Congress.

"A. M. Herring's 'Mobike'." *Horseless Age* 5 (October 4, 1899): 19.

Albertson, Catharine. *Roanoke Island in History and Legend*. Privately printed, 1934.

————. *Wings over Kill Devil Hill and Legends of the Dunes of Dare*. Elizabeth City, N.C.: privately printed, 1928. This contains a reprint of William Tate's *Brochure of the Twenty-Fifth Anniversary of the First Successful Airplane Flight, 1903–1928.*

Alexander, John, and James Lazell. *Ribbon of Sand: The Amazing Convergence of the Ocean and the Outer Banks.* Chapel Hill, N.C.: Algonquin Books of Chapel Hill, 1992.

Allward, Maurice F. "Some Russian History." *Flight* 64 (17 July 1953): 80, 84.

Ballance, Milford R. *The Hands of Time.* New York: Vantage Press, 1972.

Barefoot, Daniel W. "The North Carolina Coast: Treasure of the Atlantic." Unpublished manuscript.

———. *Touring the Backroads of North Carolina's Upper Coast.* Winston-Salem, N.C.: John F. Blair, Publisher, 1995.

Biggs, Walter C., Jr., and James F. Parnell. *State Parks of North Carolina.* Winston-Salem, N.C.: John F. Blair, Publisher, 1989.

Brown, Aycock. *The Birth of Aviation, Kitty Hawk, N.C.* Winston Salem, N.C.: Collins Company, 1953.

Bryant, H. E. C. "Who Killed Nellie Cropsey?" *The State* 2 (23 February 1935): 7, 21.

Burgess, Robert F. *Ships Beneath the Sea: A History of Subs and Submersibles.* New York: McGraw-Hill Book Company, 1975.

Carpenter, Thomas. *Inventors: Profiles in Canadian Genius.* Camden East, Ontario: Camden House Publishing, 1990.

Chanute, Octave. *Progress in Flying Machines.* 1894. Reprint, Long Beach, Calif.: Lorenz and Herweg, Publishers, 1976.

———. "Some Manuscript Material." This typescript, available through the Chicago Historical Society, contains Chanute's travel diaries.

———. "Wright Brothers' Flights." *Independent* 64 (4 June 1908): 1287–88.

Chester, Ralph. "Astonished Reporters and Skeptical Editors." *The State* 21 (18 July 1953): 6–7.

Combs, Harry, with Martin Caidin. *Kill Devil Hill: Discovering the Secret of the Wright Brothers.* Boston: Houghton Mifflin Company, 1979.

Craig, Barbara. *The Wright Brothers and Their Development of the Airplane.* Raleigh: North Carolina Division of Archives and History, 1986.

Crouch, Tom. *The Bishop's Boys: A Life of Wilbur and Orville Wright.* New York: W. W. Norton and Company, 1989.

———. *A Dream of Wings: Americans and the Airplane, 1875–1905.* Washington, D.C.: Smithsonian Institution Press, 1989.

———. "In a Flight of Words: Robert Frost's Outer Banks." *Outer Banks Magazine* (1991–92): 28–31, 74–75.

Da Costa, Fernando Hippolyto. *Alberto Santos-Dumont: The Father of Aviation.* Translated by Hercilio A. Soares. Rio de Janeiro, Brazil: VARIG Maintenance Base, 1973. Available from the National Air and Space Museum.

Davenport, William Wyatt. *Gyro! The Life and Times of Lawrence Sperry.* New York: Charles Scribner's Sons, 1978.

Davis, Chester. "North Carolina's Twelve Great Seconds." *The State* 21 (18 July 1953): 3–5, 50.

DeBlieu, Jan. *Hatteras Journal.* Golden, Colo.: Fulcrum, Inc., 1987.

Drinkwater, Alpheus W. "I Knew Those Wright Brothers Were Crazy." *Reader's Digest* 69 (November 1956): 188–89, 192, 194.

East, Omega G. *Wright Brothers National Memorial.* U.S. National Park Service Historical Handbook Series, no. 34.

Engel, Leonard. "Between Wind and Water; in Forty-Five Years as a Telegrapher . . ." *True Magazine* 24 (January 1949): 54–55, 57.

Everette, Michael Lewis. "Reginald Aubrey Fessenden, American Communications Pioneer." Master's thesis, North Carolina State University, 1972.

Fessenden, Helen M. *Fessenden: Builder of Tomorrows.* New York: Coward-McCann, 1940.

Flott, Leslie W. "Augustus Herring . . . Aviation Pioneer." *Chronicle* (Third Quarter 1974): 2–8. Available through the Maud Preston Palenske Memorial Library, St. Joseph, Michigan.

Fowle, Frank F. "Octave Chanute, Pioneer Glider and Father of the Science of Aviation." Speech made at the dedication of a marker to Chanute in Marquette Park, Gary, Indiana, in 1936. Available through the Chicago Historical Society.

Francillon, René J. *Lockheed Aircraft Since 1913.* Annapolis, Md.: Naval Institute Press, 1987.

Frost, Robert. "A Trip to Currituck, Elizabeth City, and Kitty Hawk (1894)." *North Carolina Folklore* 16 (May 1968): 3–8.

Gradeless, R. M. "John H. Smith—The Inventor of the Airplane." Manuscript dated July 1, 1976, in the North Carolina Collection at UNC-Chapel Hill.

———. "Mystery Guests of the Isaiah Smiths'—Airplane Thieves of 1897." Manuscript dated September 5, 1979, in the North Carolina Collection at UNC-Chapel Hill.

Griffin, William A. *Ante-Bellum Elizabeth City: The History of a Canal Town.* Elizabeth City, N.C.: Roanoke Press, 1970.

Hallion, Richard P., ed. *The Wright Brothers: Heirs of Prometheus.* Washington, D.C. : Smithsonian Institution Press, 1978.

Harris, Sherwood. *The First to Fly: Aviation's Pioneer Days.* New York: Simon and Schuster, 1970.

Hegener, Henri. "An Unknown Aviation Pioneer: Alexander Fjodorowitsch Moshaiski." *Journal of the International Aviation Service of the British Petroleum Co., Ltd.* (June 1961): 6-9. Available from the National Air and Space Museum.

Howard, Fred. *Wilbur and Orville: A Biography of the Wright Brothers.* New York: Alfred A. Knopf, 1987.

Huffaker, E. C. "On Soaring Flight." In *The Smithsonian Report for 1897.* Washington, D.C.: GPO, 1898.

Husting, Eugene E. "Augustus M. Herring." *WWI Aero* (November 1990): 3–20.

———. "The Contribution of Augustus Herring." *Soaring* (September 1976): 37–40.

Johnson, F. Roy, and E. Frank Stephenson, Jr. *The Gatling Gun and the Flying Machine.* Murfreesboro, N.C.: Johnson Publishing Co., 1979.

Kelly, Fred C. "They Wouldn't Believe the Wrights Had Flown: A Study in Human Incredulity." *Harper's Magazine* 181 (August 1940): 286–300.

"And Kitty Hawk It Will Remain." *U.S. Air Services* 40 (January 1955): 6.

"A Lighthouse Keeper's Connection with Pioneering in Aviation." *Lighthouse Service Bulletin* 3 (2 January 1929): 272–73.

MacNeice, Jill. *A Guide to National Monuments and Historic Sites.* New York: Prentice Hall, 1990.

Maddry, Lawrence. "Man Will Never Fly." *Outer Banks Magazine* 10 (1992–93): 34–35, 84–86.

Marden, Luis. "She Wore the World's First Wings." *Outer Banks Magazine* (1984): 23–25, 27, 29.

McMahon, John R. "An Extra Spectator at the First Flight." *Aero Digest* 17 (July 1930): 73, 202, 204.

Millar, Thomas J. "Augustus Moore Herring: Aviation Pioneer (1867–1926)." Unpublished paper available from the Maud Preston Palenske Memorial Library, St. Joseph, Michigan.

Mobley, Joe A. *Ship Ashore! The U.S. Lifesavers of Coastal North Carolina.* Raleigh: Division of Archives and History, North Carolina Department of Cultural Resources, 1994.

Mooney, James L., ed. *Dictionary of American Naval Fighting Ships.* Washington, D.C.: Naval Historical Center, Department of the Navy, 1991.

Newton, Byron R. "They Said it was Neither Fact nor Fiction and

Promptly Turned it Down." *U.S. Air Services* 17 (July 1932): 20–24.

―――."Watching theWright Brothers Fly." *Aeronautics* 2 (June 1908): 6–10.

Nolan, Patrick B., and John A. Zamonski. *The Wright Brothers Collection: A Guide to the Technical, Business and Legal, Genealogical, Photographic and Other Archives at Wright State University*. New York and London: Garland Publishing, 1977.

"Notable Flying Men: Mr. Alec Ogilvie." *The Motor* (July 1910): 16. Available from the National Air and Space Museum.

"OrvilleWright GoesAgain to Kitty Hawk." *U.S.Air Services* 24 (May 1939): 12–15, 40.

Parramore,Thomas C. *Triumph at Kitty Hawk:The Wright Brothers and Powered Flight*. Raleigh: Division of Archives and History, North Carolina Department of Cultural Resources, 1993.

Poyer, Dave, and Mary Marcoux. *The Insiders' Guide to North Carolina's Outer Banks*. Manteo, N.C.: The Insiders' Guides, Inc., 1992.

Raby, Ormond. *Radio's First Voice: The Story of Reginald Fessenden*. Toronto: Macmillan of Canada, 1970.

Regis, Ed. "Spratt, Schmittle, and Freewing." *Air and Space Smithsonian* 9 (January 1995): 56–65.

Renstrom, Arthur G. *Wilbur and Orville Wright: A Bibliography*. Washington, D.C.: Library of Congress, 1968.

―――. *Wilbur and Orville Wright: A Chronology Commemorating the Hundredth Anniversary of the Birth of OrvilleWright,August 19, 1871*. Washington, D.C.: Library of Congress, 1975.

―――. *Wilbur and Orville Wright, Pictorial Materials: A Documentary Guide*. Washington, D.C.: Library of Congress, 1982.

"Reporting First Flight of Wright Bros." *Aero and Hydro* 7 (December 27, 1913): 155.

Ruhl, Arthur. "History at Kill Devil Hill." *Collier's* 41 (May 30, 1908): 18–19, 26.

Saunders, W. O. *A Souvenir Handbook of the Wright Memorial.* Elizabeth City, N.C.: The Independent, 1935.

———. "Then We Quit Laughing." *Collier's* 80 (September 17, 1927): 24, 56.

Schoenbaum, Thomas J. *Islands, Capes, and Sounds: The North Carolina Coast.* Winston-Salem, N.C.: John F. Blair, Publisher, 1982.

Shank, Joseph. "Raw Materials on the History of the Norfolk Newspapers." Seven-volume typescript available in the Norfolk Public Library.

Simpson, Bland. *The Mystery of Beautiful Nell Cropsey.* Chapel Hill: University of North Carolina Press, 1993.

Stewart, Susan C., ed. "Sky High: Celebrating the 90th Anniversary of Flight." *Outer Banks Magazine* (1993–94): 28–31, 74–76.

Stick, David. *Dare County: A History.* Raleigh: North Carolina Department of Archives and History, 1970.

———. *Graveyard of the Atlantic: Shipwrecks of the North Carolina Coast.* Chapel Hill: University of North Carolina Press, 1952.

———. *The Outer Banks of North Carolina: 1584–1958.* Chapel Hill: University of North Carolina Press, 1958.

———, ed. *Aycock Brown's Outer Banks.* Norfolk, Virginia Beach: Donning Company Publishers, Inc., 1976.

Tate, William. "I Was Host to the Wright Brothers at Kitty Hawk." *U.S. Air Services* (December 1943): 29–30.

———. "With the Wrights at Kitty Hawk." *Aeronautic Review* (December 1928): 188–92.

U.S. Congress. House. *Twenty-fifth Anniversary of the First Airplane Flight.* 70th Cong., 2d sess., 1929. H. Doc. 520.

Walsh, John Evangelist. *One Day at Kitty Hawk: The Untold Story of the Wright Brothers and the Airplane.* New York: Thomas Y. Crowell Company, 1975.

West, Rupert E. "When the Wrights Gave Wings to the World." *U.S. Air Services* 12 (December 1927): 19–23.

Whitnah, Donald R. *A History of the United States Weather Bureau*. Urbana: University of Illinois Press, 1965.

Williams, Henry Smith, and Edward H. Williams. *The Conquest of Time and Space*. New York and London: Goodhue Company, 1912.

Williamson, W. H. *Octave Chanute: Aviation Pioneer*. Rantoul, Ill.: Illinois Writers Project, Works Progress Administration, 1940.

Wright, Hamilton M. "Chaining a Mountain of Sand." *Popular Mechanics* 54 (July 1930): 99–100.

Wright, Orville. *How We Invented the Airplane*. Edited with commentary by Fred C. Kelly. New York: McKay, 1953.

———. "How We Made the First Flight." *Flying* (December 1913): 10–12.

———. "Our Life in Camp at Kitty Hawk." *U.S. Air Services* 28 (December 1943): 12–18.

Wright, Wilbur, and Orville Wright. *Miracle at Kitty Hawk: The Letters of Wilbur and Orville Wright*. Edited by Fred C. Kelly. New York: Farrar, Straus and Young, 1951.

———. *The Papers of Wilbur and Orville Wright: Including the Chanute-Wright Letters and Other Papers of Octave Chanute*. Edited by Marvin W. McFarland. 1953. Reprint, Salem, N.H.: Ayer Company, Publishers, 1990.

———. "The Wright Brothers' Aeroplane." *Century Magazine* (September 1908): 641–50.

Young, Pearl I. "Octave Chanute and His Connection with Chicago." Typescript available through the Chicago Historical Society.

Index